PHOG ALLEN

THE FATHER OF
BASKETBALL COACHING

By Blair Kerkhoff

MASTERS PRESS

A Division of Howard W. Sams & Company

Published by Masters Press
(A Division of Howard W. Sams & Company)
2647 Waterfront Pkwy. E. Dr., Suite 100
Indianapolis, IN 46214

Published 1996

Printed in the United States of America

96 97 98 99 00 01 02   10 9 8 7 6 5 4 3 2 1

Library of Congress Cataloging-in-Publication

Kerkhoff, Blair, 1959-
    Phog Allen: the father of basketball coaching / by Blair
Kerkhoff.
          p. cm.
    ISBN: 1-57028-111-4
    1. Allen, Forrest Clare, 1885-1974. 2. Basketball coaches--
United States--Biography. I. Title.

GV884.A44K47 1996
796.323'092--dc20   96-34944
                                                      CIP

To Karen, and our reasons for living —
Nathaniel, Benjamin and Anna.

CREDITS

Cover Photos © Rich Clarkson, University of Kansas Archives
Inside Photos © as credited
Cover design by Suzanne Lincoln
Edited by Kim Heusel

ACKNOWLEDGMENTS

Phog Allen lives in the memories of his family, players, coaches, rivals and friends, and also in the libraries and museums in the towns where he lived.

A special thanks to those who allowed me to visit them in their homes or offices or take as much time as was needed over the telephone. Tusten Ackerman, Bob Allen, Ernie Barrett, Rich Clarkson, Paul Endacott, Howard Engleman, Jack Gardner, Bill Grigsby, Dick Harp, Clyde Lovellette, John McLendon, Ted O'Leary, Dean Smith, Phil Snowden and Jerry Waugh were especially gracious. I'm thrilled to have some of Clarkson's photographs in the book.

The University of Kansas Archives at the Spencer Research Library provided a treasure of information, and Ned Kehde and Barry Bunch kept the boxes of files rolling.

Steve Jansen, director of the Watkins Community Museum of History in Lawrence, got me started on the right track and provided valuable information about early years of basketball at Kansas.

From their offices in Allen Field House, Kansas assistant athletic director Doug Vance and sports information director Dean Buchan were their usual cooperative selves and provided access to files and photographs.

A tip of the hat to the staffs of the American Osteopathic Association and libraries at Central Missouri State and Baker University, the Mid-Continent Public Library in Independence, Mo., and the records division in the Johnson County, Mo., courthouse for providing valuable information.

Art McClure, chairman of the Department of History and Anthropology at Central Missouri State, kindly shared information he had collected on Phog's years in Warrensburg.

Thanks to the *Kansas City Star* for its encouragement, to Bob Snodgrass of Addax Publishing for making things happen, and Masters Press editor Kim Heusel for molding the project into its final shape.

And were it not for the patience and understanding of my wife, Karen, this book never would have happened.

TABLE OF CONTENTS

Whence the Name Phog ix

Foreword xi

Introduction xiii

1 — Independence Days 1

2 — The Amazing Allen Brother 9

3 — Here a Coach, There a Coach 19

4 — Mending Friends and Foes 29

5 — Normal Phog 41

6 — Dreaming Touchdowns and Stadiums 49

7 — 1923: The Legend Begins 59

8 — Dr. Naismith 69

9 — The Entrepreneur 79

10 — Rules, Rules, Rules 95

11 — Olympic Rise and Fall 105

12 — Phog's Folly 115

13 — NCAA Tournament 121

14 — The Patriot 131

15 — Smelling a Rat 141

16 — Friends and Enemies 153

17 — Brass Rings and Gold Medals 165

18 — Wilt and Statutory Senility 177

19 — Retirement 193

Epilogue 205

Phog's Career Coaching Record 209

Appendices 213

Notes 225

WHENCE THE NAME PHOG

Sports followers sometimes wonder what is the significance of my nickname "Phog". The story is very simple. As a young man, I used to umpire baseball games. In those days, the baseball umpire would bawl out the word "B-A-L-L" just as he now cries out the word "STR-I-K-E".

Evidently I executed this word "B-A-L-L" in a foghorn voice and thus acquired the nickname, Foghorn. Soon, as a time saver, the fellows shortened this name to just plain Fog.

Later I picked up a sports page and found that "Fog" had been spelled "Phog". I inquired of Ward Coble, the sports writer responsible, where he had acquired this name for me. "Oh," he said, "Fog was too plain. I thought I would doll it up a little."

Coble's nickname was "Pinhead".

From *Phog Allen's Sports Stories for You and Youth*, 1947

Editor's note: The nickname was pinned (or pinheaded) on Allen in the summer of 1905, just before he enrolled at the University of Kansas. In 1940, Phog received a letter from a New Jersey college student who claimed to have the same name.

Letter to Mr. Frank "Phog" Allen
Phi Epsilon Kappa
State Teachers College
Trenton, N.J.

Dear Mr. Allen:

I am very happy to have your letter of December 6 and I assure you that the moniker is an unusual one.

The nickname gradually hung on and gathered momentum, and I still get letters addressed to Fog, Pfog, Pffog, Poag, Ffog, and actually got one addressed 'silent P' hog. So you see they come in all shapes and sizes.

Sincerely yours,

Forrest "Phog" Allen
Director of Physical Education and Recreation
Varsity Basketball Coach

"It didn't bother him being called Phog. The boys all called him Doc, all the players. He didn't mind the professors or people he knew calling him Phog, but if a student or somebody he didn't know came up to him and called him Phog, he'd say `Young man, my name is Dr. Allen. You didn't go to school with me, so you don't call me Phog.' He thought of it as a name of endearment to his own age group."

Bob Allen, Phog Allen's son, 1995 interview

FOREWORD

It is indeed an honor to be invited to write the foreword to the biography of Dr. Forrest C. "Phog" Allen, who was my college coach at the University of Kansas.

Dick Harp, co-captain of the 1940 team, longtime assistant to coach to Dr. Allen and his successor as head coach, had intended to write a biography of Dr. Allen with the help and expertise of Don Pierce, an All-American football player while a student at Kansas and later the school's sports information director. Dick and Don had taken notes for years to write about Dr. Allen. After Don died in a tragic accident in 1965, coach Harp chose not to do the book.

Those two knew Dr. Allen as well as anyone outside the family. Their in-depth biography would have been a fitting tribute to a life well-lived. I am pleased that Blair Kerkhoff has now chosen to bring the wisdom and influence of Dr. Allen's greatness to the public. Once you have read this book, you will understand why Dr. Allen was called the "father of basketball coaching."

Dr. James Naismith, who invented basketball, told his KU colleague, D. Allen, that "basketball should simply be played; you do not coach it." But Dr. Allen did coach it, and he coached it extremely well! Each Kansas team was well grounded in the fundamentals of the game. Believe me; I did learn how to pivot correctly after a pivot drill that lasted 20 minutes every other day during preseason workouts. I remember coach Adolph Rupp's great Kentucky teams still running some out-of-bounds plays which he learned as a player at Kansas. Dr. Allen's influence was still evident.

At the Final Four in 1991, I made the remark to the opening press conference that each of the teams at Indianapolis — the University of Nevada-Las Vegas coached by Jerry Tarkanian, the University of Kansas coached by Roy Williams, Duke University coached by Mike Krzyzewski and out North Carolina team — were all there because of outstanding pressure man-to-man defense, which was started by Dr. Allen and coach Harp in 1952. The zone press was started by Gene Johnson in Wichita, Kan., in the mid-30s, but our University of Kansas team was the first man defensive team to have a defender play between his man and the ball. All four coaches may have learned this defense from different sources, but the defense itself originated with Dr. Allen and coach Harp.

The year after I graduated, I had the opportunity to serve as assistant coach with Dick Harp to Dr. Allen. Those two had a tremendous influence on my thinking as a beginning basketball coach and it continues to this day.

I could never be the motivator that Dr. Allen demonstrated to be time and time again. Well before I became one of his students in the early 1950s, he served as a hero to thousands and thousands of Kansans. My father, Alfred Smith, coached all sports at Emporia (Kan.) High School. When I was in junior high, Dad invited Dr. Allen to speak at the athletic banquet. I had never heard a man talk the way he could and move people to action as he did in that banquet speech.

Approximately nine years later, however, in our meeting prior to playing Washington in the NCAA Final Four in 1953, Dr. Allen talked about his son, Dr. Bobby Allen, the great player Ralph Miller, and Dick Harp, all players on the 1940 team who had missed winning the NCAA championship. With tears in my eyes, I looked around the dressing room to find my teammates also overcome with emotion and inspired to play. Our team promptly went out to a big lead and won over an excellent University of Washington team following that so-called "pep talk."

Dr. Allen was a gifted individual who made the most of his gifts to help others in his many, many years of influence. Readers of this book will gain a greater appreciation of this unique man, as well as the game of basketball, thanks to this work by Blair Kerkhoff.

Dean Smith
Head Basketball Coach, University of North Carolina

INTRODUCTION

Phog Allen never got around to writing his life story. There was talk of such a book toward the end of his career in 1956 and in the early years of his retirement, but it never came off. That's a shame because Phog would have penned an entertaining autobiography, and most of it would have been true.

Phog wrote three books about basketball and embellished the truth in all of them. Not the parts about basketball tactics, treating injuries or philosophical beliefs, but the stories. The man could spin a yarn. He loved to tell the story about listening for the droning plane, a 1932 game against Oklahoma that the Jayhawks needed to win to have a chance for the Big Six championship. Bill Johnson was the team's star player but had to attend his father's funeral in Oklahoma City on the day of the game. Phog pushed the game time back and arranged for a booster to fly Johnson to Lawrence. According to team members, that's how it happened.

But the players weren't consulted when Phog dramatized the incident, and he wasn't averse to using his poetic license. Phog remembered how anxiety gripped Hoch Auditorium and fear grew in his players' hearts. Then Phog cupped his hand to his ear. Listen! The airplane had arrived! Bedlam! Adulations of joy! A conquering spirit answers the call of duty! Out and at 'em, fight your hearts out!

Phog replayed the story, hand gestures and all, in pregame pep talks through the years. The part where Johnson fouled out in the first half and really wasn't a factor in the Jayhawks' victory conveniently escaped Phog's recollection.

Such stories were staples in Phog's motivational menu. Players laughed, they cried, but they never tired of hearing the fiction. The tales, which he also shared at athletic banquets and graduation on the public speaking circuit, were only one example of Phog's remarkable power of expression, a part of his life he took seriously.

In his office Phog kept files of magazine articles, poems, short stories, newspaper editorials and 10 pages of descriptive words, typewritten, single-spaced, three columns wide. Thousands of words. He was a longtime subscriber to *The Kiplinger Washington Letter*, *Harper's* and *The Sporting News*. His favorite books were biographies of Abraham Lincoln. Some of Phog's pet lines to the press originated from his file cabinet. Tall players were "mezzanine peeping goons." Amateur Athletic Union officials were "quadrennial oceanic hitchhikers," because they "chisel" their way to the Olympics.

Phog could name-call with the best of them. Some of his favorite lines:

- On a poor performance by center B.H. Born, "He stood around like a Christmas tree, and out of season at that."
- On Philadelphians, "They're taller and fairer than the Chinese, but not nearly as progressive."
- On a New Yorker, "When he gets as far as Philadelphia, he thinks he's on a Lewis and Clark expedition."
- On his detractors, "If the postman kicked at every dog that barked at him, he'd never get the mail delivered."
- On inspiration: "A boy must say 'No' a thousand times to temptation before he can say 'Yes' once to victory."
- On vices, "I'm against betting, bribery, booing, box office, big-time and booze."

Well, about the latter. Phog stopped smoking and heavy drinking as a teenager but his evenings as a Kansas coach often included a nightcap. When the Jayhawks were on the road — Phog loved traveling by train — he kept small, unmarked liquor bottles in his training kit. When he resumed smoking later in life, players young and old were flabbergasted.

To say Phog coached as well as he talked is a compliment. He won 746 games in 48 years at four schools, coaching two teams at the same time for three straight years. He coached before coaches were paid to coach and when his career ended in 1956 had won about every event and honor available in his profession, including an NCAA Tournament and Olympic gold medal. When he stepped down, nobody was within 100 career victories of Phog.

Unfortunately, Phog is better remembered for his sharp-tongued criticisms than his achievements. Not only would Phog not back down from a fight, he started them. He blind-sided college basketball in 1944 when he supplied the names, dates and places where point-shaving was occurring. The AAU, NCAA, sportswriters, rival coaches, even his own school incurred his wrath. "I've never been accused of being a shrinking violet," Phog once said.

Phog picked his causes and never mellowed with age. Well into retirement, headlines started with the same two words they had for decades: "Phog Blasts (fill in organization, cause or individual)."

While it's fitting that Phog was inducted into basketball's Hall of Fame as a member of the original 1959 class as a contributor, it's somehow inappropriate that he's not listed among the game's greatest coaches. He was, after all, one of the first — if not the first — paid to coach college basketball. Even James Naismith, whom Phog knew better than anybody in the sport, called him "the father of basketball coaching."

Nobody in basketball was closer to the game's inventor than Phog. But they often disagreed in their approach to basketball. Phog's version was spelled out in a 1940 letter to a reporter:

> *"It was Dr. Naismith's theory that fifty or one hundred people could play on each side and throw the ball into this hoop. He had no conception of basketball being broken up into the small numbers and intricate passing and set plays that are now indulged in. His idea was more like the game of cage ball that used to be played in the army where the large ball was handled by a group and tossed into the net high above their heads."*

As a coach, Phog was all fundamentals. His players' excitement of starting another promising season was quickly doused by two solid weeks of monotonous drilling. Defensive positioning, hook passes, two-handed chest passes — all the stuff you see diagramed in those ancient instructional books. As the game evolved, the Jayhawks may have thrown one hook pass all season. But they spent days working on it in preseason. There was method to this madness.

"We try to develop their reactions and reflexes so that when they get into a game they will perform in a way that the rest of the teammates will know just about where every individual can be found when a play is put on," Phog wrote in 1939. "Now, do not understand me to mean that the players are robots, but we do have a fundamental style of moving the ball down the floor."

Although Phog was a remarkable shooter during his playing days, defense is what he stressed. The 'stratified transitional man-for-man defense with zone principles' was Phog's fancy title for a floating man defense. When the game was played deliberately, as it was during most of Phog's tenure, his teams played a zone — two forwards out front and the guards and center forming a triangle near the basket — while the offense was looking for a shot, then slid into a man when an opponent appeared ready to shoot. The entire defense shifted with every pass.

On offense, Phog preferred the bank shot with thumbs placed on the side of the ball. He created carom shot lanes for practice drills. Players knew where on the floor to bank shots and where to shoot directly at the goal. Phog dressed in a sweat suit and demonstrated every drill. When plays didn't work, he'd call for the ball, and as he did in his playing days, smash through the defense and flip in a hook shot.

Phog liked his offensive basketball patterned, with set plays guided by his point guard, whom Phog called his center because he was the center of the offense. It's telling that even late into his career, when scores were climbing into the 80s and 90s, Phog remained an advocate of the rule that brought the teams to a center jump after every basket.

He wasn't inflexible. It was big news when Kansas once overcame a large second-half deficit at Kansas State by driving to the basket without passing. The game ended with Kansas State fans, enraged over an official's call that nullified a late tying basket, tearing the referee's shirt off his back after the game. A few days later, a K-State fan mailed a piece of the shirt to Phog, who kept it tacked on his bulletin board.

Phog could hack 'em off. Students and fans in Big Six barns — and they were little more than that for most of Phog's career — usually sat right behind the bench and on the floor where they could pull the players' leg hairs. From just about any point at Nebraska's gym, it wasn't difficult to reach Phog's head with an apple core. Teams that included his sons Mitt (1934-36) and Bob (1939-41) were derided mercilessly by opponents.

Phog got more feisty as he grew older. There were some pushing incidents and a night at Washington University in St. Louis when he nearly came to blows with an official after getting a technical.

Phog was an easy target. He dressed flamboyantly with canary yellow ties, red socks and imported tweed jackets. A crate of milk quart bottles of water was kept under his seat. He drank up to six quarts a game to keep his throat clear. At practice or in his office, horehound candy served the purpose. He bought the stuff in 60-pound boxes.

He got his share of hate mail, answered most of it and liked to end with the line, "Assuring you I would not feel comfortable without receiving an occasional love note from you, I am, Sincerely yours,". He also invited his poison pen pals to sit on the Kansas bench for the next home game.

After home-game triumphs, Phog hung around Hoch Auditorium for an hour, greeting parents and friends. After road losses, he'd take the front seat of the bus, recline, unbutton the top of his pants and fall asleep before the team had pulled out of the parking lot. "He never took defeat personally or threw tantrums," said Dick Harp, who played and coached for Phog. "I'd be upset, and our trainer Dean Nesmith took losses even harder. But Doc could let it go just like that."

More than his tactics and strategies, Phog is remembered by his players for his motivational ploys and personal relationships with them. Before important games, Phog looked for the victory light shining in his starters' eyes. Only five men are fit to wear the Kansas uniform, Phog would say. He'd approach each one, firmly shake his hand, look deep into his eyes and solemnly ask, "Are you ready?"

Phog's halftime antics often had players shaking their heads. When he was disappointed in an effort, Phog was known to skip the locker room, leaving his players to figure out their problems. More often than not it worked, and the Jayhawks rallied for a victory.

"He could manipulate you to succeed," former Kansas guard and assistant coach Jerry Waugh said. "And he was as dramatic a coach as I've ever known."

Phog believed in getting close to the players, know their problems. When grades or girls troubled them, Phog wrote a long letter of encouragement. Sometimes the letters went to parents or girlfriends. Even the players he kicked off the team continued to receive Phog's support. It wasn't unusual for Phog to contact Alcoholics Anonymous to help boys he couldn't reach. He counseled not only his players, but KU students who were sons of former teammates or players.

As a coach, Phog got his share of fan — and hate — mail, and tried to answer all of it. (Photo by Rich Clarkson)

Not every person who came out for basketball made the squad but Phog didn't turn away many. He preferred teams of 20-25 members to build unity. He never could seem to tell a friend that his boy wasn't good enough to play college ball, but only the strong survived the first few weeks of practice.

Basketball was his game, but Phog loved all sports. He believed that all sports fans should see at least one of the ultimate sporting spectacles — a World Series, Kentucky Derby, Army-Navy football game or a championship heavyweight boxing match. Phog, a former fighter and head of the Kansas boxing commission for a decade, did see title fights in the 1930s and believed Jack Dempsey was the best he'd ever seen. He also took in several World Series. His interest in baseball was so great that one summer he agreed to serve as an area scout for the Philadelphia Phillies. He also received a complementary season pass from the St. Louis Browns.

Phog was an avid golfer, a Phi Kappa Psi, a Methodist who taught Sunday school for 25 years, and a staunch Republican who briefly considered running for governor in 1956. Nearly all Kansas governors were Phog's friends, and he was closely associated with the state's top two politicians of the 20th century, Alf Landon and Bob Dole. Landon was a huge fan and a regular at games. Dole played on the freshman basketball team and stuck around on Phog's varsity team for about two months as a sophomore before turning to indoor track.

It can be argued that college basketball has known better coaches, and there's no scorebook to track who contributed most to the game. But it is fair to say that, at least in the sport's infancy, there was no more passionate supporter than Phog Allen. In 1935, he took great exception to a *Harper's* article that listed the top 10 fast-growing sports in America and didn't include basketball. Phog supplied a seven-page response, complete with statistics and enclosures from educational groups and an assurance from Naismith that the game not only was mushrooming in America but worldwide. To show there were no hard feelings, Phog invited the writer to Lawrence and a game, which was accepted. The writer was convinced.

Toward the end of his coaching days, other detractors started to come around and an appreciation for his career was spreading. A paragraph from a 1950 Associated Press story, written while the Jayhawks were playing in New York, sums Phog perfectly.

"We've known Phog since way back when, and like him and admire his ability. He's out to win, and isn't averse to seeing his name in print. You just can't be neutral about the fiery Kansan. You either like him or can't stand him, and that's all right with him, as there's nothing neutral about him, either. After all, you can't get anywhere in neutral, and Phog has gone a long way."

1

INDEPENDENCE
DAYS

Phog Allen is at least the second most famous person who grew up in Independence, Mo., and being second never appealed to Phog. But this time he didn't mind. Phog liked being associated with notable people, and he could live with playing second fiddle to a president.

Harry Truman graduated from Independence High in 1901, just as Phog was entering high school. Later in life, Phog described Truman as a friend, but they were more like acquaintances. Certainly, they were different sorts of fellows, as Phog explained in a newsletter to World War II soldiers in 1945:

> *"Bess Wallace Truman lived three blocks from me, and Harry Truman lived an equal distance. An equilateral triangle would describe the location of the homes of the Allens, the Trumans and the Wallaces. Harry Truman was not an athlete, and many of the boys thought him a sissy because he could not compete in athletics due to the fact he wore thick magnifying glasses. Harry Truman had no enemies, but many friends among the boys of his home town. Bess Wallace was at that time characterized as a tomboy. She could play baseball, and that wasn't the*

*softball kind. She swung a bat effectively and could throw
with the best skill of the boys. She could ride a bike as
well as any of the boys in the neighborhood."*

As a boy, Forrest Clare Allen shared more interests with Bess
than Harry. Forrest was the fourth of six sons born to William T. and
Mary Elexzene Perry Allen on Nov. 18, 1885. William Allen was
born in Augusta County, Virginia, and was the son of a Confederate
soldier captured by General Grant. Most of Forrest's ancestors were
soldiers who fought in the American Revolution and the War of 1812.
Forrest, who enlisted in the Army but never fought, was proud of his
family's military heritage. Mary Allen also was a Virginian. They
were married in 1874 and moved to Daviess County, Missouri, a
year later.

Forrest was born in Jamesport, Mo., a tiny town northeast of
Kansas City about halfway to the Iowa border. In the late winter of
1887, the Allens moved to an Independence house at 802 North Union,
and a few years later Forrest started his education at the Ott School,
which continues today as the oldest elementary school in the city.

The Allen boys loved the outdoors, and sports wasn't their only
diversion. They were familiar with the tales of soldier/ruffians William
Quantrill and Jesse James, who at some point in their lives had
lived in Independence, and the Dalton brothers from Kansas. The
boys would assume their identities and play neighborhood war games.
Constructing snow forts in the winter, exploring caves by the Missouri
River in the summer, the Allens rarely arrived home for supper
in clean shirts.

Fierce sibling rivalry fueled competitive spirits but the Allen
sons were still a tight-knit group. Brothers Homer, Elmer, Harry
("Pete"), Forrest, Hubert and Richard — 15 years between oldest
and youngest — all eventually moved into athletics and the brothers'
rough-and-tumble demeanor often carried over to the playing fields
with fights on the baseball diamond and football field. Sports were
crude in the 1890s with little or no protective gear in boxing, baseball
or football. Such conditions were ideal for the Allens, especially the
largest of the brothers, Pete and Forrest.

Pete Allen, three years older, became Forrest's sports idol.
Forrest was 10 when he'd watch his brother spend an afternoon winging
a baseball for hours against a knothole on the side of the Allen
barn. Later, Forrest couldn't be talked into catching Pete's fastballs
but younger brother Hubert slipped on an oversized mitt and became

a battery mate. Hubert went on to become an outstanding tennis player, winning many regional tournaments. After Forrest and Pete, Hubert accomplished more athletically as an adult than any of the other brothers.

As a youngster, Forrest became smitten with sports. He had just turned 10 when he attended his first football game, a Thanksgiving Day Kansas-Missouri contest at Exposition Park in Kansas City. Playing for the Tigers that day were two Independence sons, Adam Hill and Charley Latimer, who were friends of the Allens. After that, Forrest turned the Allens' back yard into a football field for daily games.

At an early age, Forrest determined to make a life of sports, much to his father's chagrin and expense. Legend has it dad had to buy his sons so many pairs of shoes he became known in town as "Shoe" Allen. William Allen believed his son was wasting his time with sports and wouldn't amount to much if he pursued athletics.

He wasn't the only one.

Forrest had taken up boxing as a teenager and one day was running through the streets of Independence in a sweater and shorts. A farmer, atop a load of hay, pulled alongside and asked the runner where he was headed. To a spring to get a drink of water about five miles away, was the reply. "You're a disgraceful sight," the farmer said.

At the time, Forrest didn't know the farmer was Frank Milton, father of Bessie Milton, the woman he eventually married. When they wed, Forrest was missing four teeth. As a boxer he was known as Pug Allen, and he lost a match and the teeth in the Kansas City stockyards. Socked after the bell, Forrest insisted.

For baseball and football, the young Allens needed friends to field teams and play games. But this new sport sweeping the nation in the 1890s, basketball, especially appealed to the brothers. The Allens eventually played together as a team, with one coming off the bench as a substitute. Pete got the brothers interested, first playing for the Independence YMCA team then a local lodge called the Modern Woodmen of America. Pete played for two years for the Woodmen before heading to the University of Kansas, and when he left, Forrest took his place on the team.

How crude was basketball at the turn of the century?

"Pete was a tremendous athlete, a powerfully built man," said Bob Allen, Forrest's son. "In basketball, he was called a checker. In those days they played a lot of games in places that had concrete columns on the floor. If there was a bully on the other team, it was his job to check him against one of those concrete posts."

Some of the first organized basketball games Forrest watched in person were on March 30 and 31, 1899. He sat in the hayloft of a barn in Independence to watch Pete's YMCA team take on Kansas. Lanterns provided the light. Basketball had been introduced at KU that year by a physical education director named James Naismith, and the team was making its first extended road trip — two games in Independence and one at William Jewell College in nearby Liberty, Mo. There are no accounts of a meeting between Naismith and Allen at that time.

Independence won both games, 21-15 and 22-10. After the second, Samuel Emley, captain of the Jayhawks, presented a silk banner to the Independence captain that noted "championship of Missouri and Kansas."

It wasn't Naismith's first trip to Independence. In 1895, he was brought to town from Chicago to introduce basketball to the Independence Athletic Club, founded a year earlier. Naismith selected seven men from the club, all six feet or taller, and organized the first practice at the Independence Armory. For baskets, the team used kitchen chairs with the bottoms knocked out, suspended upside down on their end of the Armory, and a medicine ball until Naismith could have a basketball delivered from Chicago.

Forrest wasn't part of this team, but he watched Pete's games for the Modern Woodmen. In 1901, the team laid unofficial claim to the national championship by winning two of three games over a team from Fond du Lac, Wis., which had been touted as the nation's best team. The games were played at the Armory and drew 600 spectators each night.

Before Forrest could lose himself in athletics, he had to win some personal battles. He grew untamed as a teenager, and by his 17th birthday had gained a reputation as a smoker, beer drinker and general hell-raiser. A scar on his forehead came from a billiards cue during a pool hall fight.

"That was his lesson to us," said Ted O'Leary, who played for the Jayhawks from 1930-1932. "He'd tell us not to do what he did — drink and smoke. He said he was doing it when he was 14 and 15 before he realized it was his ruination and saw the light."

Sports helped Forrest mature. He eventually gave up smoking, drinking and fighting, and pledged to work himself into shape. Even his odd jobs as a teenager promoted strength. In the days before ice machines and with no natural ice in the area most of the year, Forrest was an ice man. In the summers he'd peddle ice that was brought in by train from northern destinations. The block was tossed into a yard with a shout of "Ice" and the customer had to hurry to wash it and get it inside.

During Christmas vacations, Forrest harvested ice from Dickinson Lake. Icemen drove a plow onto the lake and plowed the ice both ways but not cut all the way through. The cakes were broken off with poles by workmen who floated them to a chute where they were hauled to an icehouse and stored in sawdust.

Forrest remembered one particular customer who always gave him a tall glass of cool buttermilk in the summer. "You can well imagine that they always got extremely good weight from the ice-man!" Forrest wrote.

His real incentive for working, Forrest once said, was for cloth-ing. The Allen brothers had one set for school and had to change into low-cost clothes for the remainder of the day. Forrest earned money to buy clothes he could wear all day.

In the summer of 1902 Forrest went to work for the Kansas City Southern Railroad. He was sent to Texarkana, Texas, where he served as an axeman, pounding stakes up and down the line. He also talked about having worked in Texas lumber mills about the same time. The next year, Forrest returned to Independence and sought to improve his physical prowess by joining the Kansas City Athletic Club, then located in the Pepper building at Ninth and Locust streets. Forrest was the club's best basketball player, and in 1904 was named team captain.

By then, Pete had been at Kansas for two years and had de-veloped into one of the school's first all-around athletes. He played tackle on the football team, pitched for the baseball team and was a forward on Naismith's basketball team. Frequently, Forrest made the trip to Lawrence to watch his brother play.

There were no athletic scholarships then, and the Allens, living on their father's income as a produce salesman to grocery stores, couldn't afford the tuition. Pete Allen, a strapping 200 pounds, was given $300 on the sly by some Lawrence businessmen to attend Kan-sas. With no rule against freshman participation in the earliest days of competition Pete Allen played in the 1902 game against Missouri with a broken collarbone. It was the first KU game seen by William Allen, and the Allens later said their father's attitude about sports changed that day and he became a fan.

Pete Allen's KU career ended after two years. The businessmen who had bought his services didn't come through when Pete needed more money to repay some loans. Pete withdrew from school, played some minor-league baseball, became an assistant football coach at Central Missouri State, before finally settling into a long military career.

Forrest learned two valuable lessons from Pete's experiences. First, subsidizing athletes was risky business. "I'll never forget the bitterness it caused him and the education it gave me," Forrest wrote in 1938. "I would no more accept money for attending college than I would accept money for selling my vote."

The great harm in such arrangements, Forrest believed, was outside interests conflicting with team and school loyalty. The feeling was a basis for Forrest's early suspicions about gamblers infiltrating college basketball, which proved correct.

As a coach, Forrest preached purity. But as a player, there's reason to believe he, like others, didn't resist temptation. In 1907 he was supposed to play a game for the Modern Woodmen. On a Saturday night in February, a game had been arranged in Independence between the Independence team and the Kansas City Athletic Club, the two most prestigious teams in the area. But the Kansas City team backed out when it learned Forrest was going to play, claiming he was a professional. The Woodmen played against some Independence boys in attendance and ticket-holders got a refund.

The other lesson from Pete's experiences changed the course of Forrest's life and college basketball. More than any one factor, visits to his brother's games in Lawrence persuaded Forrest to attend Kansas. He liked the town, and in 1967 explained why he chose Kansas and not Missouri:

> "I came out there to see those games and naturally became interested in the University of Kansas. I noticed that Lawrence had wide, paved streets. Columbia had muddy streets. They hadn't lifted Missouri out of the mud then. The store fronts were different. Lawrence had all glass fronts and the merchants were very progressive in appearance, while Columbia had many of their store

*fronts boarded up. I could see the difference, and I
wanted to go to a place that was progressive."*

Forrest was college-bound even though he never received a high school diploma. Independence High School yearbooks of the time list all the graduating classes and the name Forrest Allen never appears.

In the fall of 1905, Forrest enrolled at Kansas and the Jayhawkers were excited. The basketball team was getting a star player, not because he was Pete Allen's brother, but because of an event that had happened in March of that year. By the time he arrived in Lawrence, the legend of Phog Allen had been born.

2

THE AMAZING ALLEN BROTHER

James Naismith's passion was physical fitness and, as he mentioned in many of his writings, "clean living through sport." Basketball was born at the Springfield, Mass., YMCA in December 1891 because Naismith needed an indoor physical activity for bored administrators in training.

As legend goes, Naismith borrowed ideas from several games to create basketball. Mostly, he recalled a childhood activity called "duck on a pond," where kids tried to knock a large rock off a boulder by throwing small rocks at it. Naismith also remembered that a rugby team he played for kept active in the winter by throwing rugby balls into a box.

It was a box Naismith was looking for when a janitor at the YMCA, Pop Stebbins, brought him two peach baskets. They were hung 10 feet from the floor because that was the height of the balcony. There were nine men on a side because 18 were in the class.

Quickly, basketball spread across the land. In March 1892, Naismith accompanied a YMCA team on tours of New York and Rhode Island. YMCA instructors took the game with them to other parts of the nation. High schools and colleges, men and women were soon playing the new game.

The first group to organize a national tournament was the Amateur Athletic Union, and it crowned a "national" champion in 1897. The event was held in New York City, and drew only local teams. But by 1901, the championship went to a YMCA team from Chicago.

No AAU champions were crowned in 1902 and 1903, but in 1904 a team from Buffalo, N.Y., — the Germans — gained national acclaim by capturing the first AAU Tournament that was national in scope. The Buffalo Germans had won the Pan-American championship in Buffalo, then ran the table in a round-robin event in conjunction with the Olympic Games in St. Louis. Teams from New York, Chicago, Los Angeles and St. Louis also competed.

The Germans, and the publicity they generated from their triumph, fascinated Forrest, whose Kansas City Athletic Club blew out Kansas 27-10 on Feb. 18, 1904. Forrest had recruited his brother Pete to the KCAC team called the Blue Diamonds. After the Olympic Games, Forrest, confident that the KCAC was the better team, wired a challenge to the Germans, which was promptly accepted.

Forrest assured the visitors their expenses would be paid, a critical condition. Except Forrest hadn't cleared the games with the KCAC, and he was told by club officers to call off the challenge for fear of losing money. But Forrest was in too deep and had to come up with a plan to suit all parties, thus laying the foundation for his promotional genius.

First, Forrest met with Louis Shouse, manager of Convention Hall in Kansas City, to arrange use of the building. In the early part of the century, Convention Hall was one of the nation's largest structures. It held presidential conventions for the Democrats in 1900 and the Republicans in 1928. It stood on the northeast corner of 13th and Central streets until 1935 when it was merged with Municipal Auditorium. With 5,000 seats, an unheard of capacity for basketball at the time, skeptics thought Forrest had lost his mind when he promised big crowds.

Forrest contacted his friends and acquaintances in the business world to solicit financial backing. Then he went back to the KCAC with this deal: He would bankroll a three-game series with the Germans on behalf of the club with the understanding that if the event lost money the club wouldn't be responsible. But if the event made money, Forrest and the backers would pocket the profit. The club

Kansas City's Convention Hall, called 'America's greatest auditorium', was the site of Phog Allen's KCAC team victory over the Buffalo Germans in 1905.

agreed, and the series that Forrest dubbed the "World's Championship of Basketball" was scheduled for March 1905.

He planted a story in the *Kansas City Star* on March 21, a week before the games started:

> *"No athletic event has ever taken place in Kansas City in which a world's championship has been at stake and the series is therefore very important to amateur athletic interests in Kansas City. In foot ball and other branches of sport, Western institutions are seldom able to arrange games with well-known Eastern teams because the latter hold themselves aloof and apparently have the impression that anything Western is wholly unworthy of their caliber. On account of this feeling, additional interest is given to the series of basket ball games that will be played in Convention Hall Monday, Tuesday and Wednesday nights. Should the Athletics win, the victory will mean the greatest boost amateur athletics has ever had in Kansas City."*

A week before the event Forrest claimed to have received from the AAU a written sanction of the games so that the winner could own the national champion title. The buildup continued. Forrest had set up preliminary games on the first two nights between the women's teams of two Kansas City high schools, Central and Manual. The series attracted the attention of Naismith, and some enterprising *Kansas City Star* reporter sought out the game's inventor for this opinion:

> *"The Convention Hall series will be among the most important ever played in the West. Kansas City men individually are star players without question. Whether or not they have trained down to teamwork, I don't know. The Buffalo men have had opportunities to meet more varieties of teams and have been in contact where there have been many styles of play. The tendency in the East is to play a more open game than in the West and the large size of the Convention half-court may give the Easterners an advantage. If Kansas City's teamwork is on par with its individual players I think the Olympic champions will have their work cut out for them."*

Naismith also noted that the series was drawing considerable interest on the KU campus and the school would have a large contingent at the games. Finally, the event arrived. Fans flocked to Convention Hall. In terms of basketball interest Kansas City, or any place west of St. Louis, had never seen anything like it. The KCAC and Forrest Allen were the talk of the town. The first game went to the Germans, 40-36. Naturally, the home side cried foul. The *Kansas City Star* carried this report:

> *"Never has such a well-played, exciting basket ball game been seen in Kansas City. A very questionable decision by Referee Dischinger was responsible for the four points that won the contest for the Buffalo team. Dischinger is a substitute for the Buffalo team. Had it not been for this one incident the game would have been clean throughout."*

One more triumph and the Germans could return to Buffalo with the championship banner and who knows what impact the loss would have in Kansas City or in Forrest Allen's life. But the second game went to the Blue Diamonds, 30-28, and this time the Germans complained. The report in the *Star*:

> *"Unfortunately in both of the games already played there were repeated squabbles over the decisions of the referees, and the defeated team left the field of battle each night feeling that the victory had not been justly*

won. This is not meant as a criticism of the refereeing of Wood last night. There can be no questioning his honesty. Wood has officiated capably too many games in this city to permit his methods to be questioned.

"Before the game last night the Buffalo captain insisted that fouls should be called only in important cases. It certainly was a strenuous performance as many of the players can testify. Strotz got a bloody nose and one eye inclined to blackness. Pete Allen's jaw is swollen considerably and the chests and muscles of all the players are spotted with black and blue marks, the result of collisions with the elbows of opposing players."

The matter of officiating had to be resolved or the Germans were going home. For the finale, the Germans requested that Naismith, who had watched the first two games, act as the referee for the deciding contest. He agreed and warned both sides beforehand that the game would be played by the rules — his rules — and Naismith deplored overly aggressive play.

Tom Shiras, Blue Diamonds teammate of Allen who played in several games that Naismith called around the area, remembered his officiating style in this 1937 account in the *Arkansas Gazette*:

"Games in which he officiated generally went off smoothly, for he knew the game, and the players took his word as final. His regulation uniform when acting as an official in a game was a dark, tight woolen jersey and a cap."

The KCAC won the rubber game in a blowout, 45-14. Under the rules of the day, one player shot all the team's free throws and Forrest buried 17 for the Blue Diamonds. Shiras continued with his story:

"After the Blue Diamonds won that series, 'Fog' was credited by many basket ball authorities as being the best center in the United States. Whether he was may be open to argument, but take it from an old teammate, he was a great center. Graceful, quick, with a rapid-fire brain, and eyes and a steady pair of arms that seldom failed him when he tossed a free throw."

Shooting free throws was essential for success then, and nobody was better than Forrest.

"Dad would have 90 percent of the team's scoring in those days because he was a great free-throw shooter," Bob Allen said. "He had a phenomenal ability to shoot a two-handed set shot. When we'd practice, he'd call for the ball and tell us it was just a matter of using the fingers. He'd stand about 35 feet from the basket and flick the damn thing in. People would say it was luck, then he'd say 'The hell it is,' and he'd do it again. Free-throw shooting was just so simple to him."

After the series, a smug *Star* reporter stuck it to the Germans:

"The Buffalo team will go back to its home town with many excuses for its defeat. They will say they were robbed and that the game was not played as they were accustomed to play it. However, there cannot be a doubt in the minds of the thousands of spectators who saw the game last night as to which is the superior organization. It was manifest, too, that the game was being played strictly in accordance with the rules as laid down by the AAU, the governing body in amateur athletics in America. Last night, Referee Naismith was very strict and the Buffaloes were penalized again and again."

Today, a referee wouldn't comment on the outcome of a game. But then, Naismith was no ordinary referee. In an interview with the *Star*, he said:

"If the Athletic club should play as good a game as it did Thursday evening, I do not doubt they could defeat the Buffalo team on any floor in the United States. While all the rules and regulations of a championship game many not have been complied with, I certainly consider the Athletics as 'top-notchers.' The result was a great surprise to me for basing my opinion on the past record of the Buffalo team, I thought that it could defeat the Athletic club with considerable ease. But such was not the case, for while the former had the game reduced to an exact science, the Kansas City team met them at every point and beat them on account of their height. They were able to make high passes which the visiting team could not block.

"Another thing I noticed was that the Buffalo players seemed to have lost confidence in their ability to

beat the Kansas City team and so did not play with as much energy as they might have. While my duties as an official prevented me from noticing the individual work of the players, I could not help but see the fine work of both teams. For myself, I would be delighted to have the Athletic club play the Buffalo team a return game for I have a reasonable degree of confidence in their ability to win again.

"I was much delighted with the interest shown in the game and personally I believe that the time is coming when basket ball will compete successfully with foot ball for popular favor.

"In inventing the game, I worked on the following theory as a basis for the game: Foot ball is rough because the players are tackled; the players are tackled because they run with the ball. So with this idea always in mind that the players must not run with the ball, I worked out the details of the game. Certainly basket ball has a great future before it if it is played in the same manner it was the other night."

A Naismith seal of approval. The Blue Diamonds said there would be no rematch because its members worked full time. A banquet was held the next week to honor the team. "Especial credit is due Manager Forest (sic) Allen, who was largely responsible for securing the games with the Buffalo team," reported the *Star*. "Mr. Allen has been a very energetic manager and has worked hard in the interest of the team."

Forrest would benefit from the outcome in many ways, not the least of which was financially. About 10,000 total paid for the three games with the building packed for the final. Before the series the KCAC membership was 410. By the end of the year it had jumped to more than 1,000, and the club was able to finance a new home.

In 1967, Forrest recalled the triumph as one of his most proud and lucrative moments.

"We played at old Convention Hall. We chopped a hole in the concrete floor, put a six by six there, wrapped some binding around it and that was the goal. The Germans were tricky. As we would run, they would kick the back of our heels to trip us. They would run along

*beside us and would hold our thumbs. We were the
greatest 'floor men' that you ever saw. We were on the
floor most of the time.*

*"For the first two games each team had a referee.
Six men on a side so to speak. We didn't like theirs and
they didn't like ours. For the final game we got Dr.
Naismith and U.S.G. Plank of Haskell and we beat them
45-14. We beat the tar out of them. We gave them six
hundred dollars and we made five thousand dollars."*

The event marked the high point in Forrest's athletic career. He was a hero and liked how it felt. He had created a basketball event, promoted it, won it, then cashed in on it. Even Naismith was impressed. After the series he approached Allen about attending Kansas. Because of Pete Allen, KU was Forrest's destination all along.

Although Pete and Forrest wouldn't be teammates at Kansas, they continued to play together as members of the Amazing Allen Brothers. The team that included all six brothers was formed in the fall of 1904, and as their success mounted they all took nicknames. Forrest, of course, was evolving into Phog. Harry was Pete, Homer was Ham, Elmer was Jammer, Richard was Dick, and Hubert, well, he just stayed Hubert.

The design on their dark jerseys was a white circle containing a letter A followed by a number 1 through 6. Homer, the oldest, wore A1, and his son, Homer Jr., the team's mascot, also wore A1. Elmer was A2, Pete, A3, Forrest A4, Hubert A5 and Richard, at age 13, was A6.

"We played for five years and lost only one game," Hubert Allen told the *Alton*, Ill., *Telegraph* in 1974. "Forrest was one of the best players I've ever seen play basketball. He was always the best all-around athlete of them all."

The loss Hubert Allen remembered came in February 1908 at Baker University in Baldwin, Kan. There was considerable interest in the game. Forrest served as the Baker coach that year, but that night he played with his brothers. According to Hubert Allen, the Baker floor had been waxed and polished "much like the front room of the governor's mansion." The Baker team had practiced on the slick surface, perfecting the art of sliding to a stop. Opponents would just have to adjust.

But Forrest knew the situation. They arrived with resin and before the game, with the powder on their shoes walked single file

The 'Amazing Allen Brothers' in 1904. From left are Harry (Pete), Forrest, Homer (Ham), Elmer (Jammer), Hubert (Hub) and Richard (Dick). Standing in front is Homer Jr. (Little Ham). (From the University of Kansas archives)

down the middle of the floor, end to end. When the Baker students caught on, they tried sweeping the resin from the floor, but that only spread the powder. Now, at least, the floor wouldn't be a factor. The contest was close throughout. Three times the game had to be stopped so that the floor could be cleared of debris. At some point during the action the scorer lost his pencil. In the end the teams agreed Baker had won by one point.

After that basketball season, the Allen team disbanded and Forrest's athletic career was about over at age 23. The brothers remained close-knit after childhood. Hubert and Elmer got into the automobile business in Kansas City; Pete and Dick were active in the military. Pete became a lieutenant in World War I and commanded a field artillery in the Argonne. Dick's life ended tragically in October 1932. He was serving as a aeronautical instructor for the Department of Commerce and was flying to his home in New Jersey to celebrate his birthday when his plane went into a tailspin. He bailed out but his parachute didn't open.

But brotherly love did not overcome the Allens when, having lost their mother in 1904, their father passed away in 1937. Business hadn't been good for most, and when bills came due on nursing home care and funeral arrangements, Forrest resented paying more than his share and scolded his brothers. In letters to Pete, Hubert and Elmer, he said:

"Life is a paradox, isn't it, boys. We profess to care for the living, but when somebody passes away that is dear to you, cocktail parties, vacations, classification clubs and some other things, can prevent a son from taking care of the obligations of a father. It does not give me pleasure to say these things. The fourth son (Forrest), who has paid four times as much as any one of the other sons, has three or four times as many dependents as any of the others who cannot pay or do not pay . . . Some boys may not be able to pay all, but a dollar a week up to $5 a week would not be more than the cocktail parties that are so necessary to keep contact with friends, rather than to pay bills that would make me ashamed of myself if I did not at least pay something."

Forrest was a stickler for fiscal responsibility. As a coach he scolded players for late loan payments. When he was involved in an auto accident near Tonganoxie, Kan., in 1928, the damage to his car was only $20, well within his means. But the accident was the other driver's fault and he wasn't paying. Forrest hired a lawyer not to prosecute the offender, but to make sure he paid his bill.

As the years passed, Phog had less and less contact with his brothers. However, when he needed some automobile advice, which was often, Phog would stop by his brothers' shop in Kansas City. Hubert was the only surviving brother when Phog died in 1974.

3

HERE A COACH, THERE A COACH

By the beginning of the school year in 1905, Forrest Allen was one of the most popular sports figures in Kansas City, and his appearance at the University of Kansas was big news. On Oct. 18, the school newspaper, the *University Daily Kansan*, heralded his arrival like it had no other athlete:

> *"Forrest Allen made his first appearance at basket-ball in the gymnasium Thursday evening. The ceiling was too low for him to show how well he could throw long goals, but he gave the men some good ideas of how to get into the game. Allen will be able to play in the games in this year's schedule, and will make a strong addition to the team. He is one of the world's champions and is said to be the best goal thrower in the world."*

Forrest enrolled two months before his 20th birthday with the intention of becoming a lawyer, perhaps influenced by his huckster arrangement of the KCAC-Buffalo Germans series. But athletics was his main interest. Before basketball, Forrest played on the freshman football team. His season was cut short by a back injury, which ended up bothering him for the rest of the year and eventually encouraged him to switch career choices from law to medicine.

Around this time Forrest started appearing in print as "Fog" Allen, although the nickname hadn't gotten back to Kansas City and Independence. Newspapers there continued to call him Forrest. It would be a couple more years before the nickname assumed its popular spelling and universal appeal.

For the 1905-06 school year, Kansas had agreed to use the eligibility rules of the Chicago Conference, the forerunner to the Big Ten. Freshmen could not play during the first semester, so Phog and another promising newcomer, Tommy Johnson, formed the nucleus of the school's first freshman team. Phog, who played forward, was elected manager of the seven-member rookie team, which took one of three games from the varsity squad that winter.

Because there was no national body to govern college athletics then, Phog was free to pursue other basketball interests while attending Kansas, and pursue he did. Before he suited up for the Jayhawks varsity team, Phog played in five games for the KCAC and also suited up for the Modern Woodmen team of Independence during the Christmas holidays. Before the second semester started, he also officiated games, including a contest between the Jayhawks and Chilocco Indians.

On Feb. 8, 1906, Phog played his first game for the Kansas varsity in a 40-10 victory over the Wyandotte Athletic Club. He also played the next day in a 43-16 triumph over the Independence Athletic Club. Phog was used only in the second half of both games. His first starting role came on Feb. 12 against Nebraska at Lincoln, and Phog displayed his flair for the dramatic. He scored 23 points in a 37-17 victory. From then on, Phog was a starter, and he saved his best game for last. In a 60-13 triumph over the school known today as Emporia State, Phog scored 26, a school record that stood until 1915.

The final two games of the season were in Lawrence, and they were only the second and third home games of the season. Kansas' home was in the basement of Snow Hall, on a floor that measured 36 feet wide by 84 feet long. A support post on the court made for hard picks. In the first few years of the program, the distance from floor to ceiling was 11 feet. Naismith discovered unused space below the floor and eventually had it dropped five feet. The team also played games at a roller skating rink and two YMCA buildings before a new gymnasium was constructed.

As director of physical education, Naismith always wanted a new building not just for basketball but for his wrestling, fencing and

Forrest Allen was very proud of his affiliation with the Kansas City Athletic Club. Here he poses in 1906 in his KCAC sweater. (From the University of Kansas archives)

gymnastics classes. The 1905-06 basketball season, with the enthusiasm created by the freshman star, sealed the deal. Phog had become such an attraction, the bleachers in Snow Hall for those final two games were "taxed to the limit" reported the *Kansan*.

Phog had become so important to the Jayhawks that a final game against Baker, billed as the "championship of Kansas" was called off when Allen came up with an injured hand. Oddly enough, in the Kansas team photograph of 1906, eight players are wearing dark, sleeveless T-shirts with a large "K" embroidered on the front. Phog, almost defiantly, is wearing his KCAC top, white with a "KC" inside a diamond on the front.

The season was Kansas' most successful to date. The Jayhawks finished 12-7; they had never won more than seven games in a year, and Phog, had he stayed longer than his freshman season, may have evolved into one of the game's greatest players. But the 1905-06 school year was the extent of his life as a Kansas student.

That spring, Phog played for the baseball team as an infielder and pitcher. For at least one summer before he attended Kansas, he was a standout pitcher on a semipro team in Eureka, Kan.

Not only had Phog played for two basketball teams and officiated during the year, he had started his coaching career. In December
1905, Phog took a trip to Baker to speak to school officials about a
job. That somebody could get hired as a coach seemed absurd to
Naismith, and Phog, in many speeches and articles, loved telling the
story of when Naismith broke the news:

NAISMITH: I've got a good joke on you, you bloody beggar.
They wanted you to coach basketball down at Baker.

ALLEN: What's so funny about that?

NAISMITH: Why, you can't coach basketball. You just play it.

ALLEN: Well, you certainly can coach free-throw shooting.
And you can teach the boys to pass at angles and run in curves. You
can show them how to arch their shots. And pivot toward the sideline, instead of into the court where a guard can get the ball.

Phog said Naismith just shook his head. "I don't think it changed
his mind," Phog used to tell audiences. "But I thought a coach was
necessary if the game was going to grow. By this token, you can see
how many basketball coaches today are obtaining money under false
pretenses."

But did the conversation really occur? In 1941, Phog received a
letter from a Longview, Wash., jeweler who reminded the coach he
was the one responsible for getting him to Baker. Wilbur Arnett was
president of the student council and a member of the basketball team
in the fall of 1905. He knew Baker had good players who needed
instruction, so he, along with the school's faculty adviser, first sought
a coach at Haskell College. No luck there. The search continued in
Kansas City to find a certain member of the Kansas City Blues baseball team. But the person was out of town. While in Kansas City, the
Baker delegation heard about Forrest Allen of Independence, the guy
who had beaten the Buffalo Germans.

"We found you, as I remember, just before lunch at the grocery
store," Arnett wrote. "We went to lunch together and had a good steak
and put the proposition up to you and you agreed to come up to Baker
two nights a week in the fall of '05. Then in the fall of '06 you came up
and stayed all season. That's how it started. Naturally, I have always
followed your career with a good bit of interest, possibly more than anyone else since I was one of the two who got you started."

Phog replied: "Yes, I do now remember very clearly how you
and (faculty advisor) Dr. Parmenter came to Independence, Missouri,

and how we went together to a restaurant and had a fine steak and a fine visit."

Which all would have made for a fine story, except apparently it wasn't how Phog wanted to remember his introduction to coaching. The meeting in Independence was never mentioned in any biographical sketch. The Naismith conversation made for a better anecdote.

What is known is that over the next four years, Phog was a very busy man. In that time he coached at three colleges, a high school, held at least two jobs outside of basketball, played for his brothers' basketball team, got married and maintained his residence in Independence. In this period, the Allens moved from N. Union to 619 Delaware, and, in 1908, Phog moved again, to 121 Alton.

The store where the Baker fellows found Phog was his father's Haines-Allen Grocery Co. at 108 West Maple. Phog worked there as a clerk. In 1910, Phog is listed in the city directory as a deputy county assessor. He never got involved with the newest family venture, Allen Motor Car Company, which sold and repaired Studebakers. Four brothers — Elmer, Pete, Homer and Hubert — had jobs there.

The Jayhawks were crushed when Phog didn't return to play in 1906. During a team meeting in Naismith's office after his freshman season, Phog had been unanimously chosen captain. "He is a steady, consistent player who can be depended upon to do all that is possible for the best interests of the team and the university," reported the *Kansan*.

What Phog couldn't do was pay his bills. Living expenses were too great, and, hey, he wasn't a football star like his brother. Alumni weren't interested in supporting star basketball players then so Phog dropped out for work. Baker offered him room, board and a small stipend.

Phog never stopped working. His next coaching duty came at his high school. It was the second year of football at Independence High in 1907. Phog poses prominently in the team photograph, standing in coat and tie above the 10-member squad that included his youngest brother, Dick, who was listed as a quarterback. The team finished 3-4-1. Phog also coached the first Independence basketball team that year, but the school yearbook doesn't include him on the roster or in the team photograph. The team finished with a 5-1 record including several blowouts.

Between coaching stints, Phog found time to get married. He and Bessie Milton had known each other since childhood and attended the same church. The Miltons lived on 420 acres known as Sunnyside Farm on Lee's Summit Road. In 1907 Bessie was working in Blue Springs, when Phog made quite an impression.

The train usually didn't stop in Blue Springs, but it did on this December day. "A rosy-cheeked blond male of 21 disembarked, and all business stopped," Bessie Allen told the *Topeka Daily Capital* in 1955. "Little did the stolid agrarian folk know then or now how beautiful the law of love can make the hard stiff lines of daily life."

On June 25, 1908, Forrest Allen and Bessie Milton were married on the Milton Farm and thus began one of the greatest supporting roles in the history of coaches wives. Bessie bore six children — Mary and Forrest Jr. came before Phog started his coaching career in earnest — and she helped raise hundreds of Kansas basketball players.

"She tutored all kinds of athletes," Bob Allen said. "English was her strong suit, but she also taught algebra, trig, you name it. I remember growing up, seeing all the boys come over with their books, sitting in our sun room and studying. And if the fellows had girl problems, they'd come to mom with those."

A typical winter day in 1907 found Phog working as a grocery store clerk until midafternoon, when he'd coach the high school team or catch a train to Baldwin for a Baker game or practice. Although he no longer was connected with Kansas as a player, Phog didn't disappear from the scene. At least twice, he traveled from Baldwin to Lawrence after a Baker practice to work with the Jayhawks, who finished 7-8 in Naismith's final year as coach.

On Feb. 14, 1907, Phog's Baker boys knocked off Naismith's Jayhawks 39-24. Afterward, Allen praised the Kansas team, but it was apparent then that Naismith's life was crammed with activities and coaching basketball wasn't a priority.

"The great difficulties in developing a team are the lack of suitable quarters in which to train and the lack of a coach," reported the *Kansan*. "Dr. James Naismith, the inventor of the game, is so busy with his work as athletic director that he rarely finds time to give the men thorough training."

Naismith took care of both problems after the 1907 season. He stepped down as the basketball coach and oversaw the completion of a new gym. To his list of duties that year Naismith had been named full-time professor, and, thanks to his insistence, had more space to teach classes. Robinson Hall was built to look like the Springfield, Mass., YMCA, where Naismith had invented basketball. The $100,000 structure was a palace by turn-of-the-century standards. There were 1,500 lockers for men and women in the basement, a swimming pool, a training area for the football team, and most importantly, a regulation-sized basketball floor and 3,000 seats for spectators. No finer facility existed west of the Mississippi River.

Now Kansas needed a coach, and the athletic department was being run by a person who believed coaches weren't necessary. But sports were becoming more important on campus. On Jan. 12, 1907, Kansas joined Missouri, Nebraska, Iowa and Washington University of St. Louis in forming the Missouri Valley Conference. The 1907-1908 schedule included six games designated as league contests. Naismith, the person mostly responsible for the new building and the school's representative at the meeting in Kansas City where the new league was formed, never coached a game in Robinson Hall or in the Missouri Valley Conference. The gym was dedicated during the 1907 commencement, and the Jayhawks opened the floor for competition on Dec. 13, beating Ottawa 66-22 under their new coach, Phog Allen.

Playing its most ambitious schedule to date, Kansas rolled to an 18-6 record and the first Missouri Valley championship at 6-0. For the third and final year, Phog also coached Baker and guided the team to a 13-6 record. His three-year Baker career ended with a 45-9 record. A frequent visitor to Phog's Baker games was Baldwin resident Luther "Dummy" Taylor, a deaf-mute pitcher for the New York Giants.

Was Phog college basketball's first paid coach when Baker hired him in 1906? Perhaps. Yale, a leader in college sports then, hired its first basketball coach in 1907. Walter "Doc" Meanwell, who would have a major impact on Phog's career, started at Wisconsin in 1911. It seems plausible that Phog was the first person paid to coach college basketball, but there's no way to know for certain. We do know Phog had one of the first great seasons ever. The 1908-1909 team won its first 19 games and finished 25-3. Its 8-2 conference record again was best in the Missouri Valley.

Phog's record at other schools in this period was listed inaccurately throughout his life, which caused an adjustment in his career record long after his death. Good train service was said to have allowed Phog to coach three teams in one season — Kansas, Baker and Haskell — in 1908-09. But a Baker history professor later determined that Phog's career at his school was over by then.

Phog did coach Haskell, a school for Indians, that season and had one of his most successful teams. Haskell finished 27-5, and 19 of those triumphs came during a 24-game road tour. Phog figured the team not only labored under the disadvantage of performing before hostile crowds, but there weren't too many Indian officials either.

"Being faced with the problem of all white man officials I wanted to build morale among my red men players and friends," Phog wrote in 1947 of a trip to Detroit. "I said, 'Boys, I want you to have confidence in the white man official. He wouldn't steal a ballgame even if he did steal your land.' The Indians got a big wallop out of this. Now we were getting on common ground."

Road games were a rule for Haskell. The home floor included six large steel supports on the court. Before he coached them, Phog watched a game in which players would grab the post and swing off at an angle to elude defenders and receive a pass. The court also was surrounded with chicken wire. Haskell players wouldn't shoot at the basket but at a strategic point on the wire and the ball would fall directly into the basket.

With the 1908-09 season, the first part of Phog's coaching life had drawn to a close. Although nobody was counting at the time, his college coaching record stood at 115-23. Whether or not others were getting paid to coach somewhere else, it is doubtful anybody had a record as good. Phog knew he could make a living in athletics on the sidelines. But he also understood that at a time when most sports were played without protective gear and injuries were frequent that the most successful teams would be the ones that kept its best players healthy.

The point was driven home to Phog in a 1910 football game that pitted Kansas and Missouri. The Jayhawks' star was Tommy Johnson, Phog's freshman teammate. "He was clean as a hound's tooth," Phog wrote in 1947. "Tommy's habits were exemplary. Customary vices, such as late hours, smoking and wasting time were not his. To his coaches, he was a story book athlete — almost too good to be true."

In the final game of his career, Johnson was sandwiched between two Missouri defenders and his kidney ruptured. Two years to the day later, Johnson died. Phog took the news hard. He counted

Johnson among his friends and even in his later years called Johnson the school's greatest all-around athlete.

Knowing how to treat injured athletes would give a coach an advantage not many enjoyed. Phog realized this after his second year at Kansas. It was his last for a while because Phog went back to school, this time to become a better coach. His osteopathy training would serve him — and countless others — well.

4

MENDING FRIENDS AND FOES

To most everyone he was known as Phog Allen. To his players, he was Doc, as in doctor of osteopathy.

In 1910, after three years of bouncing around Kansas, Baker and Haskell, Phog left the coaching profession and entered the Central College of Osteopathy in Kansas City. There were several motivating factors for this career decision. A back injury — a bad sacroiliac sprain, Phog called it — while playing on the Kansas freshman football team in 1905 that never healed properly, and in 1965 Phog revealed to KU publicist Don Pierce that he was banged up during the 1905 series against the Buffalo Germans.

"I came out of the series with a cracked elbow and a lame back. I went to an M.D. who treated me for stomach and liver trouble and put glasses on me. But I didn't get any better and couldn't sleep. The mattresses were bad enough in those days and my back hurt all the time. I finally saw an osteopath and he cured my back in

one treatment. I'd been thinking about coaching then, and had been helping out with high school and church teams. That quick cure impressed me that if I did coach, here was a way to keep my boys in the lineup. So I decided to study osteopathy. I won more games on the training table than I ever won on the athletic field — by being able to mend players and get them back in shape."

Phog studied osteopathy for three years at the Central College, located at 729 Troost Avenue. The school was established in 1903 by Dr. George Moffett and had a faculty of 18 when Phog enrolled. At the time, it wasn't listed among medical schools in Kansas City.

Before Phog ever worked on any of his own players, he was treating high school kids in Kansas City. In 1910, one of the greatest all-around athletes at Central High was ailing. Phog went to work on Casey Stengel, who enjoyed a solid career as a player and as a New York Yankees manager rates as one of the greatest in baseball history. Stengel was the first but not the only Yankee that Allen treated. He wasn't even the only Yankees manager who received Allen's care. As a Lawrence High wide receiver in the late 1930s, Ralph Houk injured a shoulder, but Phog fixed him up in time to play a game after the coach had given up hope of his return.

In a time when newspapers carried advertisements about miracle concoctions, usually bottled potions that were about half alcohol or opium to cure everything from rheumatism to bladder disorders, Phog offered injured athletes an alternative. And whether or not his diagnosis was correct, he always sounded sure of himself, as he did in 1937:

"The way you describe it, I would not guess that it's the small growth on the point of the shoulder that is causing the trouble, but rather it is due to a strain on the neck and shoulder muscles which causes this pain, and in back of that is some predisposing cause like a wrench to the shoulder or neck muscles, and if you will go up about the middle of the neck on the same side on which her shoulder is paining her and exert some fairly deep pressure, I think you will find that there will be much more extreme pain on that side than the other."

Then Phog supplied an equally long cure, complete with massage therapy techniques, a liniment recommendation and a suggestion to forego surgery. This wasn't even a personal checkup but a response to a letter describing the problem.

After Phog completed osteopathy school in 1912 and accepted a job as coach and athletic administrator at Central Missouri State, word of this sports injury healer spread. In 1916, Phog answered a call to mend athletes at the University of Illinois. The school had heard of Phog from Kansas assistant football coach Potsy Clark, who had played quarterback at Illinois. The *Champaign, Ill., Daily News* chronicled the visit and you might recognize one of the patients.

"Dr. F.C. Allen, miracle man. At least that's the way 35 athletes at the University, formerly more or less injured, look at him. Dr. Allen comes from Warrensburg, Mo., where he is athletic director of Missouri State Normal College, and his specialties are putting dislocated bones back in place, easing strained tendons and reducing sprains on the double quick. That, in short, is what he did for the 35 injured performers.

"Here are a few of the remarkable cures he effected in an afternoon's treatment, working on several of the men but a few moments:

"Reduced a sprained ankle for Capt. Ham Alwood of the basketball team. Alwood could barely walk on the ankle Monday morning, but played against Millikin that night after Allen had worked on him.

"Put a dislocated knee back into place . . .Gave E.T. Rundquist, football tackle, full use of his left arm . . . Snapped a dislocated bone back into place for L.L. Charpier, football guard . . .Massaged the ankle of Clarence Applegran, football star, so that he was able to walk on it . . .Changed the position of George Halas' ankle bones so that he was able to play basketball the same night.

" 'I like to coach football and fix the fellows up,' said the miracle man. 'I believe I could make money practicing in some big city, but I wouldn't leave my position in Warrensburg for anything.' "

No doubt Phog liked that "miracle man" title. The clipping from Champaign became part of his files. Stengel, Houk and Halas of the

Chicago Bears found fame as coaches, but Phog, besides treating his own players, took on several professional athletes and even some rivals. In 1927, Kansas State shipped star halfback Karl Enns to Lawrence to have Phog treat him for a knee injury. The Aggies were preparing for a big game with Nebraska and Phog got Enns ready to play.

Another request from Kansas State came in a 1938 letter from football coach Wesley Fry. Perturbed with his team's off-season eating habits, Fry asked Phog for some training table recommendations. He figured he'd get a pamphlet, but instead, Phog returned a three-page, single-spaced typewritten letter full of dietary information.

Usually, an athlete from another school visited Phog to quickly patch up a wound and return to action immediately. That wasn't the case with Missouri quarterback Phil Snowden. In 1957, Snowden, the Tigers' sophomore starting quarterback in the only season of coach Frank Broyles, had such pain in his right shoulder that he couldn't lift his arm above his head. He could hardly throw a pass during the final third of the season and a promising year ended with three straight losses and Snowden's shoulder shot full of cortisone. That spring, Missouri athletic director and former coaching great Don Faurot asked Phog to see Snowden. Phog had been retired from coaching for two years and had opened an osteopathic practice when Snowden saw him for the first time in April 1958.

"I'd been to several doctors, specialists, osteopaths. I'd had my shoulder probed," Snowden said. "I was to the point where I'd go anywhere or see anyone about it."

Within five minutes of the visit, Phog had located the problem. The pain was in the shoulder but the problem was a muscle in Snowden's back. Phog pressed it. "I nearly jumped through the roof," Snowden said. "Everybody else I had seen was treating me up high. Phog found the problem and it was lower. I went home from the visit and was throwing the ball like a bullet from 20 and 30 yards."

For the next two years, Snowden visited Phog's office 25-30 times. When he returned to Missouri for his junior season, Snowden showed Tigers trainer Fred Wappel how Phog had treated him and those treatments continued in Columbia. Phog had done Kansas no favors. In 1958, the Jayhawks and Missouri tied 13-13, and in 1959, Snowden helped the Tigers secure an Orange Bowl berth with a 13-9 triumph over the Jayhawks in Lawrence.

"If I hadn't seen Phog after my sophomore season I may have been through as a player," said Snowden, who served as a Missouri

Phog Allen (left) talks with New York Yankees slugger Johnny Mize after treating Mize for a shoulder ailment in 1950. After the treatment, Mize hit 25 home runs over the final 90 games of the season. (From the University of Kansas archives)

state representative from 1976-1984. "No question Phog Allen saved my career as an athlete. Maybe somebody else eventually would have found the problem, but Phog did find it."

The most celebrated rehabilitation case occurred in 1950, when the season appeared lost for Yankees first baseman Johnny Mize with a shoulder injury. Mize said he never received proper treatment two years earlier when he dove to first base for a tag out.

By 1950, Mize couldn't lift his arm above his shoulder, and, like many broken down ballplayers of the day, he was shipped off to the minor league. Fortunately for Mize, the Yankees' top farm club was the Kansas City Blues. Peake Carroll — a *Kansas City Post-Journal* sportswriter, the Blues general manager, favorite basketball official of Phog's and his friend — made the recommendation and for two months, Mize regularly visited Lawrence.

On June 21, after six workouts with Phog, Mize was recalled by the Yankees and over the final 90 games of the season hit 25 home runs with 72 RBIs. Mize had said before the treatments that his hitting wasn't affected by the injury. But in the days before the designated hitter, Mize wasn't going to hit unless he played in the field, and he gave Allen all the credit for his recovery.

"I sure wouldn't be here if I couldn't throw and give Dr. Allen complete credit for enabling me to throw," Mize told the *Topeka Daily Capital*. "When I started going to Dr. Allen I couldn't throw at all. I saw him several times. I don't know what it was in my shoulder that kept me from throwing and nobody else seemed to. But Dr. Allen did. Whatever it was, he found it. He's quite a swell guy. I think he's one of the finest men I ever knew."

Mize said he was throwing again after one visit with Phog. His batting average in the American Association, where the Blues played, improved from .220 early in the season to .298 when he was recalled. The Yankees, with Stengel as the manager and Houk on the team, went on to win the second of five straight World Series. The 1950 American League race was close, with New York winning the pennant by three games over Detroit and four over Boston, and Mize's play helped put the Yankees on top. It certainly prolonged Mize's Hall of Fame career. He remained in the majors for three more seasons, mostly as a pinch hitter, and was named MVP of the 1952 World Series.

National attention focused on Phog and his treatments that summer. When asked what other ballplayers he'd mended, Phog fessed up to several major-leaguers, most notably Hall of Fame pitcher Grover Cleveland Alexander.

But Phog branched out to other pro sports. While teaching during the summer of 1929 at the Springfield, Mass., YMCA, Phog came across Boston Bruins defenseman Eddie Shore, a four-time National Hockey League MVP and Hall of Fame member. An injured knee forced Shore to consider retirement. Phog fixed him up, prolonged his career and Shore claimed Phog was responsible for an extra $40,000 in earnings. Shore became owner of a minor-league team and directed injured players to Phog.

Not all sore-armed ballplayers were healed. In 1950, Yankees pitcher Joe Page lost his fastball and his job. He had been an outstanding reliever, winning and saving a game each in the World Series triumphs of 1947 and 1949. When spring training ended in 1951, Page was shipped to Kansas City, and Phog was waiting. But even after a dozen visits, Page never fully recovered. He pitched nine more innings in the major leagues.

Phog Allen around 1929. (From the University of Kansas archives)

Phog, rarely shy with information about his coaching career, revealed little about the pros he treated. And he never charged them for his service. "I have them come to me from all over the United States but we don't publicize that," Phog wrote in 1940.

There was a good reason. Phog often encountered criticism from the university's medical school. Some doctors thought it embarrassed Kansas to have Phog, not a medical doctor, treat athletes. Although Phog was a licensed osteopathic physician for nearly six decades he didn't allow himself to be listed in a national directory for osteopaths until 1958, two years after he retired. He also declined speaking engagements to schools and groups of osteopaths.

"Seems too bad that in a country like ours, a person cannot take part in the activities of his own profession without first wondering what the effect would be on the dominant school," said Earl Reed, secretary of the Kansas Board of Osteopathic Examination and Registration in 1941. "I have often thought how difficult it must be for you to stay in the middle of the road and keep our opposition (the medical society) satisfied."

Phog scolded the media when reporters mentioned his practice. He wrote to the *Kansas City Star* in 1940:

"Personally, I'm not a bit ashamed of it. In fact, I believe I have been able to do a lot of things for suffering humanity that some of the other fellows perhaps might not be able to do. But the fact remains that we have a medical school here in the University, and some of them take it that I am trying to boost something against the fair practice of medicine. So I will appreciate it if you will not mention those things on account of my good medical friends who take the wrong slant on this procedure."

Bob Allen, who became a surgeon, was proud of his father's practice. "The medical people at Kansas didn't fully understand how much he was helping the athletes," Allen said. "The athletes swore by him and the Kansas medical people swore at him."

When it came to treatments, Phog's players came first, and to a man, they're convinced his medical attention not only helped them win games but formed a coach-player bond few teams enjoy.

"This wouldn't happen today," Ted O'Leary said. "But we had a game against Kansas State; it was the first time I started. Eldon Auker, he went on to pitch in the major leagues, played for them. We collided and I split open my finger. I got taped up and continued playing. At home that night, about 10:30, somebody knocked on the door. It was Doc. He told me to get a bucket of water, and he stayed with me while I soaked my hands in epsom salts. I can't imagine a current coach doing that for one of his players."

Phog treated sprained ankles, sore knees, strains, pulls, charley horses, just about anything less serious than a broken bone. He was a great believer in massage, and kept a rubdown table at his office and in his home. The Jayhawks took a table to road games, always carried by the sophomores.

"In 1923, I badly sprained both wrists in a game at Iowa State," Paul Endacott said. "We were playing four games in five days, and the last one was against Missouri for the championship. Twice, he took me to his home and fixed me up."

Players had to get their adjustments. Phog would push, pull, rub and crack bones for hours after practice.

Phog's reputation for treating injuries spread in the 1920s with the publication of his first book, *My Basket-Ball Bible*. Besides covering the usual topics in a how-to-coach manual, Phog devoted considerable space to sports medicine. He covered everything from how to raise depressed ribs to treatment for hemorrhoids.

The *Bible* wasn't the first basketball methods book but it was the most comprehensive, and by the time it was out of print, about 10 years after its 1924 completion, it had sold more than 15,000 copies, remarkable for a sports book that catered mainly to other coaches. Besides tactics, Phog received bags of letters from high school coaches wanting information on such topics as diet, exercise, sleep and coaching psychology.

Phog usually gave a short response in the specific topic and then offered a more expansive answer with the purchase of his book for $4, which included postage and an autograph.

Players from the 1920s and 1950s say Phog's medical and social advice held up through the years. Phog produced three books in 23 years — the *Bible, Better Basketball* and *Coach Phog Allen's Sports Stories*. The instructions were the same in each:

Diet: "A young athlete should watch for the three Bs. Eat baked, broiled and boiled food. A well-dressed potato wears his jacket to dinner. Milk, one or two quarts a day, and fruit juices need to be included in the diet for growing athletes. Bread is still the staff of life. Eat what you want after you've eaten what you should. Water is a must for us all. Drink six glasses a day between meals. Water is needed for flushing the system. If urine is dark and cloudy, add to the amount of your drinking water."

Phog believed the perfect food, one his players couldn't eat enough of, was the orange. Every team meal included an orange. Snacks on long train trips usually consisted of oranges and apples.

Smoking: "Unethical physicians and prominent athletes who endorse cigarettes for pay are trafficking in the health of American boys. What a cheap price are these thirty pieces of silver when compared to the misery that their endorsement of cigarettes may bring!"

Personal appearance and decorum: "Our boys were resting between halves (of a 1940 game against Fordham in Madison Square

Garden.) In my position as coach I knew they were expecting any instructions to help them turn their losing tide to victory. I was beginning my talk when I looked down their line of earnest faces and saw one of the fellows picking or gouging his nose. Perhaps because he repelled me, or because I saw him losing in his bigger game for success outside in business and society I shifted my intended remarks to a talk about other possible defeats in life, about making too many fouls in business and society.

"While I told these boys that they could lose in life's big game by pulling too many faux pas that might indicate a lack of good breeding, five of our precious ten minutes had passed."

Sleep: "Don't sleep with your worries. Or you will awaken more tired than when you went to bed. Pied Piper them away either by cant or chant. But don't put them to bed down in your subconscious stratum or they might get into your dreams and will wear you out with nightmares."

Phog also offered the advice at coaching schools and clinics that kept him on the move throughout the summers in the 1920s and 1930s. Through these events, Phog became good friends with legendary football coaches Knute Rockne, Amos Alonzo Stagg and Pop Warner. He upstaged Warner at a 1927 school in Superior, Wis., not with his coaching ideas but his lectures on treating injuries.

"Dr. Forrest Allen's wonderful personality has taken a strong hold on the coaches attending the school here," the *Pittsburgh Press* reported from a local coach attending the meeting. "He has many new and original ideas which are of much importance and interest to men who are interested in the trainer's end of the game in football and basketball."

So overwhelmed by the interest in training, especially by high school coaches, Phog attempted to cash in. In 1938, he tried to establish with a friend who worked in the publicity office at Wittenberg College in Ohio, a school for coaches that emphasized treating injuries. Phog believed he could get 100 coaches at $15 a head. But Wittenberg officials wouldn't go along.

Phog was confident such a school would work because, by 1940, he had sent about as many former students into athletic training at major schools as he had coaches: Elwyn Dees at Pittsburgh and later Nebraska, Roland Logan with the Boston Red Sox then Army, Jimmy Cox at Harvard, Milton Kelly at Texas, who developed the popular Kelly knee pad in the 1930s, and Dean Nesmith at Kansas.

Phog sucks down another quart of water during a game. Trainer Dean Nesmith (left) made sure Phog had at least six quarts of water for each game. Phog drank the water to keep his larnyx clear. (Photo by Rich Clarkson)

Nesmith came to Kansas as a football player in 1932 and remained until he retired in 1984. He became a confidant of Phog, often rooming with the coach on road trips. Nesmith knew he had found a friend from his initial meeting soon after he arrived in the heart of the Depression.

On a cold, winter day, Allen spotted the freshman Nesmith on campus without a coat. Nesmith said he couldn't afford one. Phog made a call, sent Nesmith to Ober's Clothing Store in downtown Lawrence where he picked up the $15 coat. Not a gift, mind you. Phog had Nesmith pay him 50 cents a month until it was paid off. Nesmith didn't miss a payment, and that impressed Phog.

Phog hired Nesmith as a trainer in 1938, and while he continued to oversee the health of his players, Phog soon turned over his training duties to Nesmith. In his early years, Nesmith played an important role on the Kansas bench. Before 1948, teams couldn't come to the bench during timeouts and the coach couldn't go on the floor. But the trainer could. Phog would send in instructions with Nesmith.

Nesmith also took over many administrative duties, including travel agent, and another critical job. He kept Phog's glass water bottles full during games, and Phog downed at least six quarts a night to keep his larynx cleared.

But before Nesmith, Phog took care of all injuries from the time he became a coach in 1912. It was that ability that made him an attractive candidate to become a coach for all seasons at Central Missouri State, where Phog's coaching career began in earnest.

5

NORMAL PHOG

For $1,600 a year, Phog became Normal.

In 1912, Missouri State Normal School, District No. 2, in Warrensburg, sought a physical education director and coach. Phog had just received the only degree of his life, from osteopathy school, in June. The next month, he accepted the position and started on September 1 at the school known today as Central Missouri State University.

Phog was familiar with Warrensburg. Bessie attended the school for two years and received a teaching certificate in 1907. Two years earlier, Phog arrived with the Company F of Independence team (while attending Kansas) that provided the opposition for the first game in Central Missouri's hoop history. Phog served as the referee. As a coach, his Kansas and Haskell teams of 1909 had played against the Normals at Warrensburg. Kansas won, Haskell lost.

As basketball coach at Central Missouri for seven years his winning percentage was much higher, with victories in more than two-thirds of the games. He also coached football and baseball. Phog was hired just as Central Missouri joined the newly formed Missouri Intercollegiate Athletic Association, then got the school booted out of the league two years later when allegations of cheating surfaced.

Phog never lived a dull moment at Central Missouri, on or off the field. His winning teams created resentment. One opponent accused him of poisoning the drinking water and creating a diarrhea epidemic. Also, he was involved in a messy lawsuit, signed a con-

Phog, standing in the rear in the center of the photo and wearing his Kansas sweater, with his 1913 Warrensburg Normals. The team won the Missouri Collegiate championship. (Photo courtesy Central Missouri State University archives)

tract to coach elsewhere only to have it voided, and basically was told his coaching services were no longer needed. Phog never lived anywhere he didn't kick up a fuss or kick the stuffing out of opponents, and Warrensburg was no exception.

"Athletic prospects took a great boom when Dr. F.C. Allen was appointed coach of the Normal," announced the *Normal Student*, the school's newspaper, on Sept. 21, 1912. "One cannot talk with our coach without admiring his enthusiasm. The vim with which he speaks is only second to the vim with which he works among his men."

Phog told Central Missouri officials that he had turned down an athletic position at West Point a year earlier to complete his medical training. The school justifiably was proud of its hire.

"Whether we shall have to call him Dr. Allen remains to be seen but that we need Phog here is no question and under his leadership we hope to befog opposing teams," reported the *Normal Student* of Oct. 5, 1912.

The Phog Allen era in Warrensburg started with a 127-0 gridiron triumph over Kemper Military Academy.

Central Missouri dominated in Phog's first year, winning all conference games in Phog's three sports. The season produced one of the school's first great athletes, quarterback Ray "Ug" Sermon, who went on to become North Carolina State's basketball coach for 10 years and another subject of Phog's lore.

On the eve of a big football game with Drury College of Springfield in 1913, Sermon had stayed out all night with a friend. Phog told him the next morning he was suspended, but, at the urging of his Bessie, Phog allowed the team to determine Sermon's eligibility. Naturally, the team was forgiving, and Sermon played his way into Phog's story telling world. Later in his *Sports Stories*, Phog would write:

> *"This Mercury-footed flyer with the slick pigskin tucked under his arm and defying all laws of gravitation and running at impossible acute angles, lunged, stiff-armed, pivoted, side-stepped, vaulted and plunged his way through the vicious tackling of the opposition.*

> *"Twice, he was downed and in the clutches of his opponents, and twice he squirmed and wriggled out to pursue his perilous way to the goal line. Like a phantom with winged feet, when his opponents reached for him, he was gone; when they dived at him, he side-stepped them; when they clutched his clothing, he shook them loose; when they dived under him, he vaulted their hurtling forms. Once gaining the open, he sped the remaining yards to the goal line and to glory. Sermon 6, Drury 0!*

> *"Starting on his own 15-yard line, this indefatigable myth in human form, in his mad quest for the Drury goal line, had actually traversed 130 yards of gridiron terrain."*

But Drury got revenge the next season, not on the field, but in the court of public opinion. Drury led the charge to have Phog and Central Missouri removed from the conference.

Eight days after Phog produced another winning team in 1914, the conference, at its annual meeting in Kansas City, voted to expel Central Missouri for acts of unsportsmanlike conduct and using players alleged to be non-students. The league stripped the Normals of their football crown and awarded it to Missouri Wesleyan.

The unsportsmanlike conduct charge was brought about by the Normal School at Kirksville, a 76-0 loser to Phog's team that season. Kirksville accused Phog of stealing signals and knowing precisely when it was going to fake a punt. Phog admitted knowing the stunt, but responded Kirksville was lined up illegally to begin with.

Central Missouri players also were accused of using curse words so vile that women had to leave the field. As for the ineligible play-

Phog during his days as coach at Warrensburg Normal. (Photo courtesy Central Missouri State University archives)

ers, Central Missouri president William Hawkins, the man who had hired Phog, investigated and found none.

What appeared to be a flimsy case against Central Missouri stuck. With only Phog's brother, Pete, now an assistant football coach, representing the school at the league meeting, the MIAA gave Central Missouri the boot for an indefinite period by an 8-2 vote. Only Tarkio College sided with Warrensburg. MIAA schools were forbidden to schedule Central Missouri.

The Drury student newspaper, *The Drury Mirror*, rejoiced. The sports editor, Emmett Arnold, incensed that Central Missouri refused to play Drury in a postseason game in Kansas City in 1914, pulled out his hatchet and whacked away in a language that was sure to incite.

"We hope that the Normal has fired their coach and obtained a white man in his place (so) that we may resume friendly relations with the school," Arnold wrote. "(B)y a vote of 8 to 2, they vindicated the contentions which have long been made as to the crookedness of the Normal coach."

After the football season, Drury seniors hung Phog in effigy in the school's chapel. A few days after Christmas, Phog filed a $75,000 libel suit against the student reporter. It was the first of many litigations in Phog's life, and, like most of them, this one was dismissed.

Animosity between Central Missouri and the MIAA dragged on. The school remained outside the MIAA for the remainder of Phog's tenure, even though he had the support of Hawkins, who awarded him a new contract after the 1914-15 school year, and the faculty, which passed a resolution.

> "Be it Resolved, That we have the utmost confidence in Dr. Forrest C. Allen as a coach and Athletic Director. That we believe him to be a man of honesty, integrity and upright Christian character. That his influence an example upon our athletic field has been elevating, inspiring and conducive to clean athletics and higher moral standards. That we consider his conduct, both in victory and defeat to have been gentlemanly, courteous, and sportsmanlike toward his opponents, and kind and considerate toward his men. That our confidence in Dr. Allen can be shaken only by positive proof of wrong doing, and that we will continue to give him our strongest support in the face of all insinuations, accusations and unproved charges that may be brought against him."

Phog's conduct against Kansas in a basketball game during the previous year was cited as an example. The Jayhawks were returning from a Columbia-St. Louis swing and stopped in Warrensburg in 1913. Due to injuries, Kansas was down to six players for the game. One fouled out, and with several minutes remaining, another was disqualified. The Jayhawks would have

Phog stands with his 1915 Warrensburg Normals football team. He is in the back row with the black shirt. (Photo courtesy Central Missouri State University archives)

to finish with four players. Phog won the admiration of many that day by allowing the player to remain in the game. Kansas finished with five and won 30-24.

A copy of the faculty resolution was mailed to each conference member. But the MIAA stood firm, and Phog looked to familiar haunts to fill his football and basketball schedules. Haskell and Baker became regular opponents. Emporia State, then known as Kansas State Teachers College of Emporia, was good for two or three basketball games a year. Phog picked up Missouri Valley schools when he could and beat Oklahoma twice in 1916.

Some games didn't work out. Central Missouri was set to play a home football game against an independent team from Kansas City. When Phog learned that what he was getting actually resembled a college all-star team from the area he called off the meeting. He provided the opponent a financial guarantee, paid off the officials and ran an intrasquad scrimmage.

A tarnished reputation from the expulsion followed Phog long into his Kansas tenure. Whenever he accused other schools of cheating, and it happened often in the 1940s, it always seemed some official at the targeted school had worked in the MIAA and essentially told Phog he wasn't qualified to comment on eligibility issues of other schools.

Phog had been happy at Central Missouri until the MIAA war. But those troubles and his success on the field prompted him to look elsewhere and there was demand. In 1915, Phog considered an offer to become Kansas State's athletic director. The next year his bags were packed. Phog's visit to Champaign, Ill., to mend Illinois athletes so impressed school officials that they offered him the position of assistant football coach under Bob Zuppke. Phog agreed and signed a contract.

Unfortunately, war had broken out in Europe and rumors of American involvement were spreading. Illinois put Phog on hold and called off the deal when America joined the effort in 1917. Phog never came closer to a job outside of Missouri or Kansas.

Phog joined the war effort in the summer of 1918 as an Army captain stationed at Fort Sheridan in Illinois. A remarkable thing happened on his first day. In a 1943 letter, Phog recalled the event:

"I remember distinctly the first day I arrived at camp when the boy from Northwestern University was knocked out and Dr. Sundwall, then dean of the medical school of the University of Kansas, pronounced him dead. I was the fellow who was able to revive him, but I have forgotten his name. The fellow was a teacher in dentistry at Northwestern. I remember I got a lovely letter from his mother thanking me for my effort. I had just driven in with my family and was still in 'cits' clothing, and when Dr. Sundwall said the boy was dead I asked the captain, Trickett, I believe, if I could be of any benefit. Having been an athletic coach for a great number of years and having a degree in osteopathy, I was sure I could bring the boy back."

Fort Sheridan was the extent of Phog's active military career, and changes at Central Missouri were in store upon his return. War canceled the football season of 1918, and the 1917-18 basketball season was so unstructured that Phog himself appeared in several games, naturally leading the Normals in scoring each time.

In 1919, Central Missouri introduced a new football coach, but Phog continued his duties as AD and basketball coach. The athletic program approached the end of the decade on a positive note. Central Missouri was readmitted to the MIAA on May 16. But less than two weeks later, Phog handed in his resignation.

According to one of Phog's former football players, the Board of Regents made him choose between sports and medicine.

"His last year at Warrensburg was terminated because there were two medical doctors on the Board of Regents," H.H. Russell told the *Daily Star-Journal* of Warrensburg in 1974. "They apparently disliked the fact that Doc maintained his osteopathic practice in his spare time, after school and on weekends and holidays. So they prevailed on the other members of the Board of Regents and in the spring of (1919) delivered an ultimatum to Dr. Allen. It was that he would have to give up his practice or give them his resignation, which, of course, he did."

Indeed, Phog was offered a $400 salary increase as an instructor and coach to drop his osteopathy practice. No sale. Phog finished at Central Missouri with an 84-31 record in basketball, and 29-17-2 in football. "It is with great regret that the students witness the severance of his relations with the school," reported *The Normal Student* on May 31, 1919.

The trouble with the MIAA notwithstanding, the Allens truly had grown fond of Warrensburg. Three of their six children, Jane, Milton and Robert, were born there. Bessie dabbled in school affairs, including helping edit the yearbook. Phog's brother, Dick, played football for the Normals in 1913.

Phog's warm feelings for Central Missouri continued through the years. He regularly corresponded with old friends and maintained a connection through Iowa State coach Louis Menze, his best friend in the coaching business. Phog had persuaded Menze, a Kansas City Central High athlete, to attend Central Missouri in 1914. Menze and Sermon were Phog's first major college coaching protégés.

Phog also influenced one of Central Missouri's longest tenured coaches. Tad Reid was a football player and engineering student at Kansas in 1920, when Phog coached the Jayhawks football team. On Phog's recommendation, Reid was hired at Warrensburg in 1923 and coached football for 11 seasons and basketball for 15. His final two basketball teams in 1937 and 1938 won the national tournaments known today as the NAIA.

No longer a coach, Phog continued his osteopathy practice in a Warrensburg office at the northwest corner of campus, near his home on Broad Street. But it didn't last long. Only weeks after Phog had resigned as coach, Kansas was seeking an athletic director.

6

DREAMING
TOUCHDOWNS
AND STADIUMS

During his 1907-1909 tenure, Phog had proved to Kansas the importance of coaching and when he left for his osteopathy training, the school went off campus to find a replacement. For the 1909-1910 season, Kansas hired William O. Hamilton, who had been the coach of Central High in Kansas City.

Hamilton had carved a small place in history as a coach. Before Naismith arrived at Kansas, Hamilton had formed and was coaching a basketball team as an undergraduate at William Jewell College in the 1890s. Phog may be considered the father of basketball coaching, but he did not beat Hamilton to the occupation.

From William Jewell, Hamilton went to Central High in 1902, then moved to Kansas. He remained in Lawrence for the decade and, early on, did nothing to impede the school's progress in basketball. His teams won or shared five Missouri Valley championships in 10 seasons. Three of his teams posted overall records of 18-1, 17-1 and 16-1. The era also produced one of the program's first great players in Ralph "Lefty" Sproull, whose 40 points in a 1915 game eclipsed Phog's mark of 26 and stood as a school record until 1952.

Phog in 1919, the year he returned to Kansas to become the school's athletic director. (From the University of Kansas archives)

Hamilton, also Kansas' athletic director, finished with a 125-59 career record, and in his final season, coached two players who went on to fame as coaches. John Bunn, elected to basketball's Hall of Fame in 1964, coached for 42 seasons, starting as a Kansas assistant before moving on to Stanford, Springfield (Mass.) College and Northern Colorado. In the 1930s, Bunn coached Hank Luisetti, whose running, one-handed shot revolutionized basketball.

One of Bunn's teammates was Dutch Lonborg, who went on to coach for 23 seasons at Northwestern and returned to Kansas in 1950 as athletic director. He was elected to the Hall of Fame in 1972.

Bunn and Lonborg readied for another basketball coach in 1919. Hamilton resigned to devote more time to a budding Chevrolet dealership, and that summer the Jayhawks assigned track coach Karl Schlademan to take over the basketball program.

Kansas' coaching positions for 1919 were set, but the school sought a manager of athletics. It came down to Phog and Bert Kennedy, the football coach from 1904-1910 whose winning percentage of .833 (53-9-4) is the best in school history. Kennedy, a licensed dentist who continued a practice even when he was coaching, compiled a 93-40-4 overall record in 15 seasons. Kennedy desperately wanted the job and was the early favorite. He was Naismith's choice. A letter writing campaign produced dozens of recommendations that filled two thick files. Alumni liked the idea of a football man returning to campus. It seemed Kennedy had everybody's support, except KU Chancellor Frank Strong. There had been friction between the men when Kennedy resigned 10 years earlier.

But Strong voted only if the 10-member athletic board, comprised of five faculty members and five students, was deadlocked. It wasn't. With one abstaining, the final count favored Phog 7-2. He started with a $3,500 annual salary and a $500 expense account.

Phog brought along some new ideas, foremost a football stadium to replace aging McCook Field. In his first few weeks in the athletic department, Phog appointed himself to the football staff then publicly decried the lack of student participation. Forty students went out for the 1919 team and Phog thought the number should have been twice as many.

Fewer than four months on the job, Phog was faced with his first major crisis. Schlademan resigned as basketball coach after one game to devote his energies to track. Later, Phog claimed Schlademan quit because he couldn't handle the older athletes returning from World War I. There was no time to launch a search, so Phog, who was coaching the freshman team, appointed himself to the varsity. Lonborg was the best player of the 14-member squad, but Phog didn't know many of them. In his first game he did something unheard of then by playing everybody on the roster in a 50-40 victory over Washburn. Kansas went on to finish 11-7. The Jayhawks turned over nearly the entire team in 1921 and still managed a 10-8 record. With sophomores like Paul Endacott on the squad, the program wasn't far from some of Phog's greatest teams.

Before his second basketball season, Phog faced another coaching problem. He had hired old friend Potsy Clark from Michigan State in May 1920, but Michigan State wouldn't release Clark from his contract. Phog took over the team in the late summer and served his only season as the Jayhawks' football coach. It may have been the most memorable — certainly the most glorified — season in more than 100 years of the sport at Kansas.

Kansas was expected to be good enough. Three All-Missouri Valley players returned led by Lonborg, and the first four games were scheduled for Lawrence. The Jayhawks rolled past Emporia State,

Washburn and Drake to set up an Oct. 23 encounter with Iowa State, then known as Ames College. The game was the first of two in 1920 that supplied Phog with two of his greatest stories, and this one became known as "The Dream Touchdown."

"Never have I looked over my left shoulder at the moon for good luck, nor am I afraid of the so-called hoodoo number 13. Even a black cat crossing my path has held no terrors. However, I have always played hunches. This is why the dream touchdown — the only touchdown of the game — materialized.

"Iowa State, our next opponent, heavy and aggressive, had been highly touted. Our situation looked none too promising. In fact the week's preparation had been most disappointing.

"In my earlier coaching days, I had formed the habit of putting a pencil and pad on the night table near my bed. Solutions to the knottiest problems seemed to come in the eerie hours when little gremlins from my subconscious went out for strolls. Invariably ideas so clear would vanish with the dawn. So it seemed wise to hold on by writing them down.

"Arthur 'Dutch' Lonborg was the Kansas quarterback and field general. Ten minutes before game time we were huddled in the dressing room for final instructions. I said this to the boys, 'I had a dream last night. I saw a Kansas airplane with the faces of 11 of you taking off. Five of the faces in the ship have not been seen in a starting lineup this year. But today I'm going to play you just that way. Your ship swung from the west to the north and rose above that Iowa State team as you continued eastward to the goal line. I saw Harley Little playing right halfback. And with the ball tucked under his arm, he started from near our goal line and I watched him as he crossed the Iowa State goal line with the ball in his possession.'"

Sure enough, Kansas took the kickoff and started from its 15. On the first play, Little, starting for the first time, went around left end for an 85-yard touchdown run, the only score of the game.

"'Was it magic or hokum?' wondered the players as they left the field. Perhaps they still wonder, as do I. With this victory came many interesting angles of the analysis of the dream. Morale took a new high with the football team. This mystic something! This penetrable veil between the real and the unreal! The victory was real yet it now seemed like a dream to the men who won it. Were they dreaming lives or living dreams? It is the mystery of life that lures."

The victory kept Kansas undefeated, and the Jayhawks improved to 5-0 with a triumph at Kansas State. But a 21-9 loss at Oklahoma on Nov. 6 ended hopes of a Missouri Valley championship, which was won by the Sooners. Next was a home game against Nebraska. That year, the Cornhuskers were not members of the Missouri Valley, having withdrawn after a flap over their home field. Nebraska wanted to play home games in Omaha and believed it had a right because that's where the medical school was located. Other schools protested and refused to play the Cornhuskers. In 1920, Kansas did not regret playing Nebraska.

The Jayhawks played their home games at rickety 10,000-seat McCook Field, an east-west layout that was accessible only by dirt roads. There were no dressing rooms, only a small bungalow house that Hamilton had built south of the field. When he became athletic director, Phog heard many complaints from alumni clamoring for better access and refurbished bleachers, if not a new stadium. Alumni also were angered that in 1910, the annual Missouri game on Thanksgiving Day had moved from Kansas City to the campus sites, and in Lawrence there were fewer seats than Kansas City's Exposition Park.

Phog wanted a palace for football, akin to the major structures in the East. He had traveled to New York in December 1919, along with C.C. Williams, a faculty member in the engineering school, to visit stadiums. Princeton's horseshoe design would be perfect for Kansas, Phog believed. The open end would look toward the university buildings to the south. Phog also liked the idea of a track running around the field as they had at Princeton.

The administration supported a new stadium and a student union that would serve as a monument to students who had died in World War I. But the price tag of $1 million was prohibitive, and even before ground could be broken, it would take $60,000 just to level some hills adjacent to the location for a durable stadium.

But Phog and LaForce Bailey, professor in the department of architecture and design, weren't discouraged. They raised $600 to print a prospectus. Sketches and drawings along with opinions of prominent alumni were printed and distributed throughout the state. Now, Phog needed to ignite interest on campus. It happened on Nov. 13, 1920, when Nebraska arrived for homecoming. Even then, the Cornhuskers were a powerhouse, having won or tied for five straight Missouri Valley titles in the previous decade.

"Swooping down from the north, as Attila's Huns of old, the scarlet-clad Nebraska football giants of Coach Henry "Indian" Schulte ran roughshod over the light but scrappy Kansas Jayhawkers during the first half, 20-0. Trooping exultantly off of the field at the end of the first half, the happy Huskers shouted to a small boy who was marking up the scores, 'Say, sonny, you had better lay in a fresh supply of chalk. You are apt to run out during the second half.'

"An alumnus of earlier football fame broke into the dressing quarters, swearing 'Blankety, blank, blank, etc., You boys are a bunch of white-livered so-and-so's and won't fight those blankety-blank Nebraskans like our old-timers did.' I cut him short with these words, 'Shut up! No one except a fool or a mule can be cursed. I am running this team, and I'm darned proud of these boys, even at this stage of the game.'

"Andy McDonald! Ed Sandefur! Warren Woody! George Hale! Captain George Nettles! Tad Reid! Dutch Lonborg! Harley Little! Frank Mandeville! Johnny Bunn! Kenny Welch! Severt Higgins! and Carl McAdams! You are the men I am counting on! Out and after those red-shirted devils, who would run us out of chalk in the second half!'"

The Jayhawks scored two quick touchdowns to make it 20-14. Bunn then threw a 27-yard scoring pass to Mandeville to tie the game. Sandefur missed his only extra point of the season and the game ended 20-20.

"Pandemonium broke loose! A delirium for Kansas fans! They were weeping, shouting and crying for sheer

joy. Cursing, pummeling and hugging. There was no time for manifest now. It was a courageous little team that this mad crowd was worshiping. A gamer one never wore the cleats. Pall and gloom shrouded Nebraska's followers. Nonpartisan spectators, who came only to see the great Nebraska machine grind into fine bits the underdog, Kansas, now swung into great ovations for the boys who had done the impossible. Kansas had won a great 20 to 20 moral victory."

On Monday, during convocation, Allen and the team were seated on a platform and given a 10-minute ovation. The Kansas band played two fight songs. In the next two weeks, students and faculty pledged $200,000 toward a new facility. On May 10, 1921, the male students took hammers and axes to the McCook bleachers, and only a few yards away, Chancellor Ernest Lindley donned overalls, grabbed a horse-drawn plow and broke ground on the new stadium that was to seat 38,000.

When it opened for the 1921 season, there was only enough money collected to complete parts of the east and west sides, about 18,000 seats. The formal dedication was Nov. 11, 1922, and Kansas lost to Nebraska 28-0. The horseshoe was finished in 1927 in time for an Oct. 15 game against Kansas State, and soon after the cement had dried, Phog was eager to show off his completed structure. He sent courtesy tickets to newspaper editors across the state and area.

"To Ye Editors of Kansas," the invitation read. "Be ye informed that fur and feathers will fly when your pet wild-cat and your gaunt jayhawk bird get together. (Come) party with us in our little $660,000 coliseum, and we are happy to tell you that this edifice didn't cost the tax payers of Kansas one penny. It was built entirely through donations and by bond issues payable by athletic gate receipts. We have 'dolled' up the 'arena' awaiting your coming. We think that you will like it. We know we will be glad to see you. The University of Kansas, the Athletic Department, the Coaches, the Team, the Journalism Department — we all invite you most cordially to attend the Kansas-Kansas Aggie football game on Oct. 15. Come on over and get in on the big family fuss."

Turned out to be not much of a fuss for the Jayhawks, who lost 13-2.

The drive had lost momentum throughout the 1920s. Pledges totaled $965,000, but only two-thirds of that was ever collected. The bond was paid in 1947. Only later did Phog reveal his initial motivation for constructing a stadium — to honor his old freshman teammate Tommy Johnson. In 1943 he wrote:

"When I returned to Kansas in 1919 as director of athletics, there was but one motive in my mind and that was to build a stadium in the memory of Tommy Johnson, Kansas' greatest athlete. But the World War had just finished and there were 129 Kansas men and women who made the supreme sacrifice in the first world war and naturally the stadium was given the name of the World War Memorial in the name of these heroes and heroines. But if I had it to do of my own experiences and relationships, had the war not happened, there would have been only one name on that stadium, and that would have been 'Tommy Johnson Memorial Stadium.' He deserved such an honor."

The 1920 season ended with a loss to Missouri, leaving Kansas — and Phog's KU football coaching career — with a record of 5-2-1. Phog joined Fielding Yost and John Outland as one-year Kansas football coaches. There were 12 in the first 30 years of the football program. Clark arrived from Michigan State for the 1921 season, and Phog became an assistant.

The football season of 1925 brought tragedy to the Allen household. Forrest Allen Jr., 14, the first son and second-oldest of the six children, died on Oct. 27 of typhoid fever. He was a sophomore in high school and had played football, basketball and track. At the time, the Allens and O'Learys were neighbors.

"Forrest Jr. was my best friend," Ted O'Leary said. "I was pall bearer at the funeral, and the death brought our families closer together. Bessie was devastated. She took it much harder. She resented the doctor who couldn't save him."

In correspondence the rest of his life, Phog always said he had six children. Whenever he was asked to provide a biography for a speech, Forrest Jr. was listed. But Phog never talked much about his deceased son.

Phog never again coached football after the 1920 season, and it wouldn't take long for the success of his basketball teams to over-

Phog (left) sits along the sideline in a 1932 football game. Phog's only year as head coach was 1920 but his success (5-2-1) was instrumental in getting a new football stadium built. (Photo courtesy University of Kansas Sports Information)

shadow football and create controversy on campus. As athletic director, Phog was seen by football fans to favor the basketball program at the expense of football. The feeling today that basketball is more important on campus than football has its roots in Phog's early years as athletic director.

There's no telling how long it would have taken Kansas to build a football stadium were it not for Phog's success on the field in 1920. Only one coach in the past 75 years managed a career winning percentage better than Phog's .688. Had he stayed with football, no doubt Phog would have been a success.

According to Lonborg, Phog wasn't a football coach in name only.

"He had some unique ideas and some very unique formations," Lonborg said in 1967. "He did things very unorthodox. One of the first things he did was have his backs run around and through a great long mass of barrels for elusiveness. This was one of our daily routines. He always said 'It's like a dog, be elusive like a dog. Be able to change directions.'"

Phog served on football staffs off and on for the next two decades. He often lined up in photographs of the football coaches. But as long as Phog was athletic director he never enjoyed a season as successful as the one where he served as head coach. The game built a stadium, or so Phog related.

"Like a majestic prelude to a powerful symphony was the persisting picture of that fighting group of boys who were down and out and who had the indefatigable courage to come back and to prove that 'a champ belongs.' We owe the beautiful $660,000 Memorial Stadium, which nestles in the bosom of Mount Oread at the University of Kansas largely to this valorous team."

7

1923: THE
LEGEND BEGINS

Only twice in nearly a century of Kansas basketball has the program gone more than five years between conference championships. The longest drought is seven seasons between 1979 and 1985. The second-longest started in 1916. Hamilton's final four teams went 35-37 and by the end of the decade Missouri had become the team to be feared in the Missouri Valley.

Doc Meanwell, one of college basketball's first great coaches, interrupted his career at Wisconsin to head the Tigers in 1918 and 1920. Both teams finished 17-1 and the second one retroactively was considered the nation's second-best team.

As a full-time Kansas coach, Phog trained his sights on his first prime target: Meanwell and Missouri. He bumped heads with Meanwell for only one season, and it wasn't until Phog's third year that he beat the Tigers. In his second KU tenure, he lost his first nine games to Missouri, four to Meanwell. It's the longest losing streak to one school in Jayhawks history.

Phog respected Meanwell but they weren't best of friends. Wisconsin's defeat of Washington State for the 1941 NCAA championship in Kansas City prompted Phog to recall Meanwell's teams of two decades earlier in a letter to John Bunn.

"I was not too favorably impressed with Wisconsin's playing. They reminded me of a Meanwell team of the old Missouri days. The Wisconsin team got away with murder; they held, they roughed, they pushed and made innumerable fouls, but when Washington State came back at them in the same way, the Wisconsin boys cried like Meanwell's boys used to cry.

"You remember when the Missouri outfit would push and shove and then when they were fouled, oh my, what an uproar; they looked like big cry-baby players to me. Bud Foster (Wisconsin's coach in 1941) is a Meanwell man and a fine fellow. It must be the style of play and not the fellow that we used to suspect Meanwell of being. I like Dr. Meanwell off the court, but on the court he could cry higher to high heaven than any man I have ever seen."

However, a young Phog envied Meanwell's success. Meanwell posted an unbelievable 126-11 record in his first eight years and won six conference championships. He was a native of England and a graduate of Maryland with a doctorate in public health. He also had authored a book on basketball principles. Meanwell was who Phog wanted to be and beat.

Even after Meanwell returned to Wisconsin after the 1920 season, the Tigers didn't skip a note. Craig Ruby, a Helms Foundation All-America forward in 1920, succeeded Meanwell as coach in 1921. The Tigers finished 17-1 again and this time were rated No. 1 retroactively by St. Bonaventure accounting professor Patrick Premo, who analyzed every season from 1892 until 1937 and came up with his own top 20 polls before wire services started theirs.

In 1922, Missouri and Kansas won on each other's home floors, Phog's first victory over his rival, and tied for the Missouri Valley championship. Premo ranked the Tigers first and the Jayhawks second, although the Helms Foundation recognized Kansas as the nation's top team.

Entering the 1923 season, Phog had his best team. Endacott, a Lawrence resident, had to be talked into joining the freshman team in 1919 then went on to become the program's first Hall of Fame player. Forward Tusten Ackerman, also from Lawrence, was the team's top newcomer.

Coach Phog Allen demonstrates defense in this 1929 photo. (From the University of Kansas archives)

The Tigers, likewise, were loaded. George Bond, captain of the 1922 team, became the coach. Seniors Herb Bunker and Arthur Browning were Helms All-Americans. Nobody came close to beating Missouri in the first five games that season, and while Phog was bringing his toughest bunch to Rothwell Gymnasium on Jan. 16, there was no reason to believe the Tigers wouldn't protect their home floor.

Kansas almost didn't make it to Columbia. The Jayhawks had played three games in three nights in Iowa from Jan. 11-13, winning them all but getting beat up in the process. The final game, at Drake, was particularly rugged. "It seemed like Drake's team was nothing but football players, and we felt it," Ackerman said.

The Jayhawks returned to Lawrence for only a few hours before embarking for Columbia. Today, it's a three-hour drive. In 1923, it was a two-day trip with an overnight stay in Sedalia, Mo. Columbia wasn't on the main railroad line, so passengers got off in McBain, where a "plug" train took them to campus. But on the morning of the game, there was no train. The team, scheduled to eat breakfast in Columbia, instead was forced to dine at a blacks-only restaurant in McBain.

"True to the traditions of the South, the negroes who ran the shack served only their own color. But on this morning, they were asked to serve eleven hungry

white men who had eaten only dry sandwiches for dinner the evening before. So the colored population moved out of the shack and our basketball team moved in. We sat on soap boxes for chairs and ate from dry goods boxes for tables. The menu was 'Ole Missouri sow belly and eggs,' some half-cooked oatmeal with milk — all washed down with bitter coffee."

A moving train arrived to collect the team, but it broke down nine miles from Columbia. The team hiked six miles before a truck with canvas curtains arrived and the team reached Columbia at noon. Along the way, the driver spotted a black preacher thumbing for a ride. Phog insisted he be picked up, and the preacher accompanied the team to Columbia.

Phog was dead set against heavy meals on game days but broke his rules on this day and arranged a steak and potato feast. Phog always had his team take a walk before a game. This one was longer than usual.

More than any in his early coaching years Phog wanted this game and pulled out all his emotional ploys. Ackerman, a sophomore, had established himself as one of the team's top players and this was his first encounter with Missouri. He was familiar with the Tigers and the rivalry. As a youth, his family had lived in Columbia. Phog knew this, and he also knew Ackerman, as a boy, was a fan of Tommy Johnson. The hit that eventually killed Johnson had aggravated a kidney problem he had suffered as a boy. But details weren't important as Phog hypnotized Ackerman.

"Before the game, he took me aside and told me, 'I thought they had done Tommy Johnson wrong,'" Ackerman said. "He said, 'Tonight, you're Tommy Johnson,' and he got me to believe it."

Of course, Phog, as he so often did, fudged for melodramatic effect in his books.

"Erroneously, Tus felt that some member of the Missouri football team was responsible for Tommy Johnson's death. This young hero worshiper vowed that he would some day avenge Tommy Johnson's death. For 13 years he dreamed, played, trained and lived the fine clean life of Tommy Johnson. Daily he literally steeped himself in the valorous deeds of his unfortunate hero. I reminded him, 'Tonight, you are Tommy Johnson in all

that you would have Tommy be. Go out there and play and play as Tommy would have played.'"

No telling how Tommy Johnson would have played, but Ackerman made two field goals and seven free throws for a game-high 11 points, critical in a game that wasn't decided until the final few dramatic minutes. What actually happened that night was a source of conflict. Not between Kansas and Missouri — there was no disputing the Jayhawks' 21-19 triumph — but later between Endacott and Phog.

Phog wanted a story, Endacott sought to tell the truth. In those days, a player in a jump ball situation could tip the ball to himself. Endacott did this, controlling the tip and allowing himself to be tied up. The dispute centers around the number of jump balls. Cue the background music for Phog's version:

"Less than two minutes were left when (Waldo) Bowman called Captain Endacott's signal for a smash through center. True to form Endacott took the tip from center, high in the air. Before he could alight, the Tigers divining the play drove to a clench. It was a held ball.

"Referee Quigley threw the ball again into the air. Feeling that the time to play was short, Endacott bulldogged the ball for the rest of the game, refusing to let it out of his grasp.

"Sixteen times the ball was thrown up and 16 times Endacott after the tip-off pounced on it, like a leopard upon its prey. He leapt for it, he dived, he lunged, he plunged, with no thought of himself. The ball was the thing. He was conscious only of the two points that would tie the game. A greater exhibition of man's doggedness has not been witnessed before or since. The timer's gun cracked, with Endacott and a Tiger still bulldogging the ball.

"In the dressing room later came the scene that coaches and players do not forget. The other players had helped Endacott to the basement dressing room, where, for the first time after the game I saw him. He was sitting on a bench in a crouched position, his head resting in his hands and his elbows on his knees.

"Upon examination, I found that the intercostal muscles, due to overexertion had cramped. He had played himself out. It was then that we fully realized what he had given. We worked on him for 20 minutes before we could get him comfortable."

Newspaper accounts of the game do not detail a series of jump balls at the end. After years of answering inquiries about the events, Endacott typed up a one-page recollection in 1991.

"It is certain that he greatly exaggerated that incident, and I respectfully told him so," Endacott said. "Unfortunately, he insisted that this was not the case and that he had a record to prove it, although he never showed it to me.

"As I recall the action of the Missouri coach in the last minute or two of the game, he resorted to a big gamble by positioning a couple of players far away from the jump ball and close to the Missouri goal. The idea apparently was that one of the Missouri players might score if he could get hold of the ball after a long throw from the jump spot. Phog, I believe, placed only one of our players in a position to watch both of these Missouri players, which left only three of their players in the jumping spot against our four.

"Present day fans do not understand Phog's story for the reason that held balls in those days were not alternately thrown in from outside the court, but were continuously jumped for. Thus, any player on the court might get the ball. Although I do not remember, even at the time, what happened after the first three or four jumps, the first one was with the Missouri center Bunker. I think all the rest were with different players."

It helped, Endacott continued, that he had been an acrobat in his youth, and that the Jayhawks, thanks to Allen's treatments for stamina, were in better condition that day. The starting five for both sides played the entire game.

The outcome paved the way for the Jayhawks' first perfect record in conference play — 16-0. Phog called it "ever-victorious." It was the first of his four teams to go undefeated in league play. Only a loss to the Kansas City Athletic Club spoiled a spotless record, and to clinch the Missouri Valley championship Kansas needed a season-ending 23-20 victory over the Tigers before a record home crowd of 3,000. The Helms Foundation recognized Kansas as the national champion of 1923 to follow its 1922 title. Banners recognizing the achievement still hang in Allen Field House.

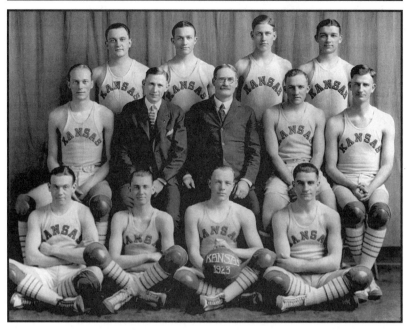

In what may be the most famous team picture in history, Phog Allen (second from left, second row) poses with his 1923 club. To the right of Allen is James Naismith. Hall of Famer Paul Endacott is holding the ball while future coaching legend Adolph Rupp is on the top row at the far left. (From the University of Kansas archives)

From 1922-1927, Kansas won a remarkable 88 percent (81-11) of its games and captured the Missouri Valley six straight years. Phog's coaching reputation and the program's fame were spreading nationally. But for the rest of his career, Phog would never coach a team like the 1923 Jayhawks. It produced three all-conference players in Endacott, Charlie Black and John Wulf. Helms named Endacott national player of the year.

That year, the torch of conference power was passed from Missouri to Kansas. In the first 15 years of the Missouri Valley, Kansas had won or shared eight titles, Missouri four and Nebraska four. Beginning in 1923 until the end of the Big Eight Conference last season, the Jayhawks had won at least part of 35 titles. Next is Kansas State with 12.

The 1923 team was Phog's favorite for several reasons. First, it may have saved his career. Some 15 years after the fact, Bessie confided to Endacott that Phog had talked of quitting coaching if the

Jayhawks didn't win the league title in 1923. Phog knew Kansas was capable and also knew that a championship meant beating the Tigers twice, which he hadn't done. Without the sweep, Bessie told Endacott that Phog was prepared to hand over his coaching duties to concentrate on his work as athletic director. "I don't know if he would have gone through with it," Endacott said. "But that's what Bessie Allen told me, and I believe it."

Probably no Kansas team, or many in college basketball history produced a greater bond or team photograph. The famous picture, snapped by longtime Lawrence photographer Duke D'Ambra, includes Phog and Naismith, whom Allen often asked to sit in on team pictures, side by side. The third Hall of Fame member is Endacott, and the fourth, top row far left, is Adolph Rupp.

Rupp was a seldom-used senior guard in 1923. Born in Halstead, Kan., a town along the Santa Fe Railroad line north of Wichita, Rupp was a star player on his high school basketball team. He made the KU freshman squad and was selected to the varsity as a sophomore. He was a member of the Meat Packers, the scrubs who played when the outcome no longer was in doubt.

In his three years on the varsity, Rupp didn't see enough action to earn a letter. But his named showed up on Phog's list of players recommended to the athletic board for a basketball "K" for 1923, with this explanation:

> "Adolph Rupp has worked for three consecutive years giving the best he had in him for the success of the team. It is an unwritten law among coaches that when a man comes out and does his stint without fail for three successive years that that man should receive a recommendation for a letter."

Rupp got his "K."

Beginning in 1948 and every five years until Phog's death, the 1923 team held a reunion, organized by Endacott and his wife, Lucille. They were gala affairs that attracted not only the players and Phog but media members, school officials and even opponents. In 1958, Bun Browning of Missouri was honored as the 1923 team's most feared opponent. A special guest at each was the game ball from the second game with the Tigers.

Endacott became president of Phillips Petroleum in Bartlesville, Okla., and everybody else on the team went on to successful busi-

Phog had already coached Kansas to two Helms Foundation national championships by the time this 1929 photo was taken. (From the University of Kansas archives)

ness careers. During the 1963 reunion, Rupp paid the squad a heart-felt tribute:

> *"I'm glad to be here because this group means possibly more to me than any other group because it proves that there is something in my profession that is worthwhile . . .You boys are tremendous to me. I am the only one who stayed in the profession. The rest of you were smarter than I and got yourselves good jobs. I guess I'm the only failure in the crowd."*

The 1923 team and especially Endacott were particularly generous in fund-raising dinners and functions that honored Phog. As plans were finalized for the dedication of Allen Field House in 1955, contributions were sought from former players to buy Phog a Cadillac. When funds were running short as the deadline approached, Endacott assured the purchase with a large contribution made on the team's behalf. He also underwrote a $1,000 portrait of Phog that was unveiled a year later.

The 1923 season had made Phog hot property. During the summer, he threw himself into his first book, *My Basket-Ball Bible*, or rather, had Bessie tied up for the summer writing it. As she did for all three of her husband's books, Bessie was the ghost writer. With his hectic traveling schedule Phog never would have had time to fill hundreds of pages. In the mornings before Phog would head off to work or travel to a speaking engagement, he and Bessie discussed chapters during breakfast. Phog would give Bessie notes he had scribbled, and she turned them into 445 pages.

Endacott is credited with writing the foreword, but Bessie wrote that, too.

Reviews were good, considering there had been nothing like it on the market. Other coaches had written basketball books but none included the treatment of injuries.

"Dr. Allen does not hold that his is the first word, nor the last, on basketball," said a report in the *Chicago Herald and Examiner*. "But he does feel, and we agree with him, that he has provided a very substantial 445 pages of the words in between."

Perhaps it was after reading that review in 1925 that an official from Northwestern University contacted Phog about becoming its athletic director. Allen was tempted. "In my opinion, Northwestern University will move steadily to the front in the Western Conference," Phog told the *Kansan*.

But in the midst of six straight conference championships, Phog knew he was better off at Kansas. And he was, if for no other reason, for his close association with the man who invented the game.

8

DR. NAISMITH

Nobody in basketball knew the game's inventor, Dr. James Naismith, better or longer than Phog.

Acquaintances for nearly four decades and colleagues for 20 years, Phog and Naismith were basketball's original odd couple. Their offices were separated by a floor in Robinson Gym but they may as well have been on different planets when considering their approach to the game.

The idea of coaching was the most obvious difference. Naismith introduced basketball at Kansas and was the program's first coach. The nine teams under his direction won 55 and lost 60, making Naismith the only losing coach in the program's history. But Naismith never considered himself a coach, and he certainly didn't act like one. He made the schedule but rarely traveled with the team. When he did, it usually was to officiate the game. To Naismith, in his early years at Kansas, basketball was merely an extension of the physical education department that he headed until 1924. He also taught his students fencing, lacrosse, gymnastics, wrestling, track and boxing.

Basketball didn't bring Naismith to Lawrence in 1898. Chancellor Francis Snow needed somebody to lead prayer in the chapel, where daily attendance was required. Snow contacted University of Chicago chancellor Williams Harper, who relayed the message to his football coach, Amos Alonzo Stagg. Naismith and Stagg played football together for the Stubby Christians of Springfield (Mass.) College and Stagg recommended his friend, who had just graduated from medical school and was working at the YMCA in Denver.

One of Naismith's first jobs at Kansas was to administer physicals to incoming freshmen.

"The first time I saw him I didn't think he was anybody at all," Paul Endacott said. "He was throwing balls to me at the Lawrence YMCA. He'd throw the ball to us and we were supposed to start dribbling. Then he'd write things down."

Naismith was forever jotting down notes. While administering the physical exams, he measured subjects from head to toe, front to back and around. He believed humans should be symmetrical in build, and if his measures found one arm to be shorter than the other Naismith encouraged the student to lift weights to make it even.

Hall of Fame coach Ralph Miller, who played for the Jayhawks from 1939-42, remembered Naismith yanking him off the floor as a freshman in a 1937 workout to check his heartbeat and ordered him to stop playing because Naismith believed athletes could die from overactivity.

Quietly — Naismith did everything quietly — he observed basketball's rapid changes as the game developed at Kansas. Naismith's advice to Phog was to not roam too far from the game's original rules, and for the most part Phog agreed with Naismith's basic principles. Naismith always defended his 13 original rules but it wasn't until late in his life that he made many public statements about the game. It wasn't until late in his life that anybody asked.

Just before his death in 1939, Naismith ripped the concept of zone defense to reporters in New York. "I have no sympathy with it," Naismith said. "The defensive team in stalling, lays back and waits for the offensive team to come to it. If a soccer team held back and grouped itself in front of the goal, what could the other team do? The zone is much like that."

It was a rare opinion on the game he invented. It's telling that the first of Phog's three books, *My Basket-Ball Bible*, was published in 1924. Naismith's only book about his game, *Basketball, Its Origin and Development* was published in 1941, two years after his death. Except for endorsing some equipment, Naismith never cashed in on his invention.

"Dr. Naismith was a gentleman, and as fine a Christian man as there was," said Bob Allen. "But he had absolutely no idea what he had, or what basketball could become."

When his coaching days ended and if he wasn't serving as a referee elsewhere, Naismith attended Kansas home games. He didn't cheer.

"I don't think I'm exaggerating this," said Ted O'Leary. "Naismith really didn't give a damn about basketball, the way it progressed. He came to all the games, sat in the second row in the middle of Hoch Auditorium, hardly ever changed his expression and never applauded. It was far more interesting for him to teach fencing to a small group, and, at least when I was there, he was more fascinated by wrestling."

"To me," said Dick Harp, Phog's successor in 1956 and KU letterman from 1938-40, "the biggest disagreement between those two was why basketball should be played."

Phog loved basketball's competitive nature. Naismith saw it mostly as another form of recreation. John McLendon never played for Phog as a Kansas student in the mid-1930s. McLendon is black and the color line in the conference wasn't broken until the late 1940s. But as a member of the original class of seven students who majored in physical education, nobody had a better post to view the relationship between Phog and Naismith. They were his instructors for all classes in his major.

"They had interesting arguments all the time," McLendon said. "They were not bitter. They were always friends as far as I could see. I think I learned from them that you can remain friends even when you disagree about things that are important to you.

"Dr. Allen taught me physical therapy and administration of physical education. Dr. Naismith taught me kinesiology, anatomy and a course he called principles, which was really about the psychology of coaching. That might not have been the name for it but that's what it really was. He never made any X's and O's on the board or diagrammed any plays. He only talked about the essence of the games.

"Dr. Naismith taught us more than just basketball, but we were always jumping on him to talk more basketball. He just didn't want to do it. He's the reason I went to Kansas. I heard that's where he was teaching and I wanted to learn the game from the inventor. But he was more into physical education. He couldn't imagine anybody coaching basketball unless they had studied kinesiology, sociology, social pathology, anatomy. He wanted a person prepared to develop the entire individual."

Dr. James Naismith (left) with Phog Allen in 1932. (From the University of Kansas archives)

McLendon was the only member of his class to enter basketball coaching. Naismith had assigned McLendon to coach at Lawrence Memorial High as a junior. Naismith advised him to stick with the profession. McLendon went on to a 25-year coaching career, won three straight NAIA championships at Tennessee State, became the first black coach of a professional team and the first black college coach elected to the Hall of Fame in 1978.

With Naismith's unwitting assistance, McLendon also broke another barrier. To earn a physical education degree, majors had to pass a swimming test. But while the University of Kansas was integrated, the pool at Robinson Gym was not. School officials wanted to waive the test for McLendon, who was a former lifeguard. McLendon said no.

"Dr. Allen said the only reason I couldn't go swimming is that he was afraid for my safety," McLendon said. "He said some people just don't know how to act. I made a deal with him. I asked him to keep the pool open for two weeks (for everybody). If there's no incident, then open the pool for the colored. He went to Dr. Naismith and they agreed to do it."

What Phog and Naismith didn't know is that McLendon then called a meeting of all black students and told them not to go to the pool for two weeks. They didn't. All Phog and Naismith knew was that there were no incidents during that time. At the end of two weeks, Naismith posted a sign that said the pool was opened to colored. McLendon figured the word would spread and asked Naismith to take it down. "It wasn't in good taste," McLendon said.

Rumors spread that after McLendon took his test, the pool was drained. Half-true. "I just saw half of it gone," McLendon said. "Then I reminded them how big the water bill would be if they kept draining it." It didn't happen again.

The incident proved to McLendon that the common interests in Allen and Naismith clearly surpassed their differences, and it's true that their divergent personalities did not prevent a friendship. Twice, Phog was Naismith's guest on fishing expeditions in Naismith's native Ontario. The first time, in 1926, Phog met Peter Naismith, the bachelor uncle who raised James Naismith.

"I even saw the casket which Uncle Peter, after the fashion of Canada's frugal pioneers in their northern woods, had skillfully built and polished so that it would be in readiness for the time which would inevitably overtake him," Phog wrote in 1941. "Of late, Uncle Peter had taken to sleeping in his casket, perhaps to get accustomed to it."

Although they expressed it differently, Phog and Naismith shared a deep concern for the students and athletes. Naismith was more popular with the student body. Having given them physicals as freshmen he knew everybody. The 1925 edition of the *Jayhawker*, the student yearbook, is dedicated to him: "(A) true friend of KU," it read.

In *My Basket-Ball Bible*, Phog describes the ideal coach as one who "gets into the players' hearts; he must know their folks, he must find out what interests them, he must study their different temperaments as he would study the temperaments of his own sons. In short he must feel their sorrows."

There's no telling how much, if any, sorrow Naismith felt when he was demoted from head of the physical education department in 1924. The job had been given to Phog. Naismith carried on as a senior member. In 1936, his salary of $2,960 was the highest in the department. But Phog supplemented his professor's salary of $2,735 with an additional $2,327.50 from the Athletic Association as the basketball coach and athletic director.

Naismith wouldn't have needed to work if he had Phog's vision of the game. As it was, Naismith owned little when he died in 1939. A few years earlier, he had been forced to move into a smaller home during the Depression because he couldn't afford mortgage payments.

"Had Dr. Naismith patented some of his paraphernalia he might now have an income that would free him from the chores of teaching Kansas freshmen how to stand up straight," said a *Time* magazine story in 1933.

What *Time* didn't know was that Naismith thoroughly enjoyed such banal chores. Money was never his motivation. A cigarette company once offered Naismith a lucrative contract to endorse smoking. Naismith didn't approve of the habit and turned it down. He once took a drink but only in the name of science. Henry Shenk, a KU physical education department head, studied under Naismith in the 1920s and preserved this story for a 1970 paper:

> *"Being an M.D., Naismith was always intrigued with research on athletics. One time he became interested in finding the effects of drinking alcoholic beverages upon athletic performance. However, he knew that in Carrie Nation's dry Kansas, there would be trouble if students were used as subjects for such an experiment. He decided to be the subject himself and let someone else record the performance after imbibing various amounts of alcohol.*
>
> *"He developed a target of concentric rings of metal applied to wood with a bull's-eye in the middle and wired it up with electricity. The idea was that he would lunge at the target with a fencing foil a certain number of times and a light would flash each time he succeeded in scoring a bull's-eye. The performance was to be repeated several times after the consumption of increasing amounts of alcohol before each trial. History does not record the results of this noble experiment."*

Shenk seconded the motion of Naismith as a popular instructor, not because of his invention but his relationship with the students.

"He imbued his students with a love of physical education and athletics," Shenk wrote. "Not only was he popular with the students but he was highly respected by his colleagues on the University faculty. He was never interested in amassing a fortune or making large sums of money by endorsing products in advertisements."

It is true that while Phog proved Naismith wrong about the need for coaching he also possessed a deep respect for Naismith's accomplishments and his place in history. Phog's most cherished possession was a Naismith sketch by physical education professor Edwin Elbel inscribed, "With kindest regards to F.C. Allen, the father of basketball coaching from the father of the game — James Naismith, 1936."

As basketball grew in popularity, Phog wanted people to know that the person who invented the sport resided in Lawrence. Phog also wanted to make sure Naismith got to the 1936 Games in Berlin, where Olympic basketball was introduced. Phog's fund-raising idea was to denote a week in which one penny from all gate receipts collected from college and high school games throughout the country would be donated to the Naismith Fund.

The National Association of Basketball Coaches (NABC), an organization Phog helped create a few years earlier, approved and area chairmans were established. At some games, tin cans were passed through the crowd.

"At Kansas, it was every game that winter," Bob Allen said. "When it came to me I used to shake it up to see how much was there. People gave pennies, nickels, dimes, damn few had extra quarters in those days."

But Kansas fans gave enough to make the school's total of $125 the largest from any one university. In some areas "Naismith Night" went smoother than others. The Midwest sector that included mostly Kansas, Missouri and Oklahoma collected $1,386.39 with the largest sum of $640.60 coming from the contributions pooled by Kansas high schools through the state's activities association.

Originally, Phog wanted to send Naismith and his wife, Maude, to the Olympics and have enough money left to purchase them a new home. The NABC countered and approved an Olympic trip, a tour of Europe, an annuity and a Naismith Memorial to be erected either in Lawrence or Springfield, Mass. The memorial had to wait but Naismith had enough money to make the trips, however without Maude who had become ill, and purchase the home of former KU Chancellor Frank Strong.

The Naismith Night was successful enough to inspire a Chanute, Kan., native named G.F. Alcott to propose another fund-raising plan for a Naismith Memorial — this one in the form of a new gymnasium at Kansas. Alcott's idea was to have every college give a portion of a

*Dr. James Naismith
in a picture taken for
the Jayhawker
Annual in either
1937 or 1937.
(Photo courtesy
University of Kansas
Sports Information)*

home gate to the fund. The Jayhawks needed a new building but nothing came of this plan.

A different building took Naismith's name. The Naismith Memorial, which evolved into basketball's Hall of Fame, opened in Springfield, Mass., in 1941 — the game's 50th anniversary — and Phog's speech at the dedication ceremony carried the day:

> *"This game, the only international game that is the product of one man's brain, stamps Dr. Naismith as a great educator, a kindly humanitarian and a practical Christian. He loved youth. The youth of the world will arise and call Dr. Naismith blessed.*

> *"And you sitting tonight in comfortable seats in this building dedicated to a wonder sport doubtless can make a small contribution which will keep alive the memories and traditions of a young man who struggled and who gave of himself the finest qualities that he had. He gave them to youth, and youth can pass along the durable things of life to the next youthful generation.*

> *"Please remember that the youth of 52 nations of this world are playing basketball. It is not a national sport — it is an international one. And the United States is the mother country of this game, to whom it was given by her foster son, James Naismith."*

Whatever warm feelings Naismith may have had for Phog apparently weren't shared by his children. In 1950, Naismith's son, Jack, saw a photograph in the *Kansas City Star* that showed the Kansas basketball team and Phog grouped at Naismith's grave. The cutline said the grave had not been decorated and it was necessary for Phog and the Jayhawks to do so. The photo must have been taken in the morning because at 12:30 that day, Jack and his wife had arrived from their Wichita home to lay flowers.

"The whole deal smacks of a publicity stunt at the expense of the Naismith family," Jack Naismith wrote to Kansas athletic director Dutch Lonborg. Phog explained that he didn't know the Naimsiths were coming, and that the request was made by a faculty member. It was not Phog's first disagreement with the Naismith children.

Two years earlier Phog had written to Naismith's daughter, Hellen Naismith Dodd of Fulton, Mo., about obtaining the copy of James Naismith's 13 original rules for the Helms Foundation Hall of Fame in Los Angeles. Dodd said the family had many requests, including private collectors who would pay a ransom. Dodd also took the opportunity to unload on Phog.

> *"I have been to Lawrence a number of times in the past five years as all three of my sons have been in school there. It's really no pleasure to go back because it only makes me realize how very little the University appreciated what my father did for it in the forty years he spent there.*
>
> *"As far as I know there isn't even a plaque to show he was ever there. I was in hopes when the basketball team had its (1923 team) reunion last spring they would find a way to say 'Thanks, Doc' but he was only an empty chair to them. This probably seems a little bitter to you but I'm not bitter. I'm only disappointed that people who have received so many benefits from Basket Ball can take it so for granted. To be quite frank I wonder if the name, Phog Allen, would mean as much to the country if there had been no game of Basket Ball."*

Ouch.

Kansas responded. At future 1923 team reunions Naismith was recognized. At the 1963 reunion, Dick Harp represented Naismith.

What the Naismith children probably didn't fully understand were Phog's efforts to promote and protect their father's image. When the *Chicago Herald-American* ran an ad in 1940 for Old Underoof whiskey in which Naismith's photo was used, Phog fired off letters of protest.

When the Hall of Fame was planning its 1941 dedication, Phog let it be known to officials in Springfield, Mass., that Naismith had wished any tribute to him be erected in Lawrence. Phog recalled this conversation in letters to Hall officials:

"Twelve years before Dr. Naismith passed on I went to him and said, 'Dr. Naismith, if and when somebody plans a great memorial to your honor, as they should, just where would you like that memorial to be placed?'

"'Well,' he said, 'I had thought some of Springfield, and then I thought of going to California to spend my latter days, but since I have lived in Kansas most of my life, my family was raised and educated here, I am determined to spend the rest of my days in Kansas, and, of course, I would like to see anything that is done for me placed at the University.'"

Today, Naismith is represented in several ways. Naismith Drive leads to Allen Field House. Naismith Hall is where many Kansas athletes reside. Naismith and his wife Maude are buried at Lawrence Memorial Park, and a large Naismith Memorial greets visitors at the entrance. Appropriately, he's depicted holding school textbooks in one arm and a basketball in the other. Memorial Park is located on 15th Street, east of campus. Across the street is another cemetery, Oak Hill, where the Allens rest.

Current Kansas coach Roy Williams often jogs to the cemeteries and, in 1993, made headlines when he revealed he patted the grave sites for luck. It must have worked; the Jayhawks advanced to the Final Four. Perhaps hoping for the same effect when her basketball team played a women's 1996 NCAA Tournament game in Lawrence, Texas coach Jody Conradt bussed her team to the grave sites to show her players basketball history.

9

THE

ENTREPRENEUR

A top college coach today can command hundreds of thousands of dollars for signing with a shoe company like Nike or Converse. Phog had a shoe contract of his own, but he didn't merely endorse a product, he helped create and market one of his own — the Phog Allen Basketball Shoe.

In May 1929, two years after the shoe hit the market, Phog received a quarterly royalty check for $194.40. Not a bad take, if it were just for the shoes. But the money also included sales of three additional items that carried the Phog Allen name: basketball, rule book and medicine kit.

Phog, who often claimed to be one of the poorest-paid coaches in the nation — and for his stature, he was — forever looked to make a buck on the side, and throughout most of his career, he was engaged with two or three major projects for outside income. Books, free-lance articles, instructional films, radio programs, coaching schools and clinics, medical inventions, and even a game related to basketball, Phog was one of college sports' first major entrepreneurs. It was his misfortune that the most energetic period of his creative life came during the Depression years of the 1930s.

To his credit, Phog didn't sell his name or likeness to just any product, and there was demand. Usually, the idea had to be his and the ware had to be related to his profession. He summed up his philosophy in a 1938 letter to the advertising company that represented General Mills Inc., which produced the breakfast cereal Wheaties. General Mills sought a series of basketball instructions by some of the nation's top coaches for the back of its Wheaties boxes. It had been a success in baseball and General Mills was so confident Phog would accept, it sent along a contract and offered to pay him $100 just for signing the following affidavit that he promotes Wheaties for his players.

"I get a cheer out of watching my boys eat plenty of good, nourishing food. For breakfast especially, I recommend this Breakfast of Champions set-up — a big bowlful of those whole wheat flakes called Wheaties, with plenty of milk or cream, and some fruit. There's a hearty, well-rounded meal that's fine for athletes in training. What's more, I notice that Wheaties flavor gets a big hand from just about everybody who eats that dish. Signed_____."

Phog, an oatmeal man, would have none of it. Not that he didn't appreciate the offer. His response:

"I have never sold my name by the way of endorsements. Whenever it has been possible for me to originate, invent or improve upon a basketball commodity — whether shoes, ball, basket, scorebook or write a text on basketball — that I have been glad to do. But my name has never appeared on 'banana ads' or Postum endorsements. I trust that you will not think that I am going high-hat, or giving your idea a slap in the face."

A slap in the face is what some of the manufacturers of Phog's products probably felt like giving him on occasion. Phog wasn't about to put his name on a shoe or ball that was something less than his idea of perfect. For more than a year, he carried on a feud with the Servus Rubber Company of Rock Island, Ill. Servus made his shoe and sold it through one of the nation's largest sporting goods companies of the day, Lowe & Campbell, whose corporate headquarters were in Kansas City.

At the time, Servus was also making the Walter Meanwell Shoe and the Ralph Jones Shoe. Meanwell had coached at Wisconsin and Missouri, Jones at Purdue and Illinois. Phog wanted his shoe to be distinctive. When the first shipment arrived from Servus to Lowe & Campbell in 1927, Phog was furious with the quality. Converse made

"Phog" Allen

Basketball Shoe

Here Are a Few "Phog" Allen Features

—A light weight, sturdy, wear-resisting shoe.
—Made over a special last providing greatest foot protection and comfort.
—Back stay prevents breaking at counter top.
—Narrow cut shank with built-in normal-arch feature, reinforces arch and insures proper support.
—Stubber toe guard lengthens life of shoe and gives toe protection from floor dragging.
—Sponge rubber cushion in heel absorbs shocks and eliminates blistered, bruised or "pounded" heels.
—Compounded pure red gum sole is extremely fast and will not burn, scuff off or slip on smooth floors.
—Narrow, snug fitting heel eliminates chance of blistered feet.
—Non-heat insole prevents foot-burn.
—Heavy gray duck top is loose-lined and shaped so that tight lacing will not bind ankle.
—There is no back seam in back of shoe to rub and cause discomfiture to the Achilles tendon.
—The shoe fits around the arch of the foot so that when player rises on toes for a quick shift there is no lost motion between the foot and shoe.
—SPECIAL REINFORCED CONSTRUCTION assures that the arch of the foot is supported at all times regardless of the player's position.
The "Phog" Allen Shoe has been designed and produced with painstaking care of details—and the result is here for you to enjoy.

Designed for Fast, Sure Footwork

Shape, color or weight give no indication of real merit in a basketball shoe—even the maker's name may be misleading.

Nowhere is scientific design more important than in the construction of a basketball shoe—

It must be made of good materials.

It must give the wearer foot comfort.

It must provide definite safety.

It must give long wear.

You find all these features in the "Phog" Allen Model plus—a certain "built-in" speed that permits a player to start quickly—sprint rapidly—pivot accurately and stop instantly.

No man is better prepared to design the perfect basketball shoe than Dr. Forest C. Allen, Physical Director and Basketball Coach at Kansas University. "Phog" Allen knows physiology—he understands bone structure—he appreciates the playing essentials of lightness, adhesion, safety and durability and this great shoe, designed by him, embodies the result of his experience as a foot expert and successful coach.

The poor showing of many a player of championship calibre can well be blamed on his shoes for the foot is the only part of the body that must be fitted perfectly to avoid sluggishness and fatigue.

Be sure — be safe — be fast — wear "Phog" Allen Basketball Shoes.

"Basketball Injuries and Their Care" and "Taping and Bandaging for Basketball Players," two new booklets written by "Phog" Allen will be sent to you free upon request. Write for them.

The "Phog" Allen Shoe is made in a complete range of men's sizes, from 5 to 12.

SERVUS RUBBER COMPANY, Rock Island, Illinois, U. S. A.

This is from a copy of a 1928 brochure for the Phog Allen Basketball Shoe.

a much better shoe, he asserted. Phog also was perturbed that the first flyer that went out about the shoe misspelled his name on the cover — Forest C. Allen.

The Phog Allen Shoe sold for $3 in 1928 — $3.75 in 1933 — and sales were disappointing, but it wasn't Phog's fault. He arranged for sales representatives to meet him at summer coaching clinics, had pairs shipped gratis to referees, newspapermen and fellow coaches. In return and not surprisingly, the shoe got a glowing report. Phog went so far as to have pairs shipped to his fellow Big Six coaches. Even Naismith found a pair in his mailbox one day with this note:

"The thought occurred to us that a considerable amount of the profit we are deriving from the sale of basketball shoes is due, in part, to your having originated this wonderful game."

In part?

Phog got Servus to create a shoe for kids ($1.85) and women. He had to have those; Meanwell also had shoes for kids and women. To help pump up sales, Phog wrote two booklets on treating injuries, which also happened to mention his recommendation for the proper athletic shoes — his.

The Phog Allen Basketball Shoe didn't last long. Less than a decade after making its debut, not even his own players were wearing it. By the late 1930s, Servus was out of business, and Phog had taken a liking to shoes produced by Wisco, a Wisconsin-based company. However, he did have his players wear the Phog Allen during practice.

All shoes displayed Phog's stitched signature. When Big Six coaches received the No. 202 Phog Allen basketball most said they feared a negative psychological effect using a ball signed by a rival coach. Phog agreed to remove his name from some but made sure he collected the royalties on those.

Phog's ball had distinctive black and red lacing. It was made the official ball of the 1927 AAU Tournament in Kansas City, but it didn't have much of a future. Servus produced the ball with Phog's signature for five years, then started removing the signatures from its products. Phog didn't know this. Servus continued to ship him orders with his signature.

When a 1937 letter from Servus informed him his name had been removed with a curt note, "You are the only one to whom we

In a photo taken around 1935, Phog Allen holds a Phog Allen basketball and wears a pair of Phog Allen shoes. (From the University of Kansas archives)

Phog Allen shows the Phog Allen basketball in 1928. (From the University of Kansas archives)

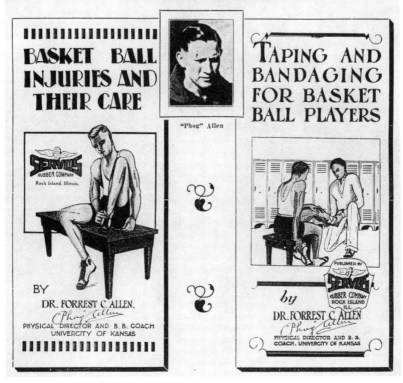

"Phog" Allen Authorizes Publication of New Books

BASKET BALL INJURIES AND THEIR CARE

"Phog" Allen

TAPING AND BANDAGING FOR BASKET BALL PLAYERS

SERVUS RUBBER COMPANY
Rock Island, Illinois.

BY
DR. FORREST C. ALLEN.
Phog Allen
PHYSICAL DIRECTOR AND B. B. COACH
UNIVERCITY OF KANSAS

PUBLISHED BY
SERVUS RUBBER COMPANY
ROCK ISLAND ILL.

by
DR. FORREST C. ALLEN
Phog Allen
PHYSICAL DIRECTOR AND B. B.
COACH. UNIVERCITY OF KANSAS

Phog used these two books he wrote about injury care to recommend his own brand of shoes.

sell a basketball nowadays with the Phog Allen name on it," Phog flew into a rage and fired back:

> *"You can rest assured that I would not have had your firm put my name on your ball for the mere vanity of it. If I am the only one that you sell a basketball nowadays with the Phog Allen name on it, please cancel the remaining order, as I would not want to play solitaire with myself."*

Servus and Phog parted ways when their second five-year contract expired in 1937, and the Jayhawks switched to a seamless ball signed by Naismith.

One of Phog's more lucrative ventures seemed like one of his silliest ideas. In the 1930s, he had heard of a government report that basketball had become the largest spectator sport in America with more than 80 million people paying to watch high school, college or professional games during the year surveyed. Phog's idea was to tap into that pool by getting spectators off their rumps and interested in an offshoot of basketball, a game he called Goal-Hi.

Basically, it was basketball without a backboard and the basket at the center of the playing floor, not at the ends. The court was a circle and not a rectangle. You shot the ball into the hoop and it would return through a chute in one of three directions.

Phog liked the game for several reasons: it was less strenuous than full-court basketball, which made it easier to promote to women's teams, youth clubs and kids. Phog believed running up and down the floor was too much for elementary school-aged kids. In Goal-Hi nearly all of the action took place around the basket. If players tended to congregate around the basket, Phog had the answer: a three-point shot. A basket made from beyond 15 feet counted for three — maybe the first time a three-pointer ever appeared in a rule book.

Phog also wrote the rule book. It came free with the official Goal-Hi equipment, which amounted to an adjustable pole, base and basket. The stuff was produced by Fred Medart Manufacturing Company of St. Louis, which even created the official leather Goal-Hi ball. For $29.50 you got the top-of-the-line standard, the mobile version. The $22.50 standard was cemented in the ground. The official ball was a costly $12. Phog was convinced Goal-Hi had a place in playgrounds and school yards.

The game was test-marketed in Lawrence, naturally, in the summer of 1939, and Phog had publicity shots made of kids, women and college students playing the game. For one photo, he dressed up high school coaches attending his summer coaching clinic in Kansas basketball uniforms. For other shots, Phog set up goals at the football stadium and planted spectators around the court.

Early sales of Goal-Hi did nothing to discourage Phog from thinking of himself as the next Naismith. Phog's deal with Medart was for five percent. His first check arrived in January 1940 for $42.27 on sales of $845.40. Goal-Hi was doing well in Texas and Richmond, Va. To spur sales, Phog called a few of his newspaper buddies in Kansas City and the national wire services, and in 1940, Goal-Hi took off.

"New game sweeps city," read a headline in Sioux Falls, South Dakota.

"Cage Coach Becomes Inventor of New Sport," cried the *St. Louis Star-Times*.

"Goal-Hi, New Game Developed by Noted Basketball Authority," reported *The Athletic Journal*.

"Se trata del Goal-Hi parecido al basketball," said a newspaper in Montevideo, Uruguay.

The next sales report was five, single-spaced legal-sized sheets of purchases made throughout the nation. Everybody was buying Goal-Hi. In the first three months of 1940, Medart sold $5,436.85 worth of equipment, netting Phog $271.84. The next three months were even better, as Phog cleared more than $400. It helped that Phog's basketball team was prominent in the news at the time. The 1939-40 season was the second for the NCAA Tournament, and the 1940 Western finals and championship game were scheduled for Kansas City in March. The Jayhawks won their way to the finals, losing to Indiana.

A month after the championship game, Phog and team dined at the mansion of Gov. and Mrs. Payne Ratner, and Phog sold them on Goal-Hi, promising to have a standard shipped. And maybe Phog could show the governor and his kids some shooting tips for the photo boys. When Medart replied no free Goal-Hi's, Phog bought a top-of-the-line model at the company discount price of $20.65 and had it delivered.

Another significant development for Goal-Hi was personally arranged by Phog. He smoothed over a long-standing feud between Medart and Lowe & Campbell and got Goal-Hi into the stores that used to carry his balls and shoes. Phog cleared more than $1,000 on his game in 1940, and 1941 started on an optimistic note. He had gotten former heavyweight boxing champion Gene Tunney, now a lieutenant commander in the Navy who was in charge of recreation for several air stations, to endorse Goal-Hi. The Medart sales force pushed hard, and the company offered a $50 bonus for the top Goal-Hi salesman for the year.

Phog and Medart withstood challenges from imitators. Some schools sent Phog shots of an apparatus that looked similar but not exactly like a Goal-Hi and claimed it had been around for years. One such item was called Uni-Goal. Rawlings' 1941 spring and summer catalog included an item called Pole-Goal, which duplicated Goal-

High school coaches at a 1939 summer clinic in Lawrence put on Kansas uniforms and demonstrate the game of Goal-Hi. Dimensions of the playing area are shown below. (Photo from the University of Kansas archives)

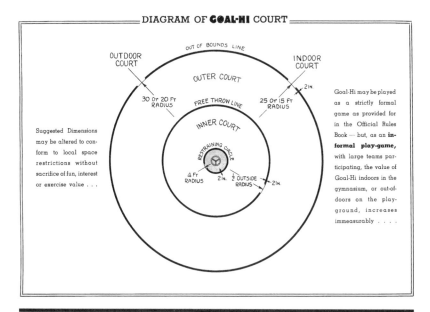

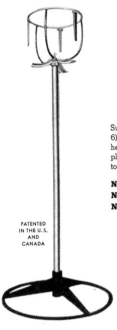

OFFICIAL **GOAL-HI** NON-ADJUSTABLE STANDARDS

- *Movable Type*
For Indoor and Outdoor Use

Substantially constructed and finished exactly the same as No. 907 (see Page 6) except that the height adjustment feature has been eliminated. Three fixed height standards available. These types are recommended for use where players of only one age group are likely to play Goal-Hi and it is not necessary to accommodate older or younger players. Order by number and description.

No. 908 — 8 ft. Height — for Elementary Use
No. 909 — 9 ft. Height — for Junior High Use
No. 910 — 10 ft. Height — for High and College Use

} $ **28** 75 YOUR NET COST

DELIVERED — (WE PAY THE FREIGHT)

PATENTED IN THE U.S. AND CANADA

No. GH 600 Goal-Hi Floor Protectors
The underside of the circular base of the official Goal-Hi standards are drilled to permit attachment of six special rubber buttons that eliminate any possibility of highly finished gym floors becoming marred or scuffed. Buttons are easily snapped into place.
No. G-H 600 (set of six) **75cNET** Delivered

OFFICIAL **GOAL-HI** NON-ADJUSTABLE STANDARDS

- *Permanent Type*
For Permanent Out-of-doors Installation

Three standards of 3 different heights available. Same high quality construction and finish as No. 917 (see Page 7) except for the adjustable height feature which is not included in these three standards. Recommended for use when players of only one age group are to be considered. Order by number and description.

No. 918 — 8 ft. Height — for Elementary Use
No. 919 — 9 ft. Height — for Junior High Use
No. 920 — 10 ft. Height — for High and College Use

} $ **21** 75 YOUR NET COST

PATENTED IN THE U.S. AND CANADA

DELIVERED — (WE PAY THE FREIGHT)

1939 Goal-Hi brochure showing some of the equipment available.

Hi. The difference between these and Goal-Hi, Phog contended, was his game had rules. Besides, Phog already had visions for expanding his game, perhaps a 12-foot Goal-Hi for taller players; a Goal-Hi for the swimming pool. Those could open up the YMCA and athletic club markets. Phog conducted a Goal-Hi tournament in Kansas City in 1940, and actually presented a trophy for the winning team.

GH 100 OFFICIAL LEATHER GOAL-HI BALL
. . . . Moulded — With Channeled Seams . . . .

Adapted as the official Goal-Hi leather ball. 'Tops' in stamina and correct action in all phases of the game. No. GH 100 has a thoroughly tested one-piece center, covered with carefully selected pebble grain cowhide, moulded and vulcanized to form a perfect, lasting sphere. Special channeled seams (Patent applied for) provide sure grip in handling. The official Goal-Hi ball is built with the utmost care, rigidly inspected and official in all details — size, shape and weight. Individually boxed. Inflating needle furnished.

Your Net Cost $12.00 Delivered

GH 200 REGULATION LEATHER GOAL-HI BALL
. . . . Moulded — With Channeled Seams . . . .

A very good quality ball. Built of pebble grain cowhide, moulded over a one-piece center forming a single sphere. Channeled seams provide correct feel and sure grip. Official in size and weight. No. GH 200 is a long wearing, moderately priced ball that will give desired service. Inflating needle furnished. Individually boxed.

Your Net Cost $9.00 Delivered

GOAL-HI RUBBER BALLS
Waterproof and Washable

SALES POLICY ON BALLS
Each Goal-Hi Ball has been carefully inspected and thoroughly tested. Each is perfect in workmanship, free from defects and will **NOT** be replaced **AFTER** being put into play.

No. GH 300 OFFICIAL	No. GH 400 REGULATION	No. GH 500 PLAYGROUND
Official in every respect—size, weight, shape, balance! Scuff-proof and virtually puncture-proof. Fabricated of 4-ply, finest grade Egyptian long-staple cotton fabric impregnated with rubber. The outside cover is of strong vulcanized rubber with simulated lacing, grooved seams and tan pebbled surface. A long-lasting, high quality ball for both indoor and out-of-door use. Equipped with all-rubber valve and STANDARD inflating needle. Individually boxed, inflated. Highly recommended!	Excellent for outdoor play under all conditions. Of 2-ply fabric, form-built construction, No. GH 400 Ball has a tan pebble - grained composition cover with simulated grooved seams. Perfect round shape, balanced—won't pull apart at seams. No bladder to replace. Weather and water-proof throughout. Equipped with all-rubber valve and STANDARD heavy duty rubber playground ball that will satisfactorily serve for a long period. Individually boxed, inflated.	Especially intended for outdoor use. Hand-built in multiple sections of 5-ply (laminated) tough rubber. Seams, stitches, pebble-grained surface texture, laceless design—even the tan color of a leather ball—are faithfully reproduced. No stitches to break and no bladder to replace. Official size, weight, and shape. Equipped with an all-rubber valve and with a STANDARD inflating needle. Individually boxed (not inflated). A highly satisfactory rubber playground ball.
Your Net Cost $6.85 Delivered	**Your Net Cost $4.25 Delivered**	**Your Net Cost $2.35 Delivered**

OFFICIAL GOAL-HI RULES BOOK

Contains all of the official rules for playing Goal-Hi, formally or informally, indoors and out-of-doors. Includes complete details and illustrations for laying out the playing courts for the several modifications of the game, as fully described by its founder, Dr. Forrest C. "Phog" Allen. Also contains a number of illustrations of various age-groups playing Goal-Hi and an extremely interesting and informative introductory article by Dr. Allen.

Per Copy $1.00 Net

RULES BOOK FREE

One Official Goal-Hi Rules Book is included Free with each shipment of any one of the Official Goal-Hi Standards illustrated and described in this brochure.

1939 brochure page showing the balls and the rule book.

In 1941, Goal-Hi earned Phog more than $1,000 in royalties, but while many small school districts placed orders, Medart couldn't interest the larger city schools. It wasn't a difficult piece of equipment to manufacture in high school shop class. Phog got many letters asking only for the rules book because the school had made its own goal. In June 1942, Medart wrote Phog informing him that after the current stock was sold the company, now heavily involved in the war effort, would produce no more, although it became a popular game in the military because it was easy to assemble and move. Phog received a settlement check for $750, and Goal-Hi slowed production. It resumed in earnest after the war. There were a couple more $1,000-plus royalty checks, but the frenzy eventually died down.

Medart hadn't heard the last of Phog. In 1945, he returned with another idea. Actually, the Foot & Arch Normalizer wasn't Phog's creation. A Georgia tax and estate counselor, Frederick Lang, invented a device intended to soothe the arch and foot muscles. Basically, it was a curved rolling pin in a box that Lang had contrived on his farm.

Phog was returning to his room from a long, hot day of teaching at a coaching school at Georgia Tech in 1936, when Lang intercepted him. Phog was in no mood to be pitched, but Lang persisted and Phog's feet were aching. After a few rolls across the normalizer Phog was sold and asked Lang to ship one to Lawrence. Phog talked up the normalizer to friends and coaching acquaintances and became something of a Midwest sales representative. His commission was $7 for every $17.50 normalizer he peddled. But Phog had bigger plans and targeted the sore-footed population: athletes, waitresses, store clerks. By 1944, Phog dreamed of selling the normalizer to foot soldiers returning from the war. Phog's recommendation of Lang's product to Georgia Gov. Eugene Talmadge helped land Lang a job in the state's treasury department.

Lang offered Phog a 10-percent share of the business. Phog wanted half of it. They never completed a deal, but Phog remained loyal to the product. Every morning before breakfast and evening before bedtime, he rolled his feet 100 times. He always traveled with his normalizer and kept one in the Jayhawks' locker room.

His books were probably Phog's steadiest source of outside income. In 1937, buoyed by the success of *My Basket-Ball Bible*, Phog wrote *Better Basketball*. Published by McGraw-Hill, *Better Basketball* was 482 pages and sold, like its predecessor, for $4. Phog got 10 percent. He was proud of the effort, which included updated coaching and injury treatment information from the *Bible*, but also a chapter on some of his favorite stories. It wasn't until the publication of *Better Basketball*, that Paul Endacott learned his effort in 1923 against Missouri was something out of the ordinary, at least to Phog.

Phog became a steadfast believer in the powers of the Lang Foot & Arch Normalizer. He helped push the product and kept one in the Kansas locker room and always took one with him on trips.

PRICE, $7.^{85}

11 inches long
6 inches wide
4 inches high
Weight, 4 pounds

DIRECTIONS

Consult your Physician, Podiatrist or Trainer for advice. Wear properly fitted stockings and shoes.

Place Normalizer on a rug on the floor. Grip roller with feet as shown on first page. Push the roller forward and backward, pushing it so as to contact only the front one-third of the foot. Then use the roller for second one-third of foot. The last one-third, or heel section, do not roll at all.

Those not excessively over weight and agile enough can get the quickest results by standing with both feet upon Normalizer, holding with the hands to bed post, highboy, etc., rolling forward and backward.

Gradually increase the amount of exercise each day, according to age and present general physical condition.

The 1936 team that finished 19-2 was used for most of the 163 photographs. McGraw-Hill pushed it nationally, taking out ads in such newspapers as the *New York Times*. As usual, local reviews were kind. The farther away from Lawrence, however, the less enthusiastically *Better Basketball* was embraced. "(Phog) thinks so much of the sport that he put almost as much effort into writing a book about it as did H.G. Wells in formulating his *Outline of History*," panned the *San Francisco Examiner*.

Seven years after it was published, *Better Basketball* had sold fewer than 7,000 copies, and more than 100 purchased by Phog who used his 40 percent discount to send autographed copies to friends.

Phog's third and final book borrowed tales from *Better Basketball*, and added some from another decade of coaching to come up with the 223-page *Coach Phog Allen's Sports Stories for You and Youth*. Allen Press (no relation) of Lawrence was the publisher in 1947 for the $3 book.

Between books, Phog frequently collected free-lance writing checks from major publications. His first job, in the mid-1920s, was writing a weekly basketball column for the Associated Press. As Phog became more well known he had stories published in *The Country Gentleman* (1934), for which he was paid $200 and *Esquire* (1940), $150.

He periodically hosted a radio program in the 1920s and 1930s on campus radio station KFKU to address primarily health issues. In 1936, he and the Jayhawks took part in an instructional film produced by Kodak that turned out to be a bust. Only 40 copies at $48 were sold during the first year. It was more successful as a $3 rental. Later that year, Phog participated in a more successful coaching film venture with Long Island's Clair Bee, John Bunn of Stanford, Notre Dame's George Keogan and Dave McMillan of Minnesota. The "talkie" film was sponsored by Converse and its representative Chuck Taylor.

Phog chose not to fleece schools and clubs for speaking engagements. Nobody in the history of sports could have traveled to speaking engagements more often than Phog. He was constantly in demand throughout Kansas and western Missouri and probably more obliging than he should have been. Beginning with postseason basketball banquets and marching through commencement addresses, Phog sometimes spoke twice a day. In 1940, his April and May calendar looked like this:

- April 2 Wathena HS athletic banquet
- April 3 Newton, Bethel College barbeque
- April 5 Abilene Rotary
- April 12 Kansas City, Kansas HS
- April 15 Topeka HS
- April 22 Lane HS
- April 23 Leavenworth HS
- April 29 Wichita Rotary Club
- April 30 Winfield HS assembly, 2 p.m.; Russell Chamber of Commerce, 7 p.m.
- May 2 Olathe HS
- May 15 Hill City HS commencement
- May 16 Seneca HS commencement
- May 21 Humbolt HS commencement
- May 22 Marysville HS commencement
- May 24 Wamego HS commencement
- May 29 Bonner Springs HS commencement

Today, top coaches are paid as much as $25,000 per speech. Phog charged $25 plus five cents a mile. If schools couldn't afford him, especially during the Depression, Phog didn't charge. The Kansas publicity office mailed a biography and photo to the school in advance, and the event always got good coverage.

In 1934, Phog nearly didn't make it to a speech. He was driving from Abilene to Kansas City when the fly wheel and the ring gear of his Buick sedan ripped through the floor board. The car ran off the road. Phog wasn't hurt, but it wasn't the first, nor would it be the last, misadventure for Phog and automobiles.

Phog also dabbled in a few ventures outside of basketball. In the early 1930s he became part owner of a Lawrence swimming pool called the Jayhawk Plunge. He also became a major stockholder in a Lawrence theater corporation, and for Christmas presents to children of athletic department staff and friends, mailed out passes. Twelve-year-old Max Falkenstien got his movie coupon book and promptly returned a thank-you letter. In 1996, Max, the son of former Kansas business manager Earl Falkenstien, began his 51st season as the Jayhawks' football and basketball radio color commentator.

Retirement didn't keep Phog from the marketplace. Late in his career, "Phog's Liniment" hit the stores. It was widely used by athletic teams but started to disappear in the early 1970s when the manufacturer pulled it off the market. When a consumer couldn't find it in 1971, a few politicos, some of Phog's old friends, got involved and "Phog's Liniment" soon returned to circulation, continuing the flow of royalty checks that padded Phog's income for decades.

As she did in most every aspect of Phog's life, Bessie figured prominently in his outside income. She wrote the books (Phog dictated his newspaper and magazine articles to secretaries) freeing Phog to pursue his interests. Bessie's reward? She got half of Phog's income. When royalty checks were delivered, he immediately cut his wife a check.

Bessie ran the household but also had her own projects. She purchased a home for the Allens' oldest son, Milton, and his family, when he enrolled in law school. The home at 831 Louisiana, which they called Peace Cottage, became Phog's and Bessie's when the last of their six children was grown.

Bessie was happy to help Milton, who had straightened out his life. Of the Allen children, he was most like his father as a youth — untamed and reckless. Mitt was a smoker, drinker and fighter. Bob Allen remembers the night his brother came home after a hard night and was ordered to the basement by Phog, who pulled on boxing gloves. Three blows and Mitt was done. Eventually, the family decided it was best for Mitt to leave and he enrolled at Iowa State, where he lived with coach Louis Menze, Phog's friend and star athlete at Central Missouri.

Mitt transferred to Kansas after a year and became a fine basketball player from 1934-36, although it would be a few more years before the run-ins would end. During a practice in his senior year, Mitt was startled to see Phog walk in wearing Mitt's overcoat. Dad fumbled through the pockets, discovered a pack of cigarettes, then dismissed his son for the day. Mitt thought he was done for the season, but Phog had him back the next day. The antics didn't stop, and Phog benched Mitt for an important game at Nebraska that season.

Eventually Mitt, like his father did decades earlier, mellowed as he matured. He became a successful Lawrence attorney, representing his father on occasion, and giving the Allens one half of the combination most families dream about: a lawyer and a doctor. Bob, often the peacemaker between his brother and father, completed the combination when he began his medical career as a surgeon-physician in Kansas City.

10

RULES, RULES, RULES

If the rules makers had listened to Phog we wouldn't recognize basketball today.

The basket would measure 12 feet from the floor, not 10. After every goal, the game would stop, the teams would be brought to center court and a possession would be gained by a jump ball. The center wouldn't jump each time, but coaches would establish a jumping lineup so centers would jump against centers, forwards against forwards and guards against guards.

Beliefs that a half-court game was more fundamentally sound and that basketball discriminated against guards — Phog never called his ball handler a point guard but a quarterback or center — guided Phog's coaching philosophy for much of his career. The center jump after every basket had been on the books until 1937. Phog wanted to bring it back with his idea of a player rotation, like a batting order in baseball.

Without the center jump after baskets, the game had become "hockey-ized," according to Phog. Too hectic, not enough strategy. Phog didn't want up-tempo, and when Stanford star Hank Luisetti scored 50 points in a 92-27 victory over Duquesne in 1938, Phog may have been the only person in basketball unimpressed. He wrote:

"Out West football is king. So the Golden Coast people, being so enamored of football, put it up to the basketball group to hockey-ize basketball to attract attention. By eliminating the center jump, they made it the rambling, scrambling, fire-wagon game, sans finesse and adroit playing. They've substituted speed for skill in ball-handling. Spectators, I'm sure, wish for a few lulls in the game. Continuous excitement is too much for those with weak hearts. To put the ball in play immediately after a successful field goal would continue the strenuous exertion giving the players no moment for relaxation."

It's a good thing that Phog's Jayhawks were good during this era. Watching paint dry sounds more exciting.

College basketball expanded rapidly in the 1920s and 1930s, and there seemed to be a major rules change about every year. A watershed moment in the sport occurred in 1927, when Doc Meanwell led a movement to eliminate the dribble. Meanwell believed the game moved better with several short passes and proposed a one-dribble-per-possession rule to basketball's joint rules committee, made up of AAU, NCAA and YMCA members. The motion passed 9-8.

Phog and other prominent college coaches like Nat Holman of City College of New York were outraged. Phog believed dribbling down the floor was as exciting as an open-field run in football and flayed the committee while speaking at the National Education Association at Drake University in April. His comments made the newspapers and in two weeks he received 169 telegrams from college and high school coaches throughout the nation supporting his stance.

At the Drake Relays the next month, Phog invited his coaching friends to meet and hash out their problems with the joint rules committee. He was elected chair of the group which agreed to meet the next month in Chicago. Word spread, and at 9 a.m., Friday, June 10 at the Auditorium Hotel, the first meeting of the National Association of Basketball Coaches was called to order. Most of the nation's top coaches showed up: Holman, Meanwell, Washington's Hec Edmundson, Ohio State's Harold Olsen, Purdue's Piggy Lambert, Notre Dame's George Keogan and Iowa's Sam Barry were among the early supporters.

Phog called the meeting to order and Creighton coach Art Schabinger, the NABC's first secretary-treasurer, read the minutes from the Des Moines meeting. A constitution was drafted, and the first stated purpose of the group was "To further dignify the basketball coaching profession." Annual dues were set at $2. The temporary labels were removed from Phog's and Schabinger's titles, and Illinois coach Craig Ruby was named vice president. Other officers in the first year of the NABC were Syracuse coach Lewis Andreas, second vice president, and California's Nibs Price, third vice president. Before the 1928 meeting, where Phog was re-elected president, the NABC — at Phog's suggestion — made Naismith the organization's honorary president.

Phog did not use his position to steamroll his proposed changes through the committee. However, he made himself heard, especially when it came to the 12-foot basket. At every NABC meeting, in coaching clinics and even high school banquets, Phog got on his soapbox for an issue that never gained much support. Even his former player and assistant, John Bunn, wasn't in his corner. At Stanford in 1931, Bunn made studies of his team's scrimmages with the basket at three heights — 10, 11 and 12 feet.

"One might draw the conclusion on the basis of this report that the raising of the goal is undesirable from practically every standpoint that was investigated," Bunn wrote. No matter. Phog forged ahead, convinced the game's dimensions should grow with the players. Phog, who also wanted to stretch the width of the floor from 50 to 56 feet, knew the 10-foot basket was accidental; that was the height of the indoor track around the YMCA balcony that Naismith had attached the peach basket.

Phog didn't like 10 feet for many reasons. By his calculation, 80 percent of the fouls occurred around the basket as smaller players attempted to prevent larger players from catching the ball or scoring easy hoops. Until 1944, four fouls meant disqualification. He abhorred the tip-in, believing it rewarded an offense for missing a shot, and had no appreciation for the dunk, which was legal although not possible for many in those days. Tall players were "mezzanine peeping toms" or "goons" to Phog.

With the hoop two feet higher, Phog reasoned the action would move away from the basket and relieve the congestion. It would eliminate goaltending by the defense, which was legal until 1944, and remove the "goalie" from basketball. The three-second lane violation rule wouldn't be necessary because taller players wouldn't stand under the basket. It's easier to make an 8-foot bank shot, Phog contended. Further, Phog believed fewer fouls would mean more field goals. In the 12-foot game, Phog wanted field goals to count three points, which he said actually was Naismith's idea. He believed there should be greater return for a field goal. In 1939, Phog wrote:

"Men 6-10 are getting to be quite commonplace. The presence of so many long fellows has reduced basketball to a freakish demonstration and has put an almost unbearable handicap on the finer athletes of a normal 6-foot height. Certainly no discrimination is asked against an exceptionally tall player. Rather, uniformity is asked so that discrimination against the little fellow is removed.

"We have seen tall players in many team line-ups born without any special gift in basketball, but who were on the team solely on the accident of extreme height. Some junior high school coach discovered this altitudinous, sky-scraping stopper cozing ethereally down the hall and the coach made for him with a pair of shorts, the stimulus being mainly his altitude and not his mobility. Only a severe cardiac insufficiency will permit that basketball monstrosity to escape that coach's tentacles."

Kansas kept a pair of 12-foot goals at its practice floor in Robinson Gym. Phog believed by firing toward those in practice his players would learn to put more arc on their shots. In 1934, Kansas actually played two games with a 12-foot basket that count in the record book. The 1934-35 season opened with Kansas and Kansas State meeting on each other's floor with the taller goal. The first game was played on Dec. 14 in Lawrence with K-State winning 39-35 in overtime. Four days later, the Jayhawks won in Manhattan 40-26.

Also in those games, field goals counted three points and the baskets were moved in four feet toward the center of the court, creating a six-foot space behind the basket. Naismith attended the game in Lawrence and didn't like the heightened goal because basketball rapidly was gaining worldwide acceptance and such a drastic change would prove unpopular, especially with the Japanese and Chinese, who didn't have many tall players. But he was so convinced basketball would see his way on this, Phog was guaranteeing victory to a friend.

"Next season is 1935," Phog wrote in May 1934. "I will buy you a good hat if by 1940 that basket is not either 11 feet or 12 feet. That goes for the best Stetson that you can wear."

No word on whether Phog paid up, but he was never deterred.

"The 12-foot basket is coming as sure as death and taxes," Phog said in 1949.

Phog had some support in the ranks. Henry Iba of Oklahoma A&M came out for the higher goal in 1940. Two years later, 7-foot Bob Kurland enrolled and Iba suddenly didn't mind the 10-foot goal, especially when he won the 1945 and 1946 NCAA championships with one of college basketball's first dominating centers. In Kurland's senior year, Phog didn't want to play the Aggies. "I'm not afraid of meeting (Oklahoma A&M) but when you have 7-footers competing against 6-footers, well, that just isn't basketball," Phog wrote.

Most other coaches scoffed at Phog's higher hoop idea. Basketball's dimensions were ideal, they contended. Also, if college goals were raised and those in high school remained at 10 feet, the newcomer would have a difficult adjustment. The rules committee never took Phog seriously on this one, and truth be known, neither did his players.

"I was never taken by it," said Ted O'Leary. "The big guys still had the advantage."

Irony abounds in all this. While Phog was moaning about unskilled giants, his 6-foot-7 Al Wellhausen, who lettered in 1935 and 1937 didn't do much except goaltend. Phog stationed him in front of the opponents' basket, and although Wellhausen was a good leaper he wasn't polished enough to help the Jayhawks on offense.

Phog didn't win an NCAA Tournament until he broke down and recruited a skilled big man, and in 6-9 center Clyde Lovellette, he got one of the best to play at Kansas. When Lovellette left after the 1952 title season, Phog nearly won his second crown with another big center, B.H. Born. And there was Wilt. Phog got the player he long complained about in Wilt Chamberlain, although he never got to coach him because of mandatory retirement.

Nor did Phog get to coach Harry Kersenbrock, who would have been college basketball's first giant. Before Phog ever mentioned a 12-foot goal, he was preparing to unleash the first 7-footer in college basketball. Kersenbrock was a gentle giant from Crete, Neb., whose high school play wasn't well known. As a junior in 1924 Kersenbrock scored 146 points for a team that finished 10-8. The next year, Crete finished 22-2 and Kersenbrock scored 444 points, including 45 in a game that today stands as a school record.

The University of Nebraska was familiar with Kersenbrock but coaches thought he wasn't coordinated enough, so he enrolled at small Doane College and started for a team that finished 11-3. That's when Phog found out about him and persuaded Kersenbrock to attend Kansas. Kersenbrock attended Doane for one more semester before transferring. He was going to suit up for the Jayhawks for the 1928-29 season, and Phog was excited. He had Servus make up a special size 13 Phog Allen Shoe for this newcomer and — quite unusual for Phog — boasted about Kansas' chances for the upcoming season.

But in the early evening of June 28, 1928, Kersenbrock and a friend were returning from a canoe ride along the Blue River. The canoe overturned. The friend swam to safety and shouted to Kersenbrock to hold on to the boat. Kersenbrock started to but lost his grip while the boat was bobbing. He slipped under the shallow but rapidly moving water. The body was recovered an hour later. "Few young lives have held greater promise than his," read the obituary in *The Crete News*.

The turn of events devastated the team. In their first full season at 2,969-seat Hoch Auditorium, the 1929 Jayhawks finished 3-15, the worst record in school history. They lost eight of 10 Big Six games, another all-time low. That season, Kansas made its first West Coast trip and managed to win one of three games from California in Oakland, but the rest of the season was a disaster.

Kansas recovered nicely the next season, winning its first 13 games before finishing 14-4, and in 1931 the Jayhawks ended a three-year championship drought.

More rules changes were affecting the game throughout the 1930s, and while Phog sounded off about many of them, the Jayhawks kept winning. Kansas won or shared seven Big Six titles in the 1930s, including his second "ever victorious" conference title team of 1936.

Whatever the rules, Phog usually made them work for him. In 1950, Kansas defeated St. John's 52-51 in Madison Square Garden when Lovellette scored on a tip-in with 15 seconds left. Kansas had been fouled seconds before, but rules at the time permitted a choice, attempt the free shots or retain possession. Phog usually waived the free throws. That season, the Jayhawks attempted 354 from the line, their fewest tries in the past 45 years. The NCAA put an end to the free-throw option rule in 1952.

Phog probably made as much a name for himself nationally by blasting the rules and the coaches supporting them as he did winning championships. It was big headlines in 1934 when Notre Dame's Keogan ridiculed the 12-foot basket. Phog's return volley: "Coach George Keogan is running true to form as a perennial objector on basketball rules."

The 12-foot goal and the jump ball were only two of Phog's lost causes. He also never won much support for his notion that the fan-shaped backboard with a white background was superior to the rectangle glass kind. Schools could decide its style of backboard, and in 1940 the NCAA approved the fan-shaped board.

This was a victory for Phog, who had them immediately installed in Hoch Auditorium and Robinson Gym. The new board was 18 inches narrower and 13 inches smaller than the old ones. Phog was a firm believer that a white background was easier to shoot against. With the 1940 change that moved the end line boundary from two to four feet behind the basket, Phog also knew the fan-shaped board could be attacked from over the top. It wasn't against the rules to flip a shot over the backboard.

But the fan-shaped board did not have much of a life span. In 1946, the NCAA authorized the transparent backboard; all the major buildings were already using them. Kansas lost to Colorado in a Western Regional game in 1942 at Kansas City's Municipal Auditorium, which used the glass. Phog squealed but to no avail.

Before the fan-shaped boards, Phog went in for a device called Bask-O-Lite, which looked like a regular basket except for the ring around the bottom of the net that tripped a red light bulb on the backboard directly behind the basket, kind of like today's hockey light after a goal. The idea was to allow spectators with lousy seats to know when goals are scored. Ultimately, fans decided their vision wasn't so poor that they couldn't see a basket and the concept died.

Phog also got few takers on his "safety zone" idea. The safety zone was a 16-foot radius around the basket. Players could dribble in and out of the circle but could not drive in and shoot if a teammate was also in the ring. The Associated Press picked up Phog's idea, and an Indiana newspaper ran the story under the headline, "'Phog' Allen Gets Another Brain Tantrum."

Phog had many more problems with the law makers than the law — the officials. He could sympathize, having been a referee earlier in his career. Phog never publicly criticized the stripes, and only rarely griped to the league office about a poorly called game. But when Phog lit up an official, he felt like Christmas. An example is this 1953 letter to a Tulsa-based official:

> *"To show your utter incompetency to handle a game of this nature, you consistently penalized the Kansas team from the very early beginning without calling fouls on the University of Oklahoma, and they were right under your eyes. In my opinion this is unforgivable on the part of an official, and personally I would not want you to work in any of our games from now on. In all of my experiences as a coach, this is but the second letter I have written to an official where I was convinced that there was either cowardice or incompetency so evident. Very cordially yours, Forrest C. Allen."*

Early in his career, Phog had a reason to feel confident in big games, like the pivotal 1923 encounter with Missouri. The lead official was E.C. "Ernie" Quigley, a native of St. Mary's, Kan., by all accounts an outstanding official and a friend of Phog's. Nobody was more of a man for all seasons than Quigley. As a major-league umpire, he worked six World Series and served as the National League supervisor of umpires. He called three Rose Bowls and officiated basketball for 37 years. Quigley probably worked more pro and college games than any person in the profession's history. And few were as colorful.

This was a man who called 13 balks in the first inning of the 1927 Japanese World Series, who once told a charging basketball coach that an opponent would get one technical free throw for every step back to the bench, then awarded seven free shots. When Quigley issued the same edict on another night, the coach was waiting. Two players came out and hoisted the coach by the elbows back to the bench. Quigley, who died in 1960 at 81, was often a showboat. His voice boomed with such lines as "You can't DO that," and "Son, I..I..I made the rules."

Fans never let him forget he was a Kansas man and football star. Lawrence is where his career in sports started and finished. In 1944, Quigley was named KU's athletic director, a position he held until 1950. When he cleaned out his desk, Quigley discovered a check from the 1924 World Series that he never cashed. The greatest accomplishment of his KU regime was engineering a $113,000 drive to retire the football stadium's debt.

"As an official he wasn't ruffled by anything," Ted O'Leary said. "One night, after some bad calls, our fans were throwing coins on the floor. I was the captain (in 1932) and went up to him and told him I could get it stopped. He turned to me and said in this booming voice, 'Young man, NOTHING bothers me.'"

While some of Phog's suggested rules changes were bizarre, some of his other visions proved remarkably clairvoyant. In 1948, Phog made two suggestions that were openly ridiculed: paying college players and playing football games in an indoor arena. Phog believed the gamblers who preyed on gullible and poor players could be run out of business if basketball players were paid a monthly stipend of $80. "Why wouldn't this be all right?" Phog told the *Kansan*. "People get paid for singing in the choirs."

As for the indoor facility, Phog didn't mention the word dome, but that's what he was talking about to a *Kansas City Times* reporter, who couldn't believe somebody was suggesting playing football under a roof.

"Sure thing, why not?" Phog said. "I mean only when the weather is just awful. Supposing it's snowing or raining so bad it's almost impossible to play outside. Why not play where it's dry and cozy. If a field house would seat 20,000 persons that would be large enough. There wouldn't be more than 20,000 turn out on a nasty day anyway."

As for growing grass indoors — Phog never mentioned anything about artificial turf — apparently that would have to be someone else's idea.

11

OLYMPIC RISE AND FALL

Nobody worked harder than Phog to have basketball included in the Olympic Games when it debuted in 1936. When a YMCA official once suggested to Phog that no one early advocate could be singled out, Phog shot back immediately. He wanted names. The YMCA official never came up with any.

Phog's ego could be Olympic-sized, and it probably cost him his chance to be remembered more vividly in the Olympic movement. In February 1936, Phog was named Director of Olympic Basketball. That job, designed to be something of a troubleshooter while the team was in Berlin, plus the two coaching positions made up the administrative staff for Olympic basketball.

But on May 5, Phog delivered his resignation to Doc Meanwell, chairman of the Olympic Basketball Committee. During those three months, Phog was embroiled in a major fiasco with the Amateur Athletic Union, which marked the beginning of a verbal battle with the organization that endured for the rest of Phog's life. The AAU, Phog announced, was nothing but a bunch of "quadrennial oceanic hitchhikers who chisel their way across the oceans every four years on the other fellow's money."

The other fellow in this case was Phog and the University of Kansas, which had cleared more than $10,000 at the gate for an Olym-

This cartoon depicting Phog's battles with the Amateur Athletic Union appeared in the Kansas City Star *May 10, 1936.*

pic playoff series with Utah State, only to have the money deposited into AAU coffers. In 1936, the AAU was the most powerful organization in amateur athletics and basically held political control over the Olympic sports. Having the AAU seize a profitable gate was one thing, but Phog was furious when he learned the AAU didn't cover all the expenses of the basketball team's trip to Berlin. Phog knew half of the team members, six of the 14 were from the McPherson, Kan., Globe Oilers, the national AAU champions. Seven players came from Universal Pictures, a California-based AAU team that beat the Oilers in a playoff game in New York, and there was one college player.

"I talked with the manager of the McPherson Oilers," Phog wrote in 1939. "He stated to me that the boys on both the Universal Picture Company of Hollywood and the McPherson Oilers actually had to put up their jewelry and borrow money to make the trip to Berlin. It was a sorry mess."

Such a sorry mess that the colleges vowed not to take part in future Olympics if the AAU was in control. There was talk that basketball would not be part of the program for the 1940 Games scheduled for Tokyo. Of course, World War II took care of that, and when the Olympics returned in 1948, so did basketball with the NCAA champion — Kentucky, that year — supplying half the roster.

Naismith was Phog's inspiration behind his Olympic push. Throughout his tenure at Kansas, Naismith corresponded with his friends from the Springfield YMCA, including many overseas who had taken the idea of basketball with them. By 1895, basketball was in France and a few years later had spread to Italy. Another of Naismith's former students had taken the game to Japan. Allied soldiers helped spread the game's popularity in Europe during World War I.

The forerunner to the International Amateur Basketball Federation was formed in 1928 with several nations represented. All this information was funneled by Naismith to Phog whose 1929 paper, "The International Growth of Basketball" opened the eyes of AAU officials. Before he had the data, AAU secretary-treasurer Daniel Ferris, second in command to AAU president Avery Brundage, scoffed at the notion of Olympic basketball.

"Personally, I feel that there will be so much objection by foreign countries to basket ball that it will be impossible to have it listed," Ferris wrote to Phog in 1929. "They will contend that so few countries are playing the game that it should not be included as one of the Olympic sports."

Phog's goal was to get basketball into the 1932 Games at Los Angeles and by the early 1930s waged a vigorous campaign through the American Olympic Committee. After receiving some early encouragement, Phog started to get some negative vibes. As the host nation, the United States had the right to introduce two new sports to the program. Phog was told it was too late to consider basketball but that it might find its way into the Games as a demonstration sport.

It didn't matter to Phog how basketball got on the program, so long as it did. The International Olympic Committee approved basketball but the final word belonged to the Los Angeles Olympic Committee. An Oct. 7, 1930, letter from Brundage discouraged Phog. "The Los Angeles Organizing Committee, which is concerned to a large extent about finances, will, of course, consider the subject of additional sports largely from the point of view of gate receipts."

Phog thought basketball would stir plenty of interest. The game was growing in the West, especially at Southern Cal, where Sam Berry had taken over in 1930 from his coaching duties at Iowa. Phog, in fact, had enlisted Berry's help at attempting to sell hoops to the Los Angeles committee. But Phog also knew that the fastest growing sport in that part of the nation was football, and in the newly con-

This Feb. 7, 1936, illustration from the Kansan *student newspaper, honored Phog for his efforts to make basketball an Olympic sport. Basketball officially became part of the Olympics in the 1936 Games in Berlin.*

structed Coliseum, Los Angeles was an ideal setting to display college football for the world and clear an enormous gate.

That's exactly what happened. Football was added as the demonstration sport with an exhibition game between players of Northern and Southern California. Pop Warner of Stanford coached the North, Harold Jones of Southern Cal the South. Phog watched the game and many other Olympic events. Most of the Allen family went to Los Angeles and rented an apartment in Glendale for a month.

While there, Phog had lunch with Karl Diem, secretary for the Organizing Committee of the Berlin Olympics, and Sohaku Ri, the lead official of a Japanese delegation and basketball enthusiast. Japan wanted to host the 1940 games, and Ri promised basketball would be included. But Berlin also was interested, and on Oct. 25, 1934, Diem telegraphed Phog.

"With further reference to our former correspondence I have the pleasure of informing you that the Organizing Committee at its meeting on Oct. 19 adopted the resolution that Basketball be included into the program of the 1936 Olympic Games at Berlin."

Phog knew before the AAU. He cabled Brundage and other national officials, who couldn't believe the news. "I was somewhat surprised inasmuch as (a German Olympic official) made a very definite statement this summer that it would be impossible to include basketball on the program," Ferris wrote. "It will be necessary for President Brundage to appoint an Olympic Basketball Games Committee to arrange America's participation. I would suggest that you drop President Brundage a line embodying any suggestions you may have to offer."

Whoosh! Out flew Phog's letter, reminding Brundage that he had appointed Phog as the AAU's representative on basketball's joint rules committee six years earlier, and, after all, Phog suggested, it was he who got the ball rolling on the Olympic movement in America. The Jayhawks had even showed their international spirit by scheduling a home game against the national team of Mexico in 1930.

Phog was as qualified as anybody to be part of the Olympic team. He had a terrific record, a basket full of league championships and because of Naismith the international contacts. What he didn't have was the clout of a governing body behind him. The colleges had less to do with the 1936 basketball team than any Olympics until the Dream Team of 1992. Power belonged to the AAU.

However, Phog's chances looked good. In September, 1935, Phog's buddy, Ernie Quigley, just happened to have lunch in Chicago with a group that included Ferris and wrote to Phog, "There was no doubt in the minds of any of them that you would be the logical one to receive this appointment."

Meanwell already had been chosen chairman of the Olympic Basketball Committee. The group met in Chicago on Feb. 2, 1936, to select a director. Phog was recommended, and he immediately got word out to the local press. Phog's job was to oversee the eight-team playoff in Madison Square Garden from April 3-6 to determine the team. The field would consist of a YMCA entry, two from the AAU and five college teams. The AAU and NCAA representatives were to be selected through regional playoffs. Teams meeting in the championship game would supply 13 of the 14-man roster. The coach would come from the winning team, the assistant from the runner-up.

Phog not only had a hand in Olympic administration, he had a chance to be the coach. The Jayhawks finished the 1936 regular season 18-0. In the Olympic District playoff in Kansas City, Kansas defeated Washburn and Oklahoma State. Now, all the Jayhawks had to do was win two of three from unheralded Utah State in Kansas City to qualify for the Madison Square Garden games. The Jayhawks nearly won by default. The idea for these pre-Olympic tournaments was to have each school pay its travel expenses, do its part for the Olympic movement. But Utah State wouldn't come without its expenses paid. Phog authorized $500 from the gate of the district playoff to bring Utah State to Kansas City. With three all-Big Six starters — Ray Ebling, Francis Kappelman and Fred Pralle — the Jayhawks looked formidable. But Kansas needed overtime to win the opener 39-37 and now the Jayhawks were less confident. They also were mad. At least their coach was.

Phog always preferred Kansas to wear its white uniforms. But the Jayhawks wore red tops in the opener because Utah State coach Dick Romney told Phog the team had only packed its white jerseys. Phog couldn't believe a team would travel to a series with only one set of tops, so he had his players wear white for the second game. Romney sent a manager back to the hotel for the second, blue set.

The Aggies got by Kansas 42-37 in the second game and won the clincher in a blowout 50-31. Phog wouldn't be the coach and his team lost its chance to reach Berlin. Now Phog's attention could be directed 100 percent toward organizing the Olympic team, but the next three weeks turned out to be some of the most tumultuous in Phog's life, and by the second week in May, he was out of the Olympic picture.

During the playoff series with Utah State, the AAU office heard a rumor that Kansas had been using a professional player, Kappelman, and would be forced to forfeit its games and Big Six championship. Not true, Phog said, and wrote to the AAU indicating Kappelman's eligibility had been cleared by the conference. As with all of his correspondence, Phog's letter was signed, "Director and Coach." It was not on University of Kansas stationery. Phog meant Director and Coach of Kansas. But AAU officials interpreted it to mean Director and Coach of the Olympic team, and they huffed that Phog had no reason to assume he was to be the coach.

By the time the misunderstanding was resolved, the AAU had told Dr. Joe Reilly, president of the Kansas City Athletic Club and an AAU official, that he would make the trip to Berlin as the director and Phog would have to pay his own way. Why Reilly? The Olympic playoffs in Kansas City were the only ones that made money, and Reilly was in charge of that district.

Except Reilly, who had to be in New York to run a Golden Gloves boxing tournament, had turned over his basketball responsibilities to Phog, and Phog put on quite a show at Convention Hall with streamers, banners, spotlights, high school bands and cheerleaders. Phog even had Lowe & Campbell make up a large Utah State pennant.

But the final straw was Phog's public criticism of the AAU. Universal Pictures and the Globe Oilers played for the AAU championship in Denver. On their way to New York for the Olympic tournament, the teams stopped in Topeka for an exhibition game to help defray Olympic expenses. Universal didn't take it seriously and lost 42-29. The team dressed only five players, and when one collected his fourth foul (that disqualified you in 1936) with plenty of time remaining, he remained in the game and finished with eight fouls. *Topeka Daily Capital* columnist Gene Kemper summed up the feelings of some 2,000 fans:

> *"That farcical exhibition Thursday night, which some of us prematurely designated as a basketball game, probably will serve as Topeka's insurance policy against future indigestion produced by AAU teams. Behind it all, as I see it, is a fundamental difference in the youth of the two states, Kansas and California. The Kansas kid has a good chance of growing up on a farm or in a small community. There, rather than go to shows and jolly around, he wrestles, plays games and has fun in competition. A game is a game with the Kansas kid and you have to whip him to beat him.*

> *"Out in California, sports are fashionable. Kids don't get into them for sheer diversion and fun. They follow the crowds. Everyone out there is trying to measure up to some Hollywood idol. The good athlete in coast schools is given an easy ride. Pleasing a paying and expectant crowd meant nothing to them. They're from California."*

(Note: Four of the five starters on the 1996-97 Kansas team are fashionable, California kids.)

Phog, too, ripped the AAU for the exhibition, but he was more angry to learn that the income from the tournament he conducted was all going to the AAU, and that organization was not contributing to the Olympic fund. Meanwell got his letter of resignation from Phog a few weeks later. Universal Pictures defeated the Globe Oilers for the Olympic championship in New York, setting the lineup for the first American Olympic team: seven players from Universal Pictures, six from the Globe Oilers and one from the University of Washington. James Needles of Universal Pictures was the head coach, Gene Johnson of the Globe Oilers was the assistant. Reilly went as the director.

As publicity from Phog's resignation grew, the AAU responded that Phog had quit a position that never really existed. Brundage claimed the director's job was simply an appointment by the NABC and never approved by the Olympic committee. But not attending the Olympics did remove Phog from defending the Games to The Committee of Fair Play in Sports, which had for three years been calling for a boycott of American participation in Germany under Nazi auspices. In 1933, Phog had told the president of the American Jewish Congress that he was against the Olympic Games in Berlin. But by late 1935, after basketball was included, Phog had changed his tune, saying Berlin had been thoroughly inspected and approved by American officials.

Upon arriving in Berlin the team learned of some rules changes. There would be no three-second violation, teams were limited to seven players and the games would be played on an outdoor court. The only problem was the roster limit. The coaches split the squad in half, seven from Universal and the remainder of the players would form teams. Each team would play a game and sit out the next. Another rule barring players 6-2 and taller was withdrawn after the United States protested. Six of the players were at least that tall, including the team's top scorer, Joe Fortenberry of the Oilers, who had played at Wichita State.

There were other problems. The United States was scheduled to play Spain in the opener, but the players returned home when the Spanish Civil War broke out. America's first Olympic outcome was a 2-0 forfeit victory. Also, the AAU suffered a public relations wound when Naismith's name had been deleted from the complimentary pass list. The AAU moved quickly to make amends. Naismith addressed the 21 teams before the basketball competition — only two teams understood what he was saying — and when he approached each group individually, their nation dipped its flag in honor.

Naismith tossed up the first ball in the opening game between France and Estonia. Among his observations: the Chinese were the best ball handlers, and Poland played the best game. Fittingly, the United States played Canada for the gold medal, and Naismith watched his adopted nation defeat his homeland. Because of the roster limit arrangement, only seven members — the Globe Oilers plus Ralph Bishop of Washington, the team that won 19-8 on a rain-soaked court — were awarded their gold medals at the ceremony. Phog followed it all through the newspapers. When the Olympics were over, he scorched the AAU, taking aim at the organization's snafus throughout the Games.

"In the early days of American sport, the AAU may have served a useful purpose," Phog told the *Topeka Daily Capital*. "Now, however, they resemble, in many respects the Chicago racketeers who do not create a business or industry but who step in and tell those who did that they are going to help run it."

Yet for all of Phog's clamoring about the AAU, he did support the idea of its "semi-professional" basketball to professional teams. For years he recommended players to the Bartlesville, Okla.-based Phillips Petroleum Company, which sponsored the perennial powerful Phillips 66 basketball team. Phog was friends with Phillips Petroleum president K.S. "Boots" Adams who helped arrange jobs for ex-players. Pralle, his first news service All-American, was named MVP of the national AAU Tournament in 1938 and 1939.

For Kansas players, Phillips continued to be a lure after the National Basketball Association was formed in 1947. Phog steered his players toward Phillips more for the company and not the AAU competition its team played against, which became known by Phog later in life as "**A**sinine **A**nd **U**nfair."

12

PHOG'S FOLLY

Phog faced a major career crisis only months after emerging from his crushing Olympic experience. Football was about to bring him down.

From Phog's first season as athletic director until the Olympic year of 1936, Kansas had chewed up three football coaches and was working on a fourth. In the first 31 years of the football program there were 17 head coaches including Fielding Yost, John Outland and Phog. But in that span (1890-1920), the Jayhawks had established an enviable 171-68-18 record. They held winning records over Oklahoma, Missouri and Kansas State and although their 9-17-1 record against Nebraska wasn't as admirable, it should be noted that since the famous 1920 tie, the school's record against the Cornhuskers through the 1995 season is 12-58-2.

This golden era of Kansas football ended and a spiraling slide into mediocrity began soon after Phog became athletic director. Football's fading fortunes eventually cost him that position. The decision in 1937 to relieve Phog of the athletic duties marked a low point in his Kansas tenure. Phog was so disgusted he offered his services to a conference rival. Had Nebraska accepted, the dynamics of the conference could have drastically changed. Imagine how the list of historically powerful basketball programs might look: Kentucky, Indiana, North Carolina, UCLA, Nebraska.

The shame is, the start of Phog's athletic director career was so promising. He got the job because he dared to dream of a new football stadium. Then, without a salary boost, took over coaching the football team and guided it to a tie against the Cornhuskers that so motivated the students and faculty that the pledge drive to build the new stadium started two days later. But the Jayhawks were never good enough to come close to filling the 38,000 seats and on Saturday afternoons when only a few thousand rattled around, the stadium became known as Phog's Folly.

In 1929, four home games averaged 6,383. Three of the crowds numbered fewer than 6,000. While taking hits for the football team's progress, Phog never seemed to get much credit for his efforts. He had taken over the basketball program in a pinch (also baseball, but that was in 1941 and 1942, after he was removed as AD). Then came the Kansas Relays, a 1923 Phog creation. He and track coach Karl Schlademan, the man Phog replaced as basketball coach, organized the first meeting of what grew to become one of the sport's premier events.

The Relays were a tribute to Phog's promotional acumen. In 1927, he recruited five Tarahumara distance runners from an Indian tribe in Mexico to stage an exhibition. A month earlier, two Indians had run 89 miles from San Antonio to Austin during the Texas Relays. Their Kansas route wasn't as difficult. Three men ran 48 miles from Kansas City, Mo., to Lawrence, and two women covered the 28 miles from Topeka to Lawrence.

In 1929, Phog threw a Relays parade and held a drawing for a Shetland pony. The next year, Phog turned Memorial Stadium into a rodeo. He had a buffalo shipped in from Colorado for a barbecue the night before the meet, an evening that also included bronco-busting, a parachuter and other daredevil stunts. The referee for the Relays was Avery Brundage.

By the 1930s, Kansas' athletic calling card wasn't football or basketball but track and field. Jim Bausch, a great all-around Kansas athlete from 1929-31 suspended for taking $75 a month from a Lawrence insurance man for living expenses, went on to win the decathlon at the 1932 Olympics. Glenn Cunningham, the world-record miler, was the school's first great athletic ambassador and a big attraction at the Relays.

The Kansas Relays had grown in stature to a point that Phog heard that officials from the older and more renown Drake Relays in Des Moines were upset that he was moving in on their turf. Track and basketball were in good shape throughout most of Phog's rule.

*Logo from the
1927 Kansas
Relays.*

Football, however, was another matter. In 1926, the Jayhawks lost a school record six football games, and in 1936 — the year the basketball team started 21-0 — the football team finished an abysmal 1-6-1. The wolves were howling.

Actually, Phog had been fighting the football fanatics for a decade. In 1927, the athletic board, responding to criticism, felt compelled to issue Phog a vote of confidence. Several Kansas City alumni had voiced displeasure with Phog's dual role as athletic director and basketball coach. Basketball always seemed to be the issue. Phog's remarkable hardcourt success embittered football followers, who accused Phog of everything from paying his players to hoarding all the school's top athletes for hoops. Phog once told a reporter that a Lawrence businessman offered all-around athlete Frosty Cox $75 a month not to play basketball.

As football became a big-time sport at many schools, Kansas found it difficult to keep up. The state could produce enough star athletes to fill a basketball squad, but not nearly enough for football. And rival Kansas State was competing for the same players. The small population problem plagued football teams in the state for years. It wasn't until the 1990s, when they spread their recruiting bases from coast to coast did the state's football programs achieve sustained success.

The Kansas board of regents had other problems with Phog. His battle with the AAU caused embarrassment to the university and in 1936, the athletic budget deficit reached $25,000. Kansas had trouble paying football guarantees to Michigan State and Washburn. Mediocre football during the Depression years was a sure formula for financial strife in the athletic department.

And, as always, medical school graduates were embarrassed that the athletic and physical education departments were headed by an osteopath at a school that graduated doctors of medicine. Never mind that Phog wasn't hired by Kansas to treat injuries even though he was doing it as well as anybody in the country. Here was an opportunity for the medical folks to get rid of Phog. They almost succeeded.

After a 21-6 loss to Oklahoma in the 1932 home opener, Phog replaced football coach Bill Hargiss with former Oklahoma coach Ad Lindsey. But when Lindsey couldn't produce a consistent winner, he took some of his frustrations out on Phog, accusing him of caring more for his basketball team than football. Then Phog's mouth, as it had a habit of doing, got him in trouble. Hearing rumors that his days were numbered as athletic director, Phog wrote a letter to the *Kansan*, ripping the school paper for its criticism of the 1936 team.

"The football season is now over and the University Daily Kansan *can do no more harm to the football team. To this editorial staff must go the major credit for the team's early debacle. (The newspaper's) early criticism was leveled at what they termed the incompetent football coaching. They now shift their untenable position and declare that the fault is in the system of director and supervision of athletics.*

"The football coaches have had every possible aid and cooperation from the director of athletics. We are now starting our basketball season and we invite our bathtub-radio Galahads, with flaming pens to hop onto us with both feet. We will answer them with a corking team — answer them with deeds, not words."

Those deeds included losses to tiny Southwestern College of Winfield, Kan., and Baker before the Big Six season had opened. The Jayhawks opened conference play at Oklahoma.

"Your talk before this game was an inspiration never to be forgotten," wrote Roy Holliday, a letterman in 1936-37, to Phog. "You pleaded with the group of boys to fight for the University and the state of Kansas even though outside pressure was being put upon you. You persuaded the boys in your true and loyal manner to play even better than their best."

And the Jayhawks did, winning 28-26. Kansas went on to tie Nebraska for the league title. But that didn't stop the students from focusing Phog in their sights. One wrote to the student newspaper, "To get Kansas out of the fog, you've got to get the Phog out of Kansas."

Indeed, some wanted Phog out of Kansas altogether. But Phog had his supporters. Passionate letters from former players, and friends and relatives of former athletes poured in from around the country. The brother of a Kansas football player, Max Replogle, claimed he twice was saved from career-ending injuries by Phog's treatments and believed an athlete could have no finer mentor.

"Dr. Allen refuses to build great castles to induce a boy to come to Kansas," Col. Wayne Replogle wrote. "He will help him with a job if there is a job to be had, but he will not pay him for his athletic services, and for this and many other reasons, I sent my brother to him . . . He will come out of the University ready to work because that is what Dr. Allen intends and the thing he expects."

But by December the school was finished with Phog as athletic director and the board of regents abolished the position. Phog stayed on as basketball coach and head of the physical education department. Athletics was operated by a three-member committee but only for three months. In March, the search for a new athletic director was on. The early favorite was Dutch Lonborg, but cries went out that the school needed somebody with a stronger football background. That summer, New Mexico athletic director and football coach Gwinn Henry got the job. He had been Missouri's head football coach from 1923-31.

When Ad Lindsey was fired after the 1938 season, Henry took over the football team. He fared worse, with a 9-27 record in four years. Phog could have said, "I told you so," but kept his mouth shut. When some newspaper columnist suggested he return to the athletic director's job in 1943, Phog said no way. He put these feelings down on paper:

"I have arrived at an age that convinces me it isn't worth a candle and I wouldn't take the job at twice the

salary. You're dealing with an emotional, slap-happy, crackpot bunch of fanatics who know all about winning football games."

For the first time since returning to Kansas in 1919, Phog seriously considered leaving. There had been offers — Pop Warner tried to get Phog to come to Stanford in the late 1920s at a large salary increase — but Phog had a home and a young family, so he recommended his assistant, John Bunn, for the job.

But by 1940, Phog was fed up. His salary wasn't cut when he lost his athletic director job, but unlike other department heads whose salaries were adjusted upward as the Depression ended, Phog's wasn't. Maybe the board of regents considered Phog's income from books, basketball equipment, shoes and his Goal-Hi invention, but Phog knew his $2,200 annual salary from coaching basketball wasn't in line with other Big Six coaches.

So Phog looked around. He read in the newspapers that Nebraska fans had been unhappy with two straight second-division finishes and wanted Harold Browne replaced. Phog wrote to Major L. McC. Jones, the Cornhuskers' athletic director, on Feb. 3, 1940:

"Three years ago when certain incidents happened here I had decided that I would not stay. My son, Bob, who was a freshman, said, 'Dad, I always wanted to play on your team, and I hope you won't quit before I finish school.' I would not be interested in anything at all for next year because I expect to stay here until Bob has graduated. After that, if you should think of giving Brownie a full-time job with the football team and his physical education work there, then I would be at least interested in discussing the situation with you.

"I am 54 years of age, but I suit up and demonstrate all of my fundamentals offensively and defensively. As far as I know I can stay here indefinitely, but I would enjoy the opportunity to put a team in the top rung of the ladder when it seems to me they have just about everything to work with. The prestige of one sport, especially football, aids the other sport considerably in the national ranking."

Nebraska did make a change after the 1940 season, but the job went to A.J. Lawandowski. Phog stuck it out at Kansas, and for the sake of the NCAA basketball tournament, it's a good thing he did.

13

NCAA

TOURNAMENT

An angry Phog didn't let his feelings about the school's administration get in the way of his coaching. He won another conference championship in 1938, with the Jayhawks finishing 18-2 overall, and by then had claimed victory in his first great recruiting battle.

While in junior high, Bob Allen informed his father that he had just scrimmaged against the finest player he'd ever seen, Ralph Miller of Chanute, Kan. It was the first of several meetings between them. Phog saw Miller play one game, a state tournament contest in Topeka and only because Chanute High played a game right after Bob Allen's Lawrence High team. Miller injured his hip during the first half of his game and E.A. Thomas, executive secretary of the Kansas State High School Athletic Association, came into the stands to ask Phog to examine Miller. Phog fixed him up and Miller scored 26 points in the second half. Chanute won the state championship.

"I knew many schools were angling for Miller's services, but I did not use my advantage to endeavor to entice him to KU," Phog wrote in 1937.

Phog didn't have to. He had every indication that Miller was coming to Kansas, including the word of Miller's father, Harold. But Stanford, and Phog's friend John Bunn, applied pressure. A wealthy Stanford alum from Wichita promised to handle Miller's tuition and books, and told him a job in the athletic office wouldn't be a problem. The alum flew Miller to Stanford for a visit and Miller stayed in Bunn's home. Miller changed his mind and decided to attend Stanford.

Miller returned to Chanute to pack for the coast and to attend the annual football all-star game in Chicago. Phog was in that part of the country speaking at a coaches clinic. He and Bob attended the game with Ralph then drove him back to Kansas. On the trip home, Miller changed his mind and decided to stick with his original plan. They arrived in Lawrence and put in a call to Chanute where John Bunn had waited for two days to take Miller back to Stanford. The group then drove to Chanute to tell Bunn personally. In the Miller house and later on their front porch, the friendship between Phog and Bunn was severely tested. Bunn was not-so-tactfully reminded that while coaching the Kansas freshman team in the 1920s Phog had paid for part of his salary from his pocket after the chancellor had cut the basketball budget, and that it was Phog who got Bunn the Stanford job.

"I own a farm in Kansas and pay taxes," Bunn told the *Topeka Daily Capital*. "Why shouldn't I have a few Kansas boys?" Then he dropped the names of former Kansas standouts from beyond the state border, Bill Johnson from Oklahoma City and Fred Pralle of St. Louis. But Bunn apologized to Phog and the Millers and headed back to Stanford, where he already had established a national power behind scoring sensation Hank Luisetti, a three-time All-American.

With Miller at Kansas, the foundation was forming for a team that helped strengthen the structure of postseason play. The Jayhawks didn't win the 1940 NCAA Tournament, but their presence in the championship game very well may have saved the event.

The idea for an NCAA Tournament originated at the 1938 NABC convention in Chicago. That spring, the Metropolitan Basketball Writers Association of New York staged the first National Invitation Tournament, which filled Madison Square Garden. Temple defeated Colorado for the championship. Kansas had declined an invitation, citing a Big Six rule that didn't allow teams to play away from campus settings. At first, Phog liked the idea of the NIT.

"I think this would be a very interesting experiment," Phog wrote to one of the organizers, Everett Morris of the *New York Herald Tribune*. "I believe the effort will go a long ways toward nationalizing

Phog's 1939-40 team may have assured the future of the NCAA Tournament. Among players on the team were Ralph Miller (4), future coach Dick Harp (20), Phog's son, Bob (9), and T.P. Hiunter (10), later killed in action in World War II. (Photo courtesy University of Kansas Sports Information)

the game and doing away with provincialism and sectional play. Ned Irish has done a great job of building up basketball as a national sport in the minds of eastern people. Of course, the western people have been conscious of this fact for years."

When the NIT's inaugural event succeeded, coaches mostly in the Big Ten, Big Six and Missouri Valley areas were envious. New York had staged a major basketball event matching teams from throughout the nation, and while it did not call its tournament a national championship, it wasn't far off, and the NABC wanted a piece of the action. It figured if anybody was going to run a national tournament, it should be the schools and not a group of sportswriters.

At the NABC meeting on April 4 at Chicago's Morrison Hotel, a committee of Phog, John Bunn and Harold Olsen of Ohio State was formed to start a national championship tournament in cooperation with the NCAA. "This committee is to communicate with and petition the NCAA to take basketball 'under its wing' in much the same way as it sponsored national collegiate championship contests in track and field, swimming, wresting, tennis and golf," Olsen, the chairman, wrote in a letter to NCAA president William Owens of Stanford on May 24, 1938. The term "under its wing" wasn't clearly defined and would be a point of contention. In Phog's mind the NABC was to control the event and the profits, although he may have been the only one to believe that.

The inaugural NCAA Tournament in 1939 included eight teams from districts split geographically, four on either side of the Mississippi River. The Eastern playoffs were scheduled for Philadelphia. Phog tried to get the Western playoffs in Kansas City, but the newly established National Association for Intercollegiate Athletics already had booked Municipal Auditorium for its tournament. Bunn came through and lined up the pavilion at Treasure Island in San Francisco Bay.

Chicago was selected as the championship site, but Olsen couldn't get an early response from Chicago Stadium officials and scheduled the March 25 title game for Patten Gymnasium at Northwestern University. After all the promotional materials were printed and distributed, Chicago Stadium became available. The committee voted not to switch.

As the regular season ended, eight district chairmen selected their tournament teams. In Phog's District Five, a one-game playoff between the Big Six and Missouri Valley conferences was planned, but first-place ties in both leagues foiled that. It got even more complicated when the faculty council at Missouri, co-champ with Oklahoma in the Big Six, voted not to allow the Tigers to participate in a playoff for fear of missing class time. The Sooners emerged from a playoff in Oklahoma City that included Oklahoma A&M and Drake.

The Fifth District playoff was the only one of eight to turn a profit. When the beans were counted shortly after Oregon defeated Olsen's Buckeyes for the first championship, the poorly attended tournament had lost $2,531. The NABC, stunned by the poor financial showing, asked the NCAA to bail it out. The NABC briefly considered dropping the idea of a college championship. But when he returned from the final, Phog went to Municipal Auditorium not only to secure the 1940 Western playoffs but also the championship game. Phog guaranteed success, boasting he had never organized a tournament in Kansas City that failed financially, citing the KCAC series with the Buffalo Germans in 1905 and the 1936 Olympic playoffs.

"You give me this tournament in Kansas City and I will not only pay back the deficit, but we will make you some money," Phog boasted in 1939.

In the previous cases, Kansas City fans were watching a familiar product. For the 1940 NCAA Tournament, there was no guarantee the Jayhawks would be there. In fact, Oklahoma was thought to have the better team in the Big Six. In his preseason letter he sent to team members — there was an inspirational two- or three-page letter every summer to the squad — Phog mentioned that the 1940 tournament would be in Kansas City and was something to strive for.

So the Jayhawks did. With Miller, Bob Allen, Dick Harp and Howard Engleman as the standouts, Kansas tied Oklahoma and Missouri for the league title. KU won a coin flip and forced the Sooners to beat the Tigers for the right to play Kansas. The Jayhawks defeated Oklahoma in Wichita to make the NCAA field. Victories over Oklahoma A&M, Rice and a one-point thriller over Southern Cal for the Western finals put Kansas in the championship game against Indiana.

Getting Oklahoma A&M involved in the NCAA Tournament was important. Major powers from the East like New York University, Long Island University and City College of New York, were beholden to Ned Irish and the NIT. The NCAA Tournament needed all the support it could get in other areas of the country. Having Hank Iba on its side enhanced the NCAA's credibility.

"...(Iba) assures me that without any question of doubt he will stay by the National Collegiate Tournament," Phog said to Olsen in February 1940. "Hank is all right. If we could have half as good cooperation from the Eastern districts east of the Mississippi River as we have had from the Western half, the NCAA would overwhelm the whole country in basketball popularity."

Municipal Auditorium and its blue leather seats sparkled on the championship night of March 30. Fans poured in from the underground tunnels that led from downtown hotels. Phog went in for pomp and circumstance and gave this event special treatment with red, white and blue banners and streamers. A pregame ceremony honored Naismith. Lights were dimmed, candles lit and Naismith's image was cast on a large screen. Phog had collected Naismith's three favorite lines and had them announced.

"I want to build character in the hearts of young men . . . Do not fail to work for humanity and await your reward . . . Basketball is a game easy to play but difficult to master."

College basketball was on display and anybody associated with the game was in Kansas City that night. Three national groups, the NABC, the National Association of Basketball Officials and the National Basketball Committee of the United States and Canada all scheduled their annual meetings around the championship game. NABC dues were up to $5 now, and $1 of that went toward purchasing a $1.60 ticket to the 1940 championship game. Municipal was charging Phog only $300 building rental. More than 10,000 stuffed the auditorium. Three times as many wanted tickets when the Jayhawks qualified for the final.

Everything about the event lived up to Phog's expectations, except the game. The Jayhawks were no match for Branch McCracken's 'Hurryin' Hoosiers and lost 60-42. Indiana killed Kansas with its fast break and even as the game started getting out of hand in the second half, Phog didn't deviate from his ball control game plan. Phog had a friend put a clock to both teams' possessions and the Jayhawks won that count by nearly a 2-1 margin. But the deliberate style failed against Indiana, whose point total in an NCAA final wouldn't be topped for a decade.

From an organizational standpoint, the 1940 NCAA Tournament went off beautifully. And while he came away a loser in the final, Phog also profited. Soon after the season the school's boosters presented to Phog a set of Kenneth Smith handmade golf clubs with the postseason scores inscribed on each club. Everybody seemed happy, including the NABC, which gushed over the championship evening in its annual newsletter.

> *"The Kansas City Municipal Auditorium . . . is tops in the opinion of the many who witnessed that memorable clash. The coaches were amazed at the beautiful entrance, its fine ramps, its marvelous seats, and the unobstructed view of the game from all seats . . . All in all the coaches were highly impressed at the excellent arrangements."*

Financial figures started coming in within days after the tournament and compared to the previous year they were astonishing. The Western playoff and championship games in Kansas City netted nearly $9,000. After figures from the Eastern playoff at Butler University — Olsen had tried to get it in New York — were turned in, the 1940 NCAA Tournament netted $9,522.55.

Before the tournament, Phog, Bunn and Olsen had met and agreed to pay back last year's deficit to the NCAA, then, after expenses, cut them in for 20 percent of the 1940 profits. The coaches wanted to create a fund for Olympic basketball traveling expenses so there would be no repeat of the 1936 financial troubles. The problem was Olsen never mentioned this to the NCAA and its executive secretary Major John L. Griffith or the NCAA's executive committee. Imagine Phog's surprise when the NCAA came up with its own financial formula: 10 percent off the top, then half of the rest to fund the NCAA office. The coaches then were free to distribute their share to participating schools.

Phog, just as he had four years earlier when the AAU took his Olympic money, went ballistic. Before a meeting between the basketball committee and NCAA officials in Chicago that fall, Bunn had written to Phog telling him it was no use to battle the NCAA establishment. Bunn had learned from his boss, NCAA president Owens, that funds from an NCAA-sanctioned event couldn't be earmarked for a specific sport or allocated to an Olympic fund. Nobody on the basketball committee knew this before the tournament, and Phog wasn't appeased. After the committee met with Griffith in November, Phog continued to stew. The reason basketball coaches wanted their own tournament in the first place was because they believed they were better qualified to conduct one than a group of New York sportswriters, led by Irish.

The NIT not only paid expenses for its eight teams but handed each a nice lump sum as a parting gift. With 16,000 cramming into the Garden, there was still plenty left for the promoters. Phog believed the only way to counter that was to be as generous to the NCAA Tournament participants. In a Nov. 30, 1940 letter to Griffith, Phog pleaded his case:

> *"My motive has been to sweeten the pot enough for these (NCAA) teams to keep them interested and make them feel that through their activity not only are they enjoying the pleasure of competition but that they are getting a small renumeration which will help just a little toward reducing a budget that does not balance. I beg of you to see if it is not possible with some mediation to forget the original 10 percent discussed and to pay the railroad, pullman, hotel and meal expenses of all teams competing in their respective play-offs, and then divide a very handsome profit."*

The NCAA gave in on the 10 percent and checks were cut. The 1940 distribution went like this: $9,522.55 minus a rounded off figure $2,500 for the 1939 losses gave the NCAA and coaches a starting point of $7,022.55. The NCAA took half, $3,511.27. The other half was separated into 14 equal shares. After traveling expenses, finalists Indiana and Kansas each took 3/14th ($752.40), sectional runners-up Duquesne and Southern Cal 2/14th ($501.60) and the four others, Colorado, Springfield (Mass.) College, Rice and Western Kentucky 1/14th ($250.80). By contrast, Kansas had received $1,000 from its Big Six playoff game at Wichita and another $1,000 for a playoff game against Oklahoma A&M in Oklahoma City, and that was after handing over 20 percent to the NCAA.

The basketball committee had sold the idea of an NCAA Tournament to their brethren on the basis of a healthy financial return and, although it turned a tidy profit in Kansas City, they couldn't come close to matching the thousands shelled out by the NIT. Phog was crushed and resigned from the committee.

"I told them that when an individual makes certain promises that he cannot uphold the only thing for him to do was resign," Phog wrote.

And then start name-calling. Before the 1941 Western finals and championship game, also held in Kansas City, Phog blew off steam at the NCAA and Olsen, who had awarded the 1941 Eastern finals to Madison, Wis., after the University of Wisconsin had qualified for the tournament. Phog didn't buy the argument that Kansas City is 40 miles from Lawrence and, in effect, a home-away-from-home floor. Also in Wisconsin's favor: The school had cleared $18,000 on the 1939 boxing championship. Madison was a good draw.

"Such a procedure gives Wisconsin an eight- to 10-point advantage and the whole idea of the playoffs is to give every team an equal advantage," Phog spouted off in the *Lawrence Journal-World*. "(Olsen) is selling fair play rights for gate receipts."

Privately, Phog was much more critical of Olsen.

"He's a toe-dancing, shadow-boxing politician," Phog wrote in 1945.

As for the NCAA, it was no better than the AAU as far as Phog was concerned. "There is only an alphabetical difference," Phog said. Both groups "want to keep all the money and spend it as they please."

It rankled Phog that football teams competing in bowl games kept most of the gate receipts but not the playoff basketball teams. His feelings for the NCAA and its purse distribution never softened. In 1943 he wrote:

"I for one do not propose to let a lot of money-grabbers take all of the income and say nothing. These same administrators in the NCAA talk about pot-hunters and gold-diggers when they speak of the athletes who want individual prizes, yet this bunch of moguls want all the cash. Would they not be hyper-pot-hunters?"

A perturbed Phog relinquished his duties as Fifth District chairman to Missouri's George Edwards, and the tournament started losing steam in Kansas City. Madison, Wis., may have proved an unfair advantage in the 1941 Eastern playoffs, but large crowds ensured another profit. At Municipal, the Badgers beat Washington State in front of 7,219. In 1942, Stanford defeated Dartmouth before 6,500. Tournament attendance was so lousy that year the finalists received a check for a miserly $93.75. Six other participants, including first-round loser Kansas, brought home a whopping $50.59.

Phog had proved the NCAA Tournament could succeed. But it would take a few more years and some adjustments and events — the move to Madison Square Garden in 1943 ensured large crowds for the next six years and the NCAA champion defeated the NIT winner in a Red Cross benefit game from 1943-45 — for the NCAA Tournament to surpass the NIT in prestige.

One other event helped swing public sentiment in favor of the NCAA Tournament. Although all of basketball suffered greatly during the gambling scandals of the late 1940s and early 1950s, basketball in New York suffered the greatest damage.

Just as Phog predicted.

●　　●　　●　　●　　●

When it came to generating publicity, Phog screamed louder some years than others. In December 1940, he seemed to stir things up about every day. The NCAA Tournament flap aside, Phog made the papers for a variety of tempests:

■ On Dec. 4, Phog used the occasion of the opening ceremonies of the Naismith basketball league in Kansas City to predict the end of college football.

"In some schools football is more professional than in the out and out professional leagues. As the football muddle now stands the hand-writing is plain. Already,

Yale, Princeton, Harvard, Cornell and Chicago have de-emphasized football or are preparing to do so."

Naturally, everybody who had anything to do with college football denounced Allen. No matter, he was on to his next harangue.

■ On Dec. 11, the *Kansas City Star* reported a Chanute businessman had accused Phog of "subsidizing" Ralph Miller during recruiting. Phog demanded an apology, and received one in the press.

■ Throughout December, rumors swirled about Phog's retirement. He had just turned 55, and an Oklahoma newspaper had misunderstood him when he said "I hope to coach at Kansas at least until Bob has finished his course work." Bob wasn't to finish until after the 1940-41 season. "Doubtless those 'Saging' Sooner Sooth Sayers have information that I do not possess," Phog wrote.

■ Then just to get 1941 off to a flying start, Phog suggested to reporters that the sport might not be far away from nine-man basketball. Courts would measure 110 feet long, 60 feet wide, he wrote.

"There is no reason why 18 men, the original numbers that started to play under Dr. Naismith's direction, should not be possible in a game at present if the floor is large enough. With more men in the game the heart strain would not be so great on any one man as it is now."

14

THE PATRIOT

More pressing issues confronted the world in 1941 than revenue sharing from the NCAA basketball tournament. When Pearl Harbor was bombed, Phog must have thought about Sohaku Ri, his Japanese friend who joined the cause for Olympic basketball a decade earlier. Phog and Ri had remained in touch throughout the 1930s and exchanged Christmas cards. Tokyo was to play host to the 1940 Olympics and Ri had put Phog on his mailing lists of Japan's monthly Olympic bulletins.

Those Games and the 1944 Olympics were canceled but college basketball, like most other sports, forged ahead through the war years. Practically every team was affected. Wyoming, which won the 1943 NCAA championship, didn't field a team in 1944. Utah started the 1944 season without a home floor. The Army had appropriated the Utes' field house. The Skyline Conference suspended operations because there weren't enough teams, but Utah went on to win the NCAA championship.

At Kansas, the close of the 1943 season brought sweeping changes. The Jayhawks had clinched the Big Six championship with a victory at Oklahoma and all that remained were games against Missouri and Kansas State in a bid for a perfect conference season and a nonconference game against powerful Creighton. The Tigers fell in overtime. The game at Creighton would determine the NCAA Tournament representative from the Fifth District. Since the Blue Jays had defeated KU in Lawrence earlier in the year, Kansas would need to win, then win a playoff game to qualify for the NCAA.

But by the first week of March, everything changed. Phog learned that four of his starters, including standouts Ray Evans, Charlie Black and Otto Schnellbacher, were to be inducted into the service immediately after the season. Phog allowed them to miss the Creighton game to be with their families and informed the Blue Jays that Kansas was withdrawing from the NCAA Tournament consideration. Creighton coach Ed Hickey then informed Kansas that he had accepted an NIT bid. The money was better and Hickey was angry that the Jayhawks got the nod over his team the previous year. In an anticlimactic game, the Blue Jays crushed Kansas 56-34. Two nights later, Kansas completed its 10-0 conference season with a victory over Kansas State with its starters in tow. Big Six runner-up Oklahoma represented District Five.

The 1942-43 season started with a 24-man roster, most of whom made the team photograph. The longer he remained at Kansas, the more Phog believed in large squads to build team morale. Many, like a sophomore candidate in 1942 named Bob Dole, never played in a varsity game. Dole had been a football, basketball and track star at Russell High and at one time thought his skills could propel him to an athletic career beyond college. He was an end on the 9-0 football team during his senior season in 1940. Dole had his heart set on attending Kansas, and had gotten to know Phog's son, Mitt, who after finishing at Kansas in 1936, was working at the Standard Oil refinery outside of Russell.

Phog was visiting his son in Russell in 1939 when Mitt, who played on an amateur basketball team there, told him about Dole. Phog invited Dole to the 1940 Kansas Relays, which besides luring many of the nation's top track athletes, was used as a basketball recruiting tool. Phog had his prospects dress up in KU sweats and work out with varsity players at Robinson Gym on the Saturday morning of the Relays. The varsity players dressed in uniforms and conducted a few drills. This was the 1940 Kansas team that had played for the NCAA championship. All very impressive to a prospective student who lived more than 200 miles away. Dole was there as a high school junior with two of his Russell teammates, Bud Smith and Leon Mai. Such an invitation was tantamount to an offer to attend Kansas and try out for the team. Phog wanted Dole at Kansas.

When Dole enrolled, he immediately dove into the fraternity scene, joining Kappa Sigma, and sports. He was a member of the freshman football and basketball teams, earning numerals, which

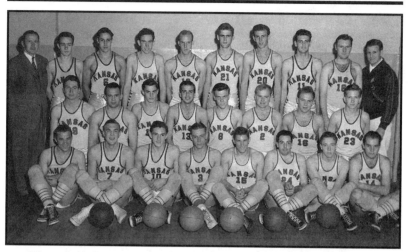

Phog, far left, with his 1942-43 team. Among the players that year was a sophomore named Bob Dole. He is third from the left (No. 6) in the back row. (Photo courtesy University of Kansas Sports Information)

freshmen received instead of a letter. A basketball award was mailed to Dole at his Lawrence address of 1045 West Hills Terrace, where he shared a room with Bud Smith.

As a sophomore, Dole didn't make much of an impression. He went out for football, had a publicity photo taken but did not earn a letter. Same thing in basketball. Dole was assigned uniform number 6, and dressed out for a preseason exhibition game. When the travel roster was posted for a Dec. 11 game in Kansas City against Rockhurst College, Dole wasn't listed. If he was discouraged, Dole didn't show it.

He made himself available for the indoor track team, and had his greatest success as a college athlete during the outdoor season. In a dual meet at Baker University on April 21, 1943, Dole won the 440-yard dash in 52.2 seconds. He also placed second in the 220 and anchored the winning 880-yard relay team. Those were Dole's only triumphs in a track season shortened by the war, but it was enough for him to earn his only college letter. Nearly 50 men were listed on the track roster for 1942-43 and Dole was one of 10 to become a K-man.

While Dole probably could have looked forward to making more of an impact in football and basketball as a junior, his grades had slipped by the spring of 1943. He had enlisted in the Army in De-

PHOG ALLEN

cember 1942 and on June 1, 1943, was called to active duty. The wounds Dole suffered when an explosion caught him in the right shoulder during a 1945 offensive in Italy ended his athletic career.

He returned from Europe on a stretcher and spent six months in Winter General Hospital in Topeka. Among his first visitors were KU trainer Dean Nesmith and Phog. Dole remembered Phog's visit in a Sept. 19, 1974, Congressional Record tribute to Phog upon his death.

> "He cleared up many things and helped me get a better perspective on what was ahead. He convinced me there was more to life than football and basketball — a large lesson for a young man with expectations like those I entertained before the war — and he helped me realize that there could be other challenges and other rewards in my future. I felt an immediate sense of personal loss when I learned of his death Monday. I shall always be in his debt."

Many from Kansas who served in World War II also felt indebted to Phog, who added several titles to his already crowded resume. During the war, Phog served as secretary of the Douglas County Selective Service Board, chairman of the county Red Cross War Fund Drive, chairman of the War Nursery Committee and chairman for various bond drives. When the St. Joseph's (Mo.) Gazette campaigned for donations of athletic equipment for Fort Leavenworth, Phog came through with sets of KU basketball and baseball uniforms, shoes and knee pads.

Everybody on the home front made sacrifices, and Phog, as KU's physical education department head, was especially burdened. Before the war, the school never had more than 450 students in physical conditioning courses. In the fall of 1942, there were 1,800 forced to take compulsory PE. The department was operating short-handed, so Phog signed up 18 football and basketball players as temporary instructors. Basketball practice, usually a late-afternoon endeavor, was pushed back to 8-10 p.m. to accommodate classes crammed in the gym in daylight hours.

Phog's greatest contribution to the war effort came from his typewriter. In the summer of 1943, the first Jayhawk Rebounds rolled off the press. Phog's monthly newsletter to players and alumni in the armed services updated the sports news at KU, the whereabouts of athletes and general area information. Rebounds often numbered up to 20 single-spaced type-written pages and continued through V-E and V-J days. By the time the final one was delivered in late 1945, several hundred, even some non-Kansans, were on the mailing list.

Phog relived some of his favorite stories, like the dream touchdown game against Iowa State in 1920, and laid it on thick when painting the enemy he called "the Japanazis." Phog poured out his heart in the 11th edition when he reported the death of Marine Lieutenant T.P. "Teep" Hunter, a letter winner from 1940-1942 who had arrived at Kansas from a broken home and had become one of Phog's favorite athletes. He started the Sept. 12, 1944, edition this way:

"Somehow this is the most difficult letter that I have ever attempted to write. Over a dozen times I have begun it and each time I have walked away from my desk because words fail me. I feel such a void. Something has gone from me. Your friend and mine — good, old honest T.P. Hunter was killed on Guam, July 21, 1944. And yet this morning he feels closer to me than at any moment that I have known him."

Phog devoted the first three pages of a 17-page report to Teep.

History's great military leaders were a favorite subject. Phog wrote about King Leonidas and his 300 Spartans at the ancient Greek battle of Thermopylae; Napoleon's Old Guard who knew how to die but not how to surrender; Washington's frozen and starving men at Valley Forge; American soldiers at Chateau-Thierry and in the Argonne Woods in World War I.

"These are the words for it — unyielding sacrifice of self for what seems a worthy cause, which in its ultimate analysis means immortality," Phog read from his script for a 1938 radio broadcast. "All athletic contests are a throw-back from the game of war."

No doubt, Phog was a patriot. His birth year of 1885 made him too young to fight in the Spanish-American War and too old to serve in World War I. Two brothers were career military men. Phog's *Basket-Ball Bible* is dedicated to Kansans lost during World War I.

A 1942 road trip to the Northeast stirred Phog's passions. The Jayhawks traveled to Buffalo, New York and Philadelphia and defeated St. Bonaventure, Fordham and St. Joseph's. Phog credited the sweep to soldiers encountered on the train. Phog wrote about the experience in April 1943.

Phog celebrated his 400th victory at Kansas in 1942. (From the University of Kansas archives)

"When we started out we didn't think were going to win a ball game. The boys played to our amazement but it was the American soldiers and sailors riding the chair cars along with our boys that caused this revolutionary psychological change in the minds of our fellows. When our boys saw such splendid morale and esprit de corps in our American soldiers and sailors then their petty differences faded away, and the big central theme was that if these service boys were willing to give their lives to their country, can ride in chair cars without beefing or belly-aching, then unconsciously, I think, they thought it was up to us to do a bigger job."

Phog even tried to get a job with the Army. In 1944, the Army Athletic Branch asked Phog if he'd be interested in coaching basketball at a military base for three months for expenses and fair compensation after V-Day. Phog said yes, even if it meant not being able to return to Kansas. Nothing came of it when the Army couldn't promise Phog a commission.

Ultimately, Phog reasoned, war was good for sports, and World War II would cure what ailed college athletics. Under-the-table payments of top athletes would cease because war sacrifices would sharpen college administrators' perspective. "Football, the game, will still be with us," Phog said. "College football, the business, will not be."

As for basketball, the war was over for only a few weeks when Phog predicted a professional basketball league on sound footing would emerge. History supported his case: professional baseball started in 1869, four years after the Civil War; pro football started two years after World War I. Returning veterans supplied most of the leagues in both cases. World War II would do the same for basketball.

Phog was right. What was to evolve into the NBA opened for business in 1946.

Oddly, the war years brought many celebrations in the Allen family. Daughter Eleanor was married in September 1943, and Bob Allen married Jean McFarland in April 1944. Phog successfully entered politics in 1945 when he was elected to the city council, gaining nearly 60 percent of the vote.

After the 1940 season, as basketball approached its Golden Jubilee season, Phog had amassed 452 career victories, and because he had such a head start in his coaching career, nobody was within 75 triumphs. Cam Henderson, who had been at Muskingum (Ohio), Davis & Elkins (West Virginia) and Marshall, collected 373 of his career 630 triumphs by then. Hec Edmundson of Washington had won 362 of his 508. In February 1943, the Helms Foundation of Los Angeles named Phog the greatest basketball coach of all time. Helms had surveyed coaches throughout the nation and came up with a candidate list of 26.

The top 10 selected: Phog, Edmundson, Sam Barry (Iowa and Southern Cal), Clair Bee (Long Island), Osborne Cowles (Dartmouth), Nat Holman (CCNY), Lon Jourdet (Pennsylvania), George Keogan (Notre Dame), Piggy Lambert (Purdue) and Walter Meanwell (Wisconsin). Those who didn't make the cut because they hadn't been around long enough were Hank Iba and Adolph Rupp.

Helms also selected the 10 greatest players from 1920-1942 and retroactively picked national players of the year from that period. Helms was generous to Kansas in both cases. Paul Endacott made the all-time team that also included Hank Luisetti and John Wooden of Purdue. Endacott was named national player of the year for 1923 and teammate Charlie Black won the award for 1924.

Phog poses with three members of his 1942-43 team. Among them is All-American Ray Evans (10). (Photo courtesy University of Kansas Sports Information)

Wooden was a favorite of Phog's. They actually met before Wooden started college. After his junior year at Martinsville, Ind., High School, Wooden and a friend hitchhiked to Kansas to harvest wheat for summer jobs. They were headed to Wichita and stopped in Lawrence with Wooden proudly wearing his all-state basketball sweater. The travelers were early for the harvest and sought jobs in Lawrence. Construction had begun on the north bowl of the football stadium. When Phog heard an all-state player was in town, he fixed them up with jobs pouring concrete. Phog also arranged to have them sleep in Robinson Gym on mattresses and set up a charge account at a local restaurant until payday. Phog asked if Wooden was interested in remaining in Lawrence for his senior year of high school. Wooden declined.

The Helms recognition was important to Kansas. Throughout most of Phog's career there were no national awards for coaches.

The first coach of the year, San Francisco's Phil Woolpert, wasn't selected until 1955. Players from the 1923 team invited Helms director Bill Schroeder to their anniversary celebrations.

But Phog certainly was appreciated locally. He didn't know how much until the evening of March 6, 1942, when more than 300 former players, friends and family toasted Phog at a supper in the Memorial Union building, commemorating his 25th anniversary as the KU coach. Phog was presented a thick scrapbook loaded with letters of congratulations from throughout the nation.

"This book is presented upon the occasion of the observance of your 25th anniversary as Coach of basketball at the University of Kansas," the book opened. "In 25 years there has never been a dull moment on Mt. Oread during the winter season. Those 19 champion basketball teams have brought countless thrills and chills to Kansas; 556 games won and only 127 lost (the record was later adjusted).

". . . Your friends and those of the University have wanted to pay tribute to you. And so, without your knowledge or permission, a committee of your old boys and admirers have arranged today's celebration in your honor. The great dinner tonight testifies to your place in the Kansas University world. But tonight, and because after 25 years you are so much a part of KU and KU is so much a part of you we announce in your honor a gift to the University of a permanent scholarship fund for needy and worthy students known as the F.C. Allen scholarship."

The goal was $500, with most giving $5, but $686.79 was raised. Phog made it an even $750 by writing a check for $63.21. The amount purchased a $1,000 war bond that matured in 10 years.

The scrapbook, hundreds of letters of stories and reminiscences, was the highlight for Phog:

- One morning in February, 1924 the squad pulled into the Union Station in St. Louis and immediately went to the dining room for breakfast. (Three) of us ate at the same table and decided to have a complete, well-balanced breakfast. The check for the three breakfasts was a little over $4.50. We handed the check to Dr. Allen and ducked. The squad had no sooner been assigned rooms at the hotel when Dr. Allen called a meeting. We were informed in no uncertain terms that we were on this trip to win a basketball championship and not an eating championship. Furthermore, it was beyond comprehension how a gorged, listless human could ever be a fighting, alert basketball player. *Vern Engel (1924-25)*

- I cannot tell you how sincerely I have appreciated knowing you from the first day that I, as a freshman, met you back on Mt. Oread in 1919. From that day on, I have always been an ardent admirer of you and one of your staunchest supporters. Sincerely, *Adolph Rupp, University of Kentucky*

- ...For a generation you have stood out in my mind, as well as in the mind of every sports-loving person, as an example and a leader of the highest type. Yours very cordially, *Dana X. Bible, University of Texas*

- Without your athletic victories we would not have had many laurels along that line. Sincerely yours, *Alf Landon (1936 presidential candidate)*

- I honestly believe that you have done more for basketball than any man, including Dr. Naismith. Very Sincerely Yours, *Gwinn Henry, Director of Athletics, Kansas*

- I know many things you have taught me that are more important than the basketball I have learned. Fraternally, *Ralph Miller*

- ...while Springfield is the birthplace of the game, Kansas is where it was nurtured in full bloom. And since you and Kansas basketball are inseparable, certainly you are due this recognition which is being given you . . .*John Bunn, Dean of Men, Stanford University*

15

SMELLING A RAT

September 6, 1944, was a Thursday. The opening of college football season was more than a week away and Sam Smith, a reporter for United Press Associates in Kansas City, wanted to stay busy. Smith was a Missouri guy, but he didn't play allegiances, not when he needed a story, anyway. Every newspaper man in the Midwest knew where to find an easy quote. So Smith banged out a letter to Phog.

"What do you look for in the way of post-war collegiate athletics?" Smith wanted to know. "When all these boys come back, battle-hardened, do you believe there may be another so-called 'Golden Age' of sports, the like of which we saw after the last war?"

Legitimate question, and a subject Phog had given a good deal of thought. Yes, the competition will be much tougher, candidates for positions will be more mature, the quality of play will be better and the country, yearning for entertainment outlets from years of war restrictions, will embrace this wave of enthusiasm.

But that was only part of Phog's response to Smith in his letter of Sept. 22. Mostly, what filled three pages was a stream of consciousness that was typically Phogian in its incisiveness. And the subject really didn't break much new ground. Phog was calling for a commissioner of college sports, like baseball's Kenesaw Mountain Landis, something he'd been clamoring about for two decades. In the fifth paragraph, Smith found his story.

"Judge Landis is fighting betting on professional baseball in his vigorous manner, but the colleges are doing nothing about it, and as sure as you live the thing is going to crack wide open sometime when they lay bare a scandal that will rock the college world. It has already happened in Madison Square Garden, but the newspapers have kept it quiet."

A line "scandal that will rock the college world" is too juicy for a newspaper man to pass up, and Phog said nothing about the letter being written in confidence. So Smith banged out the copy, using the gambling angle as his lead, and immediately shipped it to the main office in New York. But with the opening of football season and the World Series, the story didn't hit the wires until mid-October. When it did, a New York editor inserted a description of Phog as a "self-styled sage of Midwestern coaches," that burned Phog. But not many saw the story. The *Denver Post* played it big, probably because the city fashioned itself as a basketball capital since it played host to the national AAU Tournament for the past nine years. But the Eastern press just yawned.

On Oct. 20, Madison Square Garden promoter Ned Irish received a call from an International News Service reporter who read the story in Denver seeking a response about gambling on college games in New York. Irish immediately cabled Phog, insisting the Garden was working with city officials to police illegal gambling. The next day, the Associated Press picked up the story and nearly every major newspaper in the country used it. Phog was at the center of this maelstrom. Everybody was calling him and Ned Irish for comments, and these main characters volleyed telegraphs.

Irish wanted names. Phog served up a Temple player, Albie Ingerman, whose name was passed to him by sources in Philadelphia, including his son Bob, who was studying medicine at the University of Pennsylvania. Irish shot back that Ingerman, accused by Phog of shaving points in a 1943 contest, was ill during the particular game. Further, Philadelphia reporters had visited the boy in his home and verified the account.

Phog also repeated the story he heard that summer from Utah coach Vadal Peterson, who said he slammed the door on a gambler who had come to his hotel room at 6 a.m. on the day of the NCAA championship contest asking him how much it would take for him to dump the game against Dartmouth.

Irish wasn't satisfied. He had enjoyed a friendly relationship with Phog, who brought the Jayhawks to the Garden in 1940 and 1942. Phog had always praised Irish's promotional skills and, after losing the basketball tournament financial battle to the NCAA, once told New York reporters he'd rather accept Irish's invitation to the Garden for a $2,000 guarantee than play in the NCAA Tournament for $300. But this was war, and Irish, a former newspaper reporter, wasn't going to let Phog's accusations go unchallenged.

"It has not taken a statement from Lawrence, Kansas, or Denver for me to realize the seriousness of gambling on college sports," Irish wrote to Phog on Oct. 24. "Any person arrested for gambling is automatically barred from entering the building . . . It is extremely unlikely any gambling can emanate from the building here."

To the newspapers, Irish denounced Phog. "He's been doing this sort of thing for years now, and the mystery to me is that people take him seriously in light of his previous false prophecies," Irish said.

That was one of the nicer comments from the East. Newspaper columnists in New York and Philadelphia vilified Phog. Red Smith, of the *Philadelphia Record*, came out swinging.

"Dr. Phog Allen, who has made a career out of proving that he would have invented basketball if James Naismith hadn't thought of it first, is an extraordinarily fortunate man gifted with many talents, rare personal charm and a reverent admiration for the sound of his own voice. Out in Kansas, where schoolchildren are taught that Dr. Allen invented the very peach basket that Naismith first tacked up on a pole . . ."

Lawton Carver, the sports editor for the New York-based International News Service penned the harshest prose, calling Phog a "well-known loud mouth. Each year for many years this bumpkin of no particular standing and of questionable ability as a basketball coach has managed to get his name in the headlines by demanding that baskets be set higher or referees be cut shorter or some other nonsense. He has managed through phony publicity to build himself into some kind of character in basketball."

The story moved on wire services and was killed after one hour for fear of slander, but not before many papers, including the *San Francisco Call*, had included it in their editions.

Peterson, the Utah coach, was a surprising detractor. He told reporters that gambling was a New York problem and Utah didn't play there enough to worry about it. Emil Liston, the Baker University coach, executive director of the National Association of Intercollegiate Basketball and a member of Phog's Baker team in 1907, decried Phog's "deplorable lack of faith in the American youth and meager confidence in the integrity of coaches."

But support in the media and from basketball followers, which swelled in proportion to the distance from New York, proved much greater than the dissent. Pittsburgh coach Dr. Henry Carlson stood by Phog, so did columnists in the Midwest and on the West Coast.

"Phog Allen has thrown down the gauntlet," wrote Jack Carberry of the *Denver Post*. "Let the colleges of our land pick it up."

"Whether Coach Allen was right or wrong in his allegations that the gamblers of Gotham had dealt with players, he is ever so right in demanding that the college executives of the nation proceed to install a czar," wrote Cy Sherman of the *Lincoln* (Neb.) *Star*.

"No matter what the Allen episode proved, it did suggest to a lot of people that their estimate of college athletics ought to be revised again — and downward," stated the *Saturday Evening Post*.

Then there was Andy Rooney's take on the matter. Writing for *Stars & Stripes* — Phog was flooded with letters of mostly praise from soldiers — Rooney posed the question, "So what?"

> " . . .(T)he fact is, if (Irish) stamped out gambling he would stamp out a great deal of Garden basketball. Not all of those 17,000 people were at the Garden the other night because either St. Francis or Muhlenberg were dear to their hearts. They were there for the same reasons they go watch the horse races — and that ain't to watch the nags run. The hardest comment to answer about such gambling is 'So what?' But it is true that gambling makes for a bad smell and dishonesty."

The reason it persisted, Phog insisted, was the NCAA was powerless to do anything about it. Phog called it a "paper organization," which lacked the power to enforce standards. He charged that gamblers were getting to college football and basketball players, paying them for information about injuries and team morale. Even team managers and reporters from school newspapers had been approached. Phog was convinced that gamblers were buying information from sports reporters from his own student newspaper.

"The head of the department can do nothing about it," Phog said in 1944. "Of course it is difficult to prove because the individual can deny it."

The coincidences defied explanation. At times, the Garden erupted in euphoria as if a home team won on a last-second shot. Only these final points made no difference in the outcome, only the point spread. Phog said Peterson told him that in 1943, a spectator rushed on to the Garden floor and kissed a Utah player because his last-minute goal against Kentucky allowed the Utes to cover, thus winning the gentleman $15,000.

Basketball gambling had gotten sophisticated. Bookies were playing the "middle finish," that is establishing betting lines on games so they couldn't lose and sometimes win huge amounts. Say St. John's was favored by 14-16 over DePaul. The bettor who took St. John's had to win by more than 16 points to cash. The bettor who picked DePaul had to have the Blue Demons lose by fewer than 14 points. If St. John's won by 15, the bettors won nothing, and the bookies won both ends.

The hubbub was just beginning to simmer down in January 1945, when two professional gamblers and five members of the Brooklyn College basketball team were arrested for plotting to throw a game against Akron at Boston Garden. At the home of one of the gamblers, $1,000 was given to the players to let Akron win by more than the eight-point spread. Akron canceled the game. This happened three weeks after an NCAA meeting in Columbus, Ohio, where college leaders criticized Phog for spreading unfavorable publicity.

"Now, who's the bumpkin?" Phog responded to the hordes of reporters seeking his reaction to the Brooklyn mess. He offered a photo op: a handful of parlay cards, dope sheets and point spreads mailed to him over the previous three months. Only days later, flush with confidence, Phog trained his sights on another target. Informants in Lexington, Ky., told Phog about the Mayfair Bar at 224 East Main Street. Upstairs was a sports gambler's paradise operated by Lexington's kingpin bookmaker, Ed Curd. Odds were available on pro, college and local high school games, plus every horse racing track in the Western Hemisphere. The house cleaned up on the 1944 presidential election when Franklin Roosevelt didn't carry the state by as wide a margin as predicted.

Four long-distance lines kept the information flowing. More than a half-million was wagered through the bar on football weekends. Its direct number was 3730. Phog had already accused the Lexington-based *Thoroughbred Racing* magazine of becoming involved in bookmaking, and when the magazine demanded he supply names, Phog fired back a Chicago address. The *Lexington Leader* picked up on the squabble and went public with his information. The article prompted unsigned letters to Phog from Lexington citizens identifying other illegal gambling operations in town.

"You should be ashamed of yourself," opened an anonymous letter. "You have made every hand book in town close up and every one has had his phones discontinued for the present time. They have been notified by the police not to open up until further notice . . .I bet it was the first time in years they saw the sun in the afternoon. You did something that the police have never been able to do, or maybe they didn't want to."

But Phog was whistling into the wind. His public awareness campaign had a fruit fly's life span. At speaking engagements throughout the remainder of the 1940s, Phog renewed his call for a college sports czar and warned of an imminent scandal on the level of baseball's 1919 Black Sox. All he could really do was keep his players from becoming involved. It wasn't easy. Access, the Jayhawks learned on their 1940 trip to New York and Philadelphia, was remarkably easy.

"The gamblers would sit in rows behind the players on both team's benches and make contact with the substitutes," Bob Allen said. "They made contact with the outstanding players and tell them they didn't want you to throw the game, just keep the score within reason, and nobody would know the difference. Back then, one or two good players on a team could control the score."

Bob Allen, who was an outstanding player, said he never was contacted, and that it would have been difficult for gamblers to reach players while in New York. The team did everything together. Restaurants, movies, shows. If family members came to town, they could eat with the team but that's all. No one was permitted to go his own way.

But it wasn't always in New York where gamblers reached the players. Kentucky's Bill Spivey and other Wildcats were approached while working and playing in the summers at the Catskill Mountains. That continued throughout the 1940s before the bomb dropped on

Phog's son, Bob, was an outstanding player, but he said he was never contacted by gamblers when the team was in New York. Phog took extra steps to make sure access to the team was next to impossible. (Photo courtesy University of Kansas Sports Information)

college basketball. Rupp told a group in Lincoln, Neb., that gamblers "couldn't touch our boys with a 10-foot pole." How wrong he was. Kentucky's powerful NCAA championship teams of 1948 and 1949 had been infiltrated by gamblers. Ralph Beard and Alex Groza were kicked out of the NBA because of their involvement in the college scandals.

On April 19, 1952, New York District Attorney Frank Hogan announced his grand jury investigation had found that 86 games in 23 cities had been fixed. Some 33 players were said to be involved, and seven programs were cited as the greatest offenders: Kentucky, City College of New York, Long Island University, Manhattan, Bradley, New York University and Toledo. Coach Nat Holman's CCNY Beavers were less than a year removed from their unprecedented double: championships of the NCAA Tournament and NIT, when rumors of point shaving surfaced. LIU dropped basketball for six years. Kentucky closed down for the 1952-53 season.

Phog remained unconvinced gambling had ceased. In 1955, he received word from a Newark, N.J., reporter that Holman believed another scandal was on the horizon. Again, Phog sounded the horn. Again, he was right. In 1961, Connecticut, Mississippi State, La Salle, Detroit, Tennessee, St. Joseph's and 16 other schools were implicated in point-shaving schemes that involved 37 players, including Connie Hawkins of Iowa.

Phog didn't discriminate. He blew the whistle on gambling establishments in Lawrence and Kansas City as well. In 1951, Phog identified a group of oddsmakers who sat in the same box for every game at Municipal Auditorium in Kansas City. The building had received complaints of open gambling for three years. "How can we keep our own house clean when persons who are laying odds and making bets are working during the very time our college games are being staged at Municipal Auditorium?" Phog said to the *Kansas City Star* in 1951.

The crusade continued well past Phog's retirement in 1956. It burned Phog that Kentucky and CCNY were allowed to keep their crowns in spite of their convictions. Phog called them the Black Wildcats and Black Beavers. "They are there for every youth to see despite the fact some members of both teams confessed dumping and shaving points," Phog said in 1958. "The NCAA has yet not seen fit to remove the championship toga from these teams."

Among Phog's solutions was to remove the game from big city arenas and have all college contests on campus where events were run by college administrators and not professional promoters. He was even willing to give up NCAA Tournament games in such lucrative locales as New York and Kansas City. That wouldn't be a catastrophe, Phog reasoned, because outside the East, college basketball didn't need double headers in large cities to draw well. When he explained basketball's provincialism — and he did it often — Phog started with attendance. He liked to brag that "West" schools in the Big Ten and Big Six filled their arenas on a regular basis with thousands of fans, while those in the East counted attendance in the hundreds.

East teams used many former professional coaches, like Holman and St. John's Joe Lapchick of the Original Celtics, while West schools have used only college-trained instructors, who inject more action

Phog poses with some of the members of his 1949-50 team. From left are Bill Lienhard, Claude Houchin, Phog, Clyde Lovellette, Bill Hougland and Jerry Waugh. (From the University of Kansas archives)

and college spirit into games, Phog contended. West teams tried to score late in games even with the lead while East teams looked to protect their advantage, even if only a point or two, by stalling. East ball was deliberate, ball control and two-handed set shots. West ball was fast break, constant action and the running one-hander.

It really wasn't the Jayhawks' style, but Phog didn't admit that. He just pointed to the records. No team east of Indiana won the first eight NCAA Tournaments, and when the NCAA champ met the NIT champ in Madison Square Garden for the Red Cross benefit games from 1943-45, the NCAA teams won them all. It mattered to Phog that CCNY once got kicked at Bradley in one of the few instances where a New York team traveled that far west. He was thrilled when Stanford and Hank Luisetti went to the Garden in 1936 and ended LIU's 43-game winning streak. New York sportswriters set the tone for the national sports scene, and to them, nowhere in the nation was college basketball better played than in their city. At least, that was Phog's interpretation.

"Some of the boys around New York think that Philadelphia is far west and Pittsburgh is just out of this world," Phog wrote in 1945. "Eastern boys do not venture out West."

At New York in 1951, Phog coached the West team in an annual all-star encounter sponsored by the NABC. His best player was a rival, Kansas State center Ernie Barrett, who had led the Wildcats to the NCAA title game against Kentucky only a few weeks earlier.

Barrett got an earful of Phog's geography lesson during a one-on-one session in Phog's hotel room.

"I was sitting in his room so cluttered with books, notepads, clothes strewn about," Barrett said. "He got on his soapbox and talked about the differences between basketball in the West and East, and how we were homespun and down-to-earth people who had to resist the temptations of the East. Later, he addressed us in the locker room and went over the same things. We were ready to run through the wall."

Barrett was MVP in the West's victory.

East coaches took offense to Phog. "Western players wouldn't last in a tough league over a period of time like our boys have done, because our style of play is sounder," Holman told *The Sporting News* in 1943. Added New York University coach Howard Cann: "We in the East play a more spontaneous game than the boys in the West. Those boys out there just can't seem to meet the situations we do."

Phog's other anti-gambling solutions were to prohibit players from entering summer leagues in the Catskill Mountains, where gamblers had easy access. And, of course, the czar. Eastern sportswriters wrote that Phog was running a campaign for what amounted to a commissioner of college athletics. In 1945, Grantland Rice suggested Phog become a national college basketball commissioner. But Phog had no interest in the job. His first choice was Gen. Douglas MacArthur. If not him, then J. Edgar Hoover or Thomas Dewey or a Supreme Court justice.

"I am thinking of a man with college ideals and at the same time a man with the love of the game in his heart," Phog wrote to Rice. "The man should be a lawyer because he should be able to write both State and Federal statutes so they would have the laws to prosecute aggressively the gangsters and tinhorn gamblers who endeavor to chisel in all college sports."

His salary of $75,000-$100,000 would be paid by the colleges and he would be hired by the NCAA. Conference commissioners would answer to him.

"Some schools are in the athletic business, some alumni are in the athletic business and some gamblers have been getting into the college athletic business," Phog said in 1945. "Why not clean it all up and start now?"

The NCAA countered that the organization could police itself, thank you, and while you're at it, shut up. Phog and college sports never got their czar, and the gambling never really stopped. In 1982, a Boston College player went to jail for fixing games during the 1978-79 season. A few years later, Tulane dropped its program in light of a point-shaving scandal.

When Kansas athletic director Bob Frederick served as the Division I men's basketball committee chairman in 1995 and 1996, he and NCAA officials threatened to remove press credentials from newspapers that carried betting lines. Newspapers responded that the NCAA would not determine their editorial content.

If only someone had listened to Phog. Not in 1943 when he popped off about the Garden, or in 1945 when he identified gambling joints in Kentucky, or in 1955 when he warned of another major point-shaving scandal.

But in 1920, when he had been on the job as KU's athletic director for 14 months. Phog told the *Daily Kansan* for its Oct. 28, 1920, edition:

> *"Horse racing, former king of sports, is a sideline, boxing is in the gutter, and baseball, America's great national game, is kept alive only by its soul, living in the breast of a six- and seven-year-old child. All this is the result of gamblers. And now they are after our greatest intercollegiate sport — football. Don't bet on your team, don't bet against your team, assure them of your support by your undying loyalty to them.*
>
> *"It's a mean and selfish practice when one student bets that his fellow students will win a football game. He is merely profiting by the sweat of the football player's brow. I have heard much betting was being done on points — betting that Kansas would win from the (Kansas State) Aggies by so much margin. Don't limit your team. Let them alone."*

16

FRIENDS AND

ENEMIES

Phog gave Howard Engleman, a star on the 1939-41 teams, a job as freshman coach in 1946-47 to help defray law school expenses. It was to be the extent of Engleman's coaching career. But during an October practice, Phog was standing on the sideline watching the action on one end of the floor. He had a speaking engagement in Topeka that night, so instead of his usual practice sweats and sneakers he was wearing dress shoes and coat and tie. He didn't see one of his players, Ted Bean, barreling in from the opposite side. Boom! Bean leveled Phog, whose head slammed hard against the floor.

After blacking out for a minute, Phog was back on his feet conducting practice unaware he had suffered a concussion. Headaches and dizzy spells continued for the next few days. Doctors told him to cut back on his schedule but Phog was fired up for the season. The Jayhawks returned four starters from a Big Six title team in 1946 that finished 19-2. Phog wasn't about to ease up. But the headaches persisted and Phog, now 61, couldn't shake a flu he caught in December.

On Jan. 9, 1947, two days after losing to Missouri in Lawrence for the first time since 1930, Phog entered the University of Kansas hospital in Kansas City, Kan., (he had never spent a night in the hospital in his life) and a few days later, he called it quits for the season. Engleman took over the varsity.

"I had no illusions about being a coach," Engleman said. "In those days, there really were no assistant coaches, so that's why they called on me. Let me tell you, I was no Phog Allen or Knute Rockne when it came to speeches. I just wanted to finish the year."

Phog needed the rest. In that Missouri game, he and Tigers coach Sparky Stalcup — in his first game against the Jayhawks — nearly started a riot. Stalcup was on his feet asking officials Cliff Ogden and Clay Van Reem for an explanation of a foul. Phog came to the Tigers' bench and pushed Stalcup. Stalcup raised him arm as if to slug Phog but, surely to the disappointment of many fellow coaches, didn't follow through. Instead, Stalcup said, "Get the hell back on your side of the court."

Explanations but no apologies followed. It turned out to be Phog's final game that season. The Jayhawks won eight of 14 games under Engleman, who kept alive the streak of head coaches with winning records since Naismith. The team's overall record of 16-11 is credited to Allen, who followed the team's progress from his daughter Mary's home in La Jolla, Calif., where he and Bessie remained until mid-April.

In California, Phog got in plenty of swimming, some golf, started work on his third book, *Coach Phog Allen's Sports Stories*, published in November, and fended off rumors of his retirement. The buzz around Lawrence was Phog would return from the coast and run for mayor. Opponents were glad he didn't for the next two years were some of his worst ever. The 1948 team finished 9-15, and lost a school-record 10 straight. In 1949, the Jayhawks went 12-12 and Phog suffered his worst defeat, by 27 points at Kansas State.

The 1948 and 1949 teams tied for last in the conference, and opponents had to be enjoying the heck out of this. By the late 1940s, there wasn't a conference team that Phog hadn't feuded with. It was as if he had become a self-appointed Big Six investigative department.

In 1942, Oklahoma was the target. The Jayhawks lost in Norman, which created a Kansas-Oklahoma tie for the Big Six title. Phog fumed when coach Bruce Drake didn't provide the Jayhawks a new ball for pregame warmups, and was peeved when he had to shoo away photographers who set up in front of the KU bench. But it was a gesture toward the end of the game that nearly brought Phog to blows. Oklahoma star Gerald Tucker taunted Ralph Miller by pointing a finger at him and running his fingers through Miller's hair toward the end of the game.

The back cover of Phog's third book, Phog Allen's Sports Stories, *published in November 1947.*

The victory was sweet for the Sooners, accused by Phog of illegally obtaining Tucker, who originally enrolled at Kansas State. Tucker, from Winfield, Kan., got a better offer from Oklahoma, according to Phog, and transferred after seven weeks. Under league rules he should have been ineligible for the season, but Tucker played anyway.

The sparring between Drake and Phog lasted nearly a decade, and Tucker became one of the league's top players, leading the conference in scoring in 1943 and 1947 before joining some former Kansas players on the Phillips 66 AAU team. In 1956 he became the Olympic coach. Although Tucker made all-conference three times, Phog refused to vote for him.

Before Tucker, Phog picked on Missouri, claiming the Tigers had been using deep pockets for obtaining football players since 1930. "Missouri has a slush fund of $15,000 a year, and no wonder Paul Chrisman can get $60.00 a month for being private secretary to (an athletic official)," Phog wrote in 1940. "We haven't pin money compared to that. In fact we don't have a single basketball player making $20.00 a month."

Phog believed the slush fund was provided by the Missouri Legislature. "Absurd," Tigers AD and football coach Don Faurot shot back.

Some of Phog's most heated battles came at Nebraska, where the fans hated him. They loved to bonk him on the head with apple cores. He didn't make any friends in Lincoln in 1951 when he accused the Cornhuskers of paying for star halfback Bobby Reynolds. "I was told that Bobby Reynolds was offered $10,000 and a Cadillac to go to some other school," Phog said to the Associated Press. "He didn't go. That raised the question what he got at Nebraska."

Phog reminded the seething Cornhusker faithful that Kansas was the only Missouri Valley school that didn't rip up its contract in 1920 when Nebraska told opponents it was going to play home games in Omaha, then a violation of league rules. The Cornhuskers withdrew from the league but wanted to continue playing Missouri Valley foes. Only Kansas, with Phog as the football coach and AD, honored its contract. The apple cores kept coming.

On a yearly basis, Phog seemed to have a tougher time at Iowa State than any place in the league, something of a surprise because the Cyclones' coach for 18 years (1929-47) was Louis Menze, who played for Phog at Central Missouri State. Menze was Phog's best friend in the league but that didn't stop the rude treatment at Ames.

During a 1941 game, fans flung a dead chicken on the floor in front of the Jayhawks bench. That spring, an Iowa State-Kansas baseball game — Phog was coaching baseball that year — ended in a near riot when the umpire disallowed what would have been the winning run for the Cyclones. The umpire ruled an out at another base before the run scored, when it clearly had not. Fans naturally went looking for Phog, who escaped to the locker room.

Oklahoma A&M wasn't in the Big Six in the 1940s but the Aggies and Jayhawks had their skirmishes. Hank Iba was so disgusted with officials after a 1943 loss in Lawrence that he refused to substitute for a player who had fouled out and finished the game with four players on the court. Phog wrote Iba the next day asking for a cease-fire in the series. The last two games in Lawrence "have been dull, multiple-fouling contests in which the spectators have been very much displeased at the type of exhibition . . .The Kansas public simply does not like that kind of basketball."

The series took a two-year break, but Phog never lost his respect for Iba. He fired off letters of congratulations after the Aggies won their 1945 and 1946 NCAA titles. When the teams met in the 1946 district playoffs in Kansas City, Iba was incensed that radio stations in Oklahoma City and Tulsa were going to be charged a $100 fee to broadcast games from Municipal Auditorium. Phog got the fees waived. "What money we would get is chicken feed when Hank Iba's goodwill is concerned," Phog said. And nobody championed Oklahoma State's admission to the conference, the Big Seven since Colorado joined in 1947, longer and louder than Phog.

"I'm for Oklahoma A&M 100 percent plus," Phog told the *Lawrence Journal-World* in 1947. "It has been my opinion that we have needed the Aggies in our conference for a long time." After the 1947 season, Kansas alumni in Oklahoma started a petition drive urging the Aggies' admission and that summer presented it to KU Chancellor Deane Malott. But Phog never got to coach against Oklahoma State as a conference member. The Aggies weren't admitted until the 1958-59 season.

Iba presented Phog with a plaque during halftime of the 1951 regular-season finale at Stillwater. Just a friendship thing. Iba announced to the sellout crowd that, "Dr. Allen has done more for the game than any other living man." The plaque read: "To Dr. F.C. Allen

Phog Allen with Oklahoma A&M coach Hank Iba (left) after Kansas defeated the Aggies in 1952 for Phog's 700th career victory. (From the University of Kansas archives)

of Kansas. A great coach, a fighting rival, a true sportsman. In appreciation for his devoted work in basketball and his towering stature in his profession of coach. Since 1908, no man has contributed as much to the game. Presented in 1951 in Doctor Allen's 41st year of coaching by his admirers and friends at Oklahoma A&M College." It became one of Phog's prized possessions.

Phog usually didn't hold grudges. He and Stalcup got off to a bad start — Phog started calling him "Sparkle Plenty" — but Phog admired his adversary's feistiness, and a 1951 incident cemented their friendship. With three minutes remaining in the Big Eight Holiday Tournament championship game, KU center Clyde Lovellette stomped his big right foot in the gut of a sprawled out Tigers guard Win Wilfong and then walked away. Many of the 9,787 in Municipal Auditorium erupted in boos, and the yelling continued as Kansas was to accept the championship trophy.

"Win Wilfong was like a gnat that bothered my eye," Lovellette said. "You swat them but they keep coming back. He had climbed my back. I got a rebound and put it back in, then I shook him off like a dog shakes water off his back. He fell to the ground on his back. I don't know why I did it but I planted my size 14 right in his stomach. I mean to tell you, the whole place started hollering and screaming. I never heard such discord. I think even the Kansas fans were after me."

Lovellette went to the Missouri bench to find Wilfong but Stalcup greeted him instead and shook his hand. But the crescendo of boos disrupted the ceremony. Finally, Stalcup came to the microphone. "The University of Missouri enjoys this rivalry with the University of Kansas," Stalcup said. "Doc Allen is a great coach."

With that, Missouri players approached the Kansas bench with their hands extended. Wilfong and Lovellette hugged. Stalcup had seized the moment and provided one of the greatest acts of sportsmanship in the history of the bitter rivalry. "The night will never be too dark or stormy to do him a favor," Phog said after the game. He and Stalcup became friends and Phog later attended the wedding of Stalcup's daughter.

Phog didn't patch up relationships with everybody. Some remained open wounds for life. As much as it may have pained Phog to admit it, his sour association with Kansas State's Jack Gardner may have been the best thing that happened in the second half of Phog's career. While Missouri improved under Stalcup, Oklahoma remained tough and Oklahoma A&M was a regional rival, the biggest threat to Kansas' conference and area supremacy came from Gardner and Kansas State.

It would have been bad enough for Phog to lose top dog status in the league, but by the late 1940s and for the first time in any sustained period in his career, the Jayhawks did not have the best program in the state. From 1947-51, Kansas lost nine of 11 games to K-State and the coach Phog disliked more than any in his career. The feeling was mutual. From their first meeting in 1939 when Gardner got the job, he detested Phog. Gardner had been tipped off about Phog from his college coach, Sam Barry at Southern Cal, who had recommended Gardner. Barry warned Gardner that Phog would try to push him around so establish your presence immediately.

"In those days coaches drew up the schedules," Gardner said. "Phog told me he was going to play us at his place on this day and at our place on that day. I told him that wasn't satisfactory. He hit the roof, started screaming at me. But I had to let him know he wasn't going to dictate to me, that we were on the same level."

Gardner nearly pulled off a shocking upset in his first meeting with the Jayhawks. KU entered that Jan. 12, 1940, contest in Lawrence with an 8-1 record and would make the NCAA championship game. Kansas State was 4-6 and finished the year 6-12. The matchup should have been a blowout. Thanks to Gardner, it wasn't.

K-State had arrived in Lawrence early in the day. Gardner wandered over to Robinson Gym to see where Naismith had worked. A few years earlier, Gardner conducted a basketball clinic in Japan and Naismith, ever curious about the game overseas, had asked Gardner for a report.

"Nobody was in the gym," Gardner said. "But there were plays diagrammed on the floor and arrows pointing to where Phog wanted his players to go. I jotted down the patterns and decided to play a four-man zone against them, with one guy down on the other end just for offense. If he was going to be that regimented, we might have a chance. He was either going to have to play us five on four, with us knowing exactly what he was doing, or four on four. That's how he played us, four on four. I could tell he was frustrated."

The Jayhawks sweated out a 34-33 victory. To friends, Phog started calling Gardner "wonder boy." Word got back to Manhattan.

"He wasn't trying to be nice," Gardner said. "He called me that throughout my career. Phog Allen wasn't one of my favorite people. He was a great contributor to the game. Too bad he was such a jerk."

Maybe Phog would have held a greater appreciation for Gardner if he had known how difficult it had been for the rookie coach. When he arrived in September 1939, Gardner asked K-State athletic director Mike Ahearn how many recruits were in the program. Ahearn told him none but Gardner was welcome to dive into the physical education classes and pluck out a few.

Basketball didn't have a budget. Gardner wasn't allowed to make long-distance calls his first few months on the job. He didn't post a winning season and went 0-6 against Kansas during his first tour of duty. Gardner left in 1942 to become athletic director and coach of the Olathe, Kan., Naval Air Base Clippers, which were made up primarily of college stars. Among them was former Indiana standout Bill Menke, who had played for the 1940 team that defeated KU in the NCAA final.

At Olathe, Gardner had the talent to match Phog, and in four years, the Clippers won four of nine games from the Jayhawks. Gardner returned to coach Kansas State in 1946 and with him came

Dean Nesmith, Dick Harp and Phog during a game in 1952. (Photo by Rich Clarkson)

some Clippers, like Harold Howey, the team's top scorer in 1947. Gardner also did not endear himself to Phog when the Kansas coach said he possessed information that the Clippers were betting on their own games. Phog had learned that bookies in Kansas City wouldn't touch Gardner's team because the boys were in business for themselves.

The Naval Station howled in protest, but Phog pointed out that it was probable Gardner didn't know it was happening. "Clair Bee of LIU, Nat Holman of CCNY and Adolph Rupp of Kentucky all said that they could not tell whether their boys were making an honest attempt to win the game or not," Phog wrote in 1952. Phog's offer to meet with Navy officials and supply proof wasn't accepted.

The strain in the Phog-Gardner relationship continued in 1948, when Phog got on one of his eligibility crusades, this time targeting K-State standout Clarance Brannum, who played for the Wildcats that season despite having previously played in the semiprofessional AAU tournament. Phog lost this battle and several more to Gardner, who guided Kansas State to the 1948 NCAA semifinals, over the next few years.

K-State was beating Kansas in recruiting because Gardner was hitting the road, making visits, charming parents. World War II had changed the recruiting game. Now, three or four years worth of classes were stacked up and unleashed at once. There was an abundance of talent and many were mature men in their mid-20s. Phog hated the idea of recruiting. If a boy wants to come to Kansas and play, Phog would find a way to get him on the team. That was his philosophy. Gardner's interpretation: "All Phog had to do before was call somebody and they'd come."

Actually, Phog wrote letters. Prospects wrote to Phog, and the coach would respond explaining that Kansas (before World War II) doesn't offer athletic scholarships and that jobs in the towel room might be available for 35 cents an hour. And don't think of coming to Kansas just for sports. In a form letter, Phog would make the following response to prospects:

> *"You will find that I am not trying to entice you here as a student because you play basketball. I have never contacted basketball players, because I think that any coach who offers a boy a job on account of his athletic ability is doing the boy a real injury. I tell each athlete that he cannot help the University on account of his athletic skill. The University helps him."*

"For years on end, his philosophy was that young men in Kansas who wanted to play basketball should attend their state university," Dick Harp said. "He would write to prospects and tell them the good things that could happen if they came to Kansas. If they

Phog got plenty of mail, much of it from prospective players who wanted to come to Kansas. He would advise them that the reason they should come to Kansas was to get an education and there would be no special treatment because of their athletic abilities. (Photo by Rich Clarkson)

needed money, there would be jobs but strictly school-related work. For Doc, there wasn't any driving around on the weekends to watch kids play."

Then Gardner started winning and the state's enthusiasm for basketball gravitated toward Manhattan. Tiny Nichols Gymnasium on the K-State campus could no longer hold the crowds. Gardner once orchestrated a ploy to gain funding for a new building by getting students to make a straw dummy, cover it with ketchup and drop if from the ceiling during a time out. There were 100 state legislators in attendance that night. In 1950, Kansas State got its new building and more than 14,000 packed the place to see the Wildcats play Long Island in the dedication game of Ahearn Field House. Down the road, Kansas continued to play games in 3,000-seat Hoch Auditorium.

"Jack Gardner's teams ultimately changed Doc's perspective," Harp said. "K-State had become more than a worthy competitor. Doc recognized Jack Gardner was a real threat to the future, the first real threat he ever faced. Before that, Doc had gotten most of the good players out of Kansas, and his coaching ability allowed him to dominate."

Phog realized he needed a recruiter. Harp, then the coach at William Jewell College, had applied to become a Jayhawks assistant in 1947, but Kansas wouldn't approve an extra $200 in salary. In 1948, Harp got his pay bump, then his marching orders from Phog.

17

BRASS RINGS AND GOLD MEDALS

In 1948, high school basketball in Kansas was terrific. Among the top prospects, Bill Hougland was a senior at Beloit, Bill Lienhard at Newton and Bob Kenney at Winfield. Phog never lured a prospective player to Kansas by promising championships. The record spoke for itself. But Kansas State and Gardner had applied pressure and Phog needed a pitch. Promise the boys, Phog instructed Harp, that if they come to Kansas they'll not only win an NCAA championship but an Olympic gold medal. They'd be seniors in 1952, when the Summer Games were scheduled for Helsinki.

"That's what I told them," Harp said. "I really didn't believe it at the time, and I don't think they did either. But that was our challenge."

Phog saved the big fish, Clyde Lovellette, for himself. At 6 feet, 9½ inches, Lovellette had blossomed into a dominating player at Garfield High in Terre Haute, Ind., and there was no reason to expect him to leave his home state for college. Not until his junior year did Lovellette much consider life beyond high school.

"My father was an engineer on the railroad, and I thought that was a glamorous job," Lovellette said. "When I was growing up I wanted to do that or be a state policeman, but I grew too tall for that.

I wasn't too high on the academic block, but I knew there were things I could have fun doing."

Lovellette had seven brothers and sisters. Three died before making it to high school. Only he and his sister Marie finished the 12th grade. If he hadn't grown so tall, Lovellette might not have had incentive to stay in school. But grow he did, wide and strong as well as tall. He went from 6-4 as a freshman to 6-8 as a sophomore. He might not have seen his basketball potential then, but his mother, Myrtle, did.

"She told me I was clumsy and that if I was going to play sports I had to get unclumsy," Lovellette said. "She wanted me to jump rope. The only people I ever saw jumping rope were girls and I didn't want to do it. She said we could go in the back yard after supper where nobody would see us, and that's what we did. I got good at it. Mom also danced with me to help my coordination."

Lovellette became a big-time high school prospect as a senior, but there was no need for anybody to recruit him. Nearly all of the coaches at Garfield had attended Indiana. Lovellette told the Hoosiers he was coming.

"If you were from Indiana, you were going to go to an Indiana school, either IU, Purdue, or, if you were Catholic, Notre Dame," Lovellette said. "Everything I did was geared toward going to Indiana. Everybody knew who (IU coach) Branch McCracken was. I had never heard of Phog Allen."

But Phog knew of Big Clyde and set up a meeting with Lovellette around a speech in St. Louis. Lovellette, however, dispatched his brother-in-law to St. Louis to tell Phog not to bother. The Lovellettes then got their first lesson in Phog's power of persuasion.

"The next thing I know, here they are coming up the driveway," Lovellette said. "Dad and I were sitting on the front porch and I went out back. I didn't want to face him. Dad told him I was going to Indiana. But Phog came in the house, met my mom and asks where I am. Finally, he found me. We talked and talked and he wanted me to visit Lawrence. I packed my bags and we headed there."

Lovellette said he fell for the town and campus. On a subsequent visit with his parents, Phog arranged a side trip to Topeka for the family to meet Gov. Frank Carlson. At the time, the Kansas student population was much smaller than Indiana's and Lovellette, upon announcing his decision to become a Jayhawk, said he felt more comfortable in Lawrence than Bloomington. Of course, nobody believed him.

One of Phog's first major recruiting prizes was Indiana native and future All-American Clyde Lovellette. (Photo by Rich Clarkson)

"Everybody was saying they sweetened the deal for me," Lovellette said. "There were no deals. I'm not saying there weren't individuals who wouldn't take you out to dinner once in a while. But they would have done that at Indiana, too. I joined (Sigma Chi), paid my own dues, and sold programs at the football games for a quarter. I got a nickel for every one I sold."

The critics weren't convinced. After Lovellette finished at Kansas, *Look* magazine printed an article titled "How Basketball Players are Bought," suggesting illegal tactics were used to entice Lovellette and teammates B.H. Born and Charlie Hoag. Phog gruffly denied everything and called the piece "too silly to bother with."

Kansas and Indiana weren't the only schools bidding for Lovellette. Kentucky wanted him, also. But Rupp said if he couldn't get him, better Lovellette go to Lawrence. He did, and the crown jewel of the 1948 recruiting class was in place.

"There are a lot of people in (Indiana) who think Kansas cheated to get me and feel betrayed that I didn't stay home grown," Lovellette said. "I could tell there was resentment when all-time teams were picked and a lot of players who couldn't carry my jock were listed ahead of me. Phog sold me. He kept telling me he had this dream about winning a conference championship, the NCAA and the Olympics, and that he couldn't do it without me. That was pretty heavy. I thought it was impressive that he had enough confidence in me to help him do all those things. That's why I came."

And not to cure his asthma. That was Phog's line to the press; Big Clyde needed to leave Indiana for the more "rarefied atmosphere" of the Midwest. Lovellette played along for a while, until the recruiting fervor died down.

Lovellette quickly became the standout all had envisioned. He led the Big Seven in scoring as a sophomore and junior. In Lovellette's first season, Kansas tied K-State and Nebraska for the league title and represented the league in the NCAA playoffs. The Jayhawks, 3-9 in league play a year earlier, finished 8-4 in 1950. National coaches were impressed by the turnaround and voted Phog "Man of the Year" in college basketball.

Kansas was much improved, but not good enough to overcome Gardner's Wildcats. Lovellette's teams lost four of their first five games to K-State, which advanced to the 1951 NCAA title game against Kentucky. The Jayhawks also got a taste of Kentucky that season and it could not have been more bitter. Kansas was returning home after winning at St. Joseph's and St. John's. The Jayhawks stood 4-0. So were the Wildcats, who had won their games by an average of 26 points. Memorial Coliseum was packed and buzzing about the meeting between these powerhouses, mentor against pupil.

Kentucky had scouted the Jayhawks on their Eastern swing and was impressed by Lovellette. But the Wildcats believed their 7-1 center Bill Spivey was quick enough defensively to keep Kansas from making entry passes. Kansas wasn't prepared and the Wildcats went nuts, clubbing the Jayhawks 68-39. Spivey outscored Lovellette 22-10 and was credited with 10 steals. Big Clyde fouled out with 13:33

Phog won a recruiting battle with Indiana and Kentucky to bring Clyde Lovellette to Kansas. The Terre Haute, Ind., star became an All-American. (Both photos by Rich Clarkson)

to play. When he sat, Rupp pulled Spivey. Phog wanted a rematch. Rupp refused, and the teams didn't meet again until 1959.

The Jayhawks finished 1951 at 16-8 overall and 8-4 in the conference, tying Missouri for second. Kansas State had defeated Kansas twice and won its third conference title in four years. Clearly, the Wildcats ruled the Big Seven, and more importantly, the state, and they reveled in their superiority. When Phog scouted a Kansas State game at Manhattan in 1951, a fan asked him for his autograph. Just as Phog returned the signed paper, the fan struck a match and set it ablaze.

Phog Allen goes over strategy with his 1952 team which won the national championship. (Photo by Rich Clarkson)

Heading into the 1951-52 season, K-State had won 10 of the previous 12 meetings with the Jayhawks, and although Kansas won a 90-88 thriller in the December 1951 Holiday Tournament, the Wildcats returned the favor on Jan. 26 with a 17-point home triumph. Kansas followed that setback with a four-point loss at Oklahoma State. In the late 1940s and early 1950s, losing games at Manhattan and Stillwater was no sin, but this was to be Phog's season, the one he'd been building toward and talking about for four years.

The Jayhawks had lived up to the promise early, winning their first 13 games. But the successive losses had Phog worried. The nation was loaded with great teams and players; Kentucky and Cliff Hagan, Duke and Dick Groat, Rod Fletcher and Johnny Kerr at Illinois. But if Kansas couldn't get past Kansas State or Oklahoma State, there would be no chance for a national championship. After returning from Stillwater, Phog met with Harp.

"He said 'We've got to change something,'" Harp said. "I said 'What do you want to change?' We talked about it and decided to go with a pressure man-to-man, half-court defense. Probably as much as the new defense helped, the change itself gave the kids new enthusiasm. We spent most of our time in practice on it. As soon as we started playing that, opponents knew we were doing something different. They began to think when they played us they needed a different offense. It played right into our hands. We had a new enthusiasm, a new perspective."

Make no mistake, the pressure defense was critical. Phog had always been a defensive-minded coach, but the Jayhawks now were playing it with much more intensity. It probably was the most significant midseason mechanical change in Phog's career and stands as his tactical legacy in college basketball. In his retirement, UCLA legend John Wooden referred to the Kansas pressure defense of 1952 as something of a defensive turning point in college basketball.

But a technical change wasn't all that was in store for the Jayhawks after the losses. Ever the psychologist, Phog went for the emotional jugular in a team meeting. The players hushed as their coach read, of all things, *Casey at the Bat*. As he recited the final stanza, Phog's eyes grew puffy and tears streaked down his face. Casey, like the Jayhawks, had hit bottom.

Then Phog picked up a copy of his favorite piece of literature, the lesser known *Casey's Revenge*, penned by Grantland Rice. The washed-up Casey returns to boos and jeers to clout the game-winning home run. The poem ends, "He came through hell to scramble back — and prove a champ belongs."

"Then we'd start crying," Lovellette said. "And want to break through walls."

The Jayhawks went on a tear, blowing through the rest of the Big Seven schedule, highlighted by a 17-point home victory over Kansas State. Kansas also avenged the loss to Oklahoma State. The occasion was memorable. On Feb. 19, Phog won what was believed to be his 700th career game. Nobody else in the business had reached 600.

In the NCAA Tournament the Jayhawks got by Texas Christian by four, and, behind Lovellette's tournament-record 44, blitzed Saint Louis. For the first time, the NCAA advanced its regional champions to one arena, creating the first true Final Four. Second-ranked Illinois was favored to win it all at the University of Washington's Edmundson Pavilion but was defeated in a semifinal by St. John's, which had pulled off the biggest upset of the tournament a round earlier by knocking off No. 1 Kentucky.

This year, Kansas was considered a sentimental choice because of Phog. He was 66 years old and knew because of the state's retirement recommendation he'd only have four more seasons. Phog was justifiably proud of the championship honors accorded the 1922 and 1923 teams, but Kansas had never won a postseason tournament. At the NABC convention in Seattle, Phog was introduced as "Mr. Basketball."

But Mr. Basketball nearly lost his star attraction before the semifinal contest against Santa Clara. Lovellette got permission to have dinner with a fraternity friend, "Fig" Newton, on a Navy cutter. Lovellette got the grand tour as the cutter set sail on the Puget Sound. Then a thick fog rolled in. "You couldn't see your hand in front of your face," Lovellette said. "Fig said we couldn't get back. It got late, and later and later. The fog lifted early in the morning and we finally got back. It was morning when I finally got some sleep."

Somehow, Phog excused the breach of curfew.

Lovellette dominated Santa Clara with 33 points and the Jayhawks won 74-55. Kansas followed the same script against St. John's and its star center Zeke Zawoluk. Lovellette had 33 and the Jayhawks won 80-63. Phog and Kansas had their national championship.

For the coach who had contributed so much to the game, the NCAA title stands as the crowning achievement of his career, although Phog probably didn't think so at the time. This being an Olympic year, larger goals remained and promises to the recruiting class of four years earlier were to be kept. But were it not for the triumph in Seattle, Phog might be remembered as the best coach in college basketball history who won nothing beyond a load of league championships.

"It would have been a tragedy if one of his teams didn't win a national championship," Harp said.

Three days after winning the NCAA crown, the Jayhawks opened the eight-team Olympic playoff by smacking NAIA champion Southwest Missouri State 92-55 in Kansas City. Next up was a trip to New York to face NIT winner La Salle and its freshman wonder Tom Gola. But the Jayhawks, their bags packed and airplane warming up at Kansas City's downtown airport, weren't going anywhere. They sat in the lobby of the Muehlebach Hotel because Phog had learned only officials from the East were to call the semifinals and finals of the Olympic playoffs. That wouldn't do. Frantically, phones were dialed, hours passed. Finally, a Midwestern official,

Phog accepts the 1952 NCAA championship plaque. (Photo courtesy University of Kansas Sports Information)

Ronnie Gibbs, joined the crew. He wasn't Phog's first choice. That was Cliff Ogden, who had worked all of the Jayhawks' NCAA games and the Southwest Missouri State contest. But Gibbs it was, and the Jayhawks winged to New York.

The semifinal against La Salle was the critical contest. The winner would provide half the Olympic team roster and a coach. The Explorers led by 13 in the first half and took a 54-49 lead into the fourth quarter. But behind Lovellette, who finished with 40 points and 14 rebounds, Kansas roared back for a 70-65 triumph. The Jayhawks were going to Helsinki and Lawrence celebrated. Bon fires burned on campus and the main drag, Massachusetts Street. A crush of cars brought the town to a halt.

Before meeting the AAU champions, the Peoria Caterpillar Diesels, Phog announced the seven players for the Olympic team:

Clyde Lovellette led Kansas to the national championship in 1952 and then played for the U.S. in the Olympics at Helsinki. Phog was an assistant coach for the U.S. team. (Photo by Rich Clarkson)

Lovellette, Kenney, Lienhard, Hougland, Hoag, Dean Kelley and John Keller. Five from Peoria were named and two from the AAU runner-up Phillips 66, including Bob Kurland. Now, all that remained was a final game to determine the head coach.

In the title game, Kansas never led. But Dean Kelley's running one-hander, tied it at 60 with 50 seconds remaining. With Peoria operating its offense around midcourt, Lovellette stole the ball from former Oklahoma standout Marcus Freiberger with about 15 seconds remaining and had a free lane to the basket. Lovellette, already with 22 points, wanted to personally reward the coach he deared.

But Lovellette jumped too soon and was farther from the hoop than he should have been. The uncontested layup banged off the back of the rim. A Peoria player grabbed the rebound, fired it up court to ex-Purdue star Howie Williams, who sank the winning basket with five seconds left. Peoria's Warren Womble became the head coach, Phog the assistant.

"I rehash that play so many times," Lovellette said. "I've seen the film. I've got two Kansas players on either side of me, and there I am lumbering down the middle of the court. I have no reason to have the ball whatsoever. I don't dribble it well, I can't run well and I'm trying to go coast to coast. All I had to do was give it to Bob Kenney, and he lays it off the backboard and we win. I felt terrible."

When it might have been the other way around, Phog consoled Big Clyde after the game. Phog certainly wanted to be the Olympic head coach, just as he did in 1936. But Phog wasn't about to cause problems this time, not with seven of his players on the team. He filled his role as assistant and truly was excited about attending the Games. In Helsinki, he wrote postcards every day.

"He never tried to take over in practice or on the bench," Lovellette said. "But I think Womble respected Phog enough to take his suggestions. A lot of what Phog said came through on the court."

The 1952 team took its cue from the 1948 Olympic champions. The team of Phillips 66 and Kentucky Wildcats tried mixing and matching teams, but after three games found playing as a unit worked much better. The 1952 team also played in shifts, with the Jayhawks and Diesels playing together. The Russians, playing in the first Games, were thought to pose a threat. The U.S. won by 28 in their first encounter. The teams met again in the gold medal game. This time the Russians stalled, but the U.S. won again 36-25. "It was an exact copy of the stall and freeze game used by Oklahoma A&M," Phog said. Lovellette led the Olympians with a 14.1 average. Kenney was next at 10.9.

Phog had his NCAA ring and a gold medal. Never again would an Olympic team carry as many as seven players from one team, and by 1972 the AAU players were all but phased out from the selection process. Lovellette's All-America career was over. Phog's prize recruit owned every Kansas scoring record and NCAA Tournament mark. He's the only player in NCAA history to lead the nation in scoring (28.4) while playing for a national championship team.

And everybody wanted his services. But Lovellette took Phog's advice by passing on the NBA to join Phillips. Just as it did when Lovellette was recruited by Kansas, more reports of foul play surfaced: Phillips had financed Big Clyde's college career and had flown him between Lawrence and Terre Haute on vacations. Lovellette denied it all.

Lovellette turned down $60,000 for three years from the NBA team in Milwaukee and joined Phillips for $12,000. Big Clyde felt an obligation. Phillips president Boots Adams, a close friend of Phog's, was Lovellette's mentor at Kansas. Even in the early 1950s, Phog was proud that Kansas' contribution to the NBA was virtually nil. That included Phog. In 1949, he had turned down an offer to coach the NBA team in Chicago.

Lovellette bucked the trend in 1953, when he signed with the Minneapolis Lakers for $20,000 with a $5,000 bonus. He remained in the league for 11 seasons and won championships with the Lakers and Celtics. He counts among his memories as a pro breaking the jaw of another Jayhawk, Wilt Chamberlain. "I never liked him,"

Phog holds court with reporters during the Olympic playoff in New York City in 1952. (From the University of Kansas archives)

Lovellette said. "He came to Kansas and didn't stick it out. I thought he should have stuck it out. When he came into the league I didn't want him pushing me around, so that's why I did it. I felt bad about it afterwards."

The year continued to be eventful for Phog. Less than a week after returning from the Olympics, he received word that he had been inducted into the Missouri Sports Hall of Fame along with Casey Stengel. In October, he and Frank McGuire, who had just left St. John's to coach North Carolina, were selected to coach a college all-star team against the NBA champion Lakers in Chicago. And there was word that the MGM studio had visited Lawrence to lay the groundwork for a movie on Phog's life. Nothing came of it.

But perhaps the most satisfying development for Phog since returning from Helsinki came by way of a November newspaper article in which Phog blasted postseason tournaments. The NCAA and NIT events made the season too long and that a conference championship should be the goal for all teams. Pretty tame stuff by Phog's standards. The real news was the byline. The story, distributed by the International News Service, was written by Lawton Carver, the journalist who ripped Phog eight years earlier for calling attention to gambling on games in New York.

"Maybe enough hollering from such people as Dr. Allen will bring some sanity back to the college game," Lawton wrote.

Ah, a convert.

18
WILT AND STATUTORY SENILITY

"I'm sure Doc did some great coaching jobs throughout the different eras," Dean Smith said. "But this had to be one of his greatest seasons."

The season, 1953, started about the way Phog thought it would. Kansas dropped its second game, at Rice, and lost three of its first eight. The Jayhawks were in an adjustment mode. Only one starter, guard Dean Kelley, returned from the championship team, and how could Kansas replace Lovellette? Certainly not with 6-foot-9 Bertram "B.H." Born, who looked terrible in the opening two games. Smith, a senior, actually went to Harp before the season and said the Jayhawks couldn't win with Born in the middle. Harp's order: support Born.

Then it was as if the punishment Born had absorbed in practice from Lovellette — broken nose, bloody lips, bruises all over, even wet towel whomps in the shower — suddenly toughened him up. Born became a force, leading the Jayhawks to an improbable Big Seven championship with an 18.9 scoring average. Kansas got by

Oklahoma City and Oklahoma State in the NCAA playoffs to reach the Final Four at Kansas City, where favored Washington and its star center Bob Houbregs awaited. Time for more Phog ghost stories.

"At our meeting at the team hotel he started telling the story about Bobby Allen and his team in the (1940) tournament in Kansas City that didn't win it," Smith said. "He said we only had an opportunity like this once in a lifetime. He went on and I was fighting not to cry."

Phog should have saved the speech for the final. The Jayhawks blasted the Huskies 79-53 to set up a return meeting in the finals with Indiana. With mighty Kentucky not playing a competitive schedule in 1953 because of the gambling scandal, the Hoosiers were the nation's top team. The championship game was tight throughout. With a 41-41 halftime score, Kansas retired to the locker room expecting to hear a Phog classic. Instead, he was teaching Born how to gargle.

Born had sinus problems and was congested during the game. At halftime, he approached trainer Dean Nesmith, who provided some bitter tasting elixir to clear his throat. Born wasn't handling it well, which caught Phog's attention. For more than half of the intermission period, Phog and Born stood in front of a sink gargling. Phog would take some, throw his head back then spit. Born would try. Phog corrected him. On and on. Chancellor Franklin Murphy entered the locker room. Born cast a help-me look his way, but Murphy just shook his head. Finally, with about three minutes left in the half, Harp hastily drew some instructions on a chalkboard.

Kansas got some breaks in the second half. Born picked up what the official scorer believed was his fifth foul, but Phog rushed to the table in protest. The Jayhawks had Born for four. Press row was surveyed and agreed Born had only four. Indiana coach Branch McCracken flew into a rage, but lost the protest and Born stayed in only to foul out a few minutes later. Late in the game, with Indiana holding a three-point lead, a Hoosier player was charged with a technical for slamming the ball to the floor. The Jayhawks tied it at 68 with 1:05 remaining.

Indiana star Bob Leonard made a free throw with 27 seconds to play for a one-point lead, and Phog told his team to hold for a final shot. Allen Kelley was to take the final shot but was closely guarded. He fired a pass to Jerry Alberts, who had replaced Born. Alberts' shot skipped across the rim with five seconds remaining and Indiana and McCracken had their second championship victory over Kansas and Phog.

Bertram "B.H." Born drives to the basket. Born's development into a top-notch player helped the Jayhawks finish second in the NCAA Tournament the year after they had won the championship. (Photo courtesy University of Kansas Sports Information)

The Jayhawks were convinced they'd have won the title were it not for a football knee injury that kept Charlie Hoag, a top reserve and Olympian from 1952, from playing. And maybe Phog would have gotten an automobile upgrade. After the season, boosters presented him with a new Chrysler New Yorker, Harp a silver service set and Nesmith a $100 gift certificate.

Phog was presented with this Chrysler New Yorker after Kansas finished second in the 1953 NCAA Tournament. (Photo by Rich Clarkson)

The season proved to be Phog's final significant achievement on the floor. The Jayhawks tied Colorado for first place in 1954, and Phog had won his 24th and final conference championship but the Buffaloes got the postseason nod. Two years remained before Phog would hit the state's recommended retirement age of 70, and, while those were mostly uneventful on the court, the period proved to be the most newsworthy of his career.

There would be no leisurely ride off into retirement for Phog. He had big plans. Big field house, big player, another crack at the national championship. The field house was on its way. Phog had worn out one building, Robinson Gymnasium, and Hoch Auditorium was woefully inadequate to accommodate interest in the program. With Kansas State preparing to move into its spacious new home, Phog led a six-member delegation to Topeka and a legislative committee in support of a new field house in 1949. The committee already had before it a $750,000 appropriation request for a new structure, but Phog told the politicians that amount would cover a dairy barn, and not a 20,000-seat basketball gym.

Phog pushed the ante to $2 million, which was how much the state had given to Kansas State. Phog made his point, and then some. Ground was broken for the $2.65 million field house in 1951 to be constructed south of campus. Bennett Construction of Topeka, which had built Ahearn Field House, got the contract — and an earful from

Phog, who blasted the company for what he thought were unnecessary delays. Phog wanted the building, now down to 17,000 seats, to be finished in time to begin the 1954-55 season and noted that Ahearn was built in less time. Bennett's return volley included a suggestion: If Phog was so concerned why doesn't he regularly visit the construction site? Jack Gardner did. From that day on, Phog started his mornings with a hard hat.

Now, what to name the field house? It became an emotional issue even before the land was cleared. Allen Field House originally wasn't a possibility because of a school policy prohibiting naming a building for a living person. But the school had made an exception in 1954, naming a physical sciences building for former chancellor Dean Malott, who had moved to Cornell. Sentiment was growing for Phog. Former governor Harry Woodring asked the state legislature to bypass the regents and name the building for Phog while he continued coaching, and he was backed up by current governor Edward Arn. Senators and other dignitaries threw in their support.

Everybody chimed in. Missouri's Sparky Stalcup said to the *Lawrence Journal-World*, "My 1954-55 team would consider it a privilege and an honor if we could be able to help dedicate F.C. Allen Field House." Ralph Miller at Wichita State said, "How can there be any other answer?"

Chancellor Franklin Murphy held his tongue. Sentiment to name the building for Naismith wasn't as loud but nearly as strong outside of campus. But the students were squarely behind Phog. The *Daily Kansan* ran a poll and students favored naming the building for Phog over Naismith by a 924-10 vote. Another 30 voted to name it for both. The regents read all the newspaper clippings that overwhelmingly favored Phog, and in an October 1954 meeting, they determined to ignore policy and dedicate the building in Phog's honor.

Nothing was said until December. When Phog got the word, he hastily typed out a statement. "In this hour of great recognition of my services to the University of Kansas, I feel very unworthy and deeply grateful."

Then he continued to Bill Mayer of the *Lawrence Journal-World*:

*"No man could get such an honor and not be
mighty jolted, but in a mighty pleasant way. You know,
it's hard to realize that anything that big and grand will*

bear my name. It just really makes a man wonder if he's really deserving of anything that big. I've received a lot of honors at various times, but this means more than all because it comes to me at my home state. A man can get all kinds of honors, but all of them don't mean as much as the one that comes from the people he works and lives with."

The Allen Field House dedication was set for March 1, 1955, against Kansas State. Every former Kansas player that could be found was invited back. Phog turned over his coaching duties to Harp that night who told the players they had to win this one for Doc. Victory wasn't a sure thing. The Jayhawks entered the game with a 9-9 record. They had lost three straight, including the final game in Hoch to Nebraska. But Kansas didn't spoil Phog's night and won 77-67. The dedication ceremony took place at halftime, and Phog received — what else? — a new car. This time a Cadillac. "The only drawback so far," Phog noted upon receiving the blue Caddy, "is that you need an engineer's degree to figure out all the gadgets."

Phog would have one full season in his new building. He had told newspapermen as early as 1945 that he had no intention of becoming a coaching fossil like Connie Mack or Amos Alonzo Stagg, and that he planned not to coach beyond 65. He later amended that to 70. Then he got involved with Wilt Chamberlain.

It all started in 1952, when Kansas publicity director Don Pierce spotted a photograph in an out-of-town newspaper of Chamberlain, then a 6-9 sophomore. Pierce ripped out the page, circled the photo in red and passed it along to Phog, who tacked it up on his office wall. The recruiting of Chamberlain ran contrary to so many beliefs and standards long held by Phog. But the man certainly was changing. For one thing, he had taken up smoking, a practice he had quit when he became an athlete. Players and associates were stunned at the site of Phog clasping a cigarette. Phog wasn't particularly good at it, either. In 1957, he left a burning butt in his car and burned up his Cadillac at the field house parking lot.

Lovellette had proved Phog would go out of the state and personally get involved in the recruiting process. But Terre Haute, Ind., hadn't been as far as Philadelphia, an Eastern haunt Phog detested. And basketball had never seen anything like the tremendously gifted 7-foot Wilt. Phog and the school would have to push the recruiting process beyond anything he had experienced, even with Lovellette.

Phog began each morning with an inspection of the new Allen Field House. (From the University of Kansas archives)

The groundwork for landing Wilt was unknowingly laid by Phog in 1951, when he integrated the team by accepting La Vannes Squires of Wichita. The color line in the Big Seven was broken in 1949 with Kansas State football player Harold Robinson. Phog's ideas about integration in athletics were ambiguous. In the 1930s, he was a fan of Jesse Owens and one year voted for him to win the Sullivan Award. Around that time, John McLendon was a Kansas student who eventually became a Hall of Fame coach. He said he wasn't good enough to play college basketball then, but it wouldn't have mattered anyway.

"It was Dr. Allen's job to resist integration then," McLendon said. "He was the AD and the whole school knew it was an area where he'd be challenged. He practically apologized to me. But as quickly as he could he got black players on his team."

It could have been sooner. Jerry Waugh, captain of the 1950-51 team, remembers as an underclassman in the late 1940s Phog asking players to vote if the team should integrate. The team voted against it because Phog had explained to them the difficulties a black player would have in the conference. By the spring of 1955, when Wilt's

Phog (left) with Chancellor Franklin Murphy at the dedication ceremonies of Allen Field House in 1955. (Photo by Rich Clarkson)

recruiting reached its peak, Kansas wasn't automatically crossed off his list because it was integrated — Wilt didn't want to be the first black in a program. That was his response to Stalcup, who met Wilt at the Kansas City airport while on a KU recruiting trip, and offered him the chance to break Missouri's color line.

A contingent of black Kansas and Kansas City businessmen and entertainers — led by *Kansas City Call* general manager and KU alum Dowdal Davis — told Wilt his presence would improve race relations in Lawrence and Kansas City and that he'd be better off in a smaller community than a large city in the East. Their letter writing campaign started during Wilt's junior year at Overbrook High, and most of them made visits to the Chamberlain home. Chancellor Murphy, also seeking to improve race relations on campus, enthusiastically supported recruiting Chamberlain. He had talked to all of his coaches about recruiting black athletes before anyone had heard of Chamberlain.

During Chamberlain's senior year, Phog showed up at a game between Overbrook and Germantown High, and he spoke at a YMCA banquet afterwards. A home visit from Kansas chemistry professor Calvin Vander Werf, stressing Wilt's education, made a big impression on mom, Olivia Chamberlain. Wilt visited Lawrence twice. He was set up with dates, shown a good time. After the second visit — he made both with Overbrook coach Cecil Mosenson, who was rumored to be offered a job on the KU staff — Wilt said yes to Kansas. But he told Phog he'd leave if there were racial problems in town and he didn't want Kansas to schedule games in the South.

Naturally, accusations started flying, and Phog didn't defuse matters when he was quoted in a *Life* magazine story in 1957.

"Of course I used everything we had to get him. What do you think I am, a Sunday school teacher? Let's be realistic. Until 1946 I never had any help. Then alumni started to sweeten the pot. I heard another coach charge us with giving Wilt $5,000. Well, if . . .(the coach) is sore about it, why then that must mean someone was dickering for less, huh?"

Phog later identified the coach as Indiana's McCracken. The $5,000 offer was denied by Wilt, but that's the figure, in the form of a trust fund, that kept surfacing during an NCAA investigation that officially started in 1958. The NCAA had been collecting information about Kansas' recruitment of Wilt since the spring of 1955. Somehow, the NCAA didn't believe Wilt was only receiving aid allowed by the Big Seven: free board, books, tuition, room and $135 a year for selling football programs. The NCAA focused on the cash, Wilt's summer job at a Kansas City tire company, financed trips to Kansas for his high school coach, a KU scholarship awarded to one of Wilt's high school teammates and cars, cars, cars. Wilt loved his wheels and Kansas boosters made sure he had them.

Wilt arrived on campus in a 1950 Buick but by the end of his freshman season in 1956, he was driving a 1953 Olds. Wilt said he was making regular payments on the car. Only a year earlier, NCAA investigators had learned from Olivia Chamberlain that the family's income was $60 a week. By 1957, Wilt was driving a 1956 Olds valued at more than $2,500. Wilt had made two payments totalling $75 on the car. In 1958, he received a check from *Look* magazine for exclusive rights to the announcement that he was skipping his senior season. This bought another car, a two-toned Olds 98.

But the NCAA couldn't pin much on Wilt, who twice interviewed with NCAA officials. After the second meeting, Wilt, after he'd left Kansas, told a reporter in New York that NCAA inquisitor Art Bergstrom said, "It was nice talking to you but I don't believe a word of it."

In 1960, Kansas was found guilty of providing Wilt with new tires for his car. During the investigation, the NCAA also found violations in the recruitment of football player Bert Coan. The penalty was two years of no NCAA basketball tournament or bowl game. Notice Kansas wasn't penalized for recruiting Wilt. The NCAA found nothing there, and Phog emerged unscathed. He had gotten in more trouble in 1954 for driving a prospect from Kansas City to Lawrence to take a standardized test — Phog said he didn't know the rules and was helping a stranded kid — than with anything that happened with Wilt.

But Phog couldn't exalt in victory. He had missed out on the opportunity to coach the greatest player in college basketball because the school stuck to its retirement guidelines and survived an ugly public relations battle with its legendary coach. When the Jayhawks landed Wilt, Phog's amusing reaction to the press was "That's great news. I hope he comes out for basketball."

Privately, Phog was working to extend his career. He wanted to coach Wilt for at least one year, and Wilt wanted Phog as his coach. Chamberlain often said he believes Kansas would have had two or three national championships if he had played for Phog. But Chancellor Murphy wouldn't allow it and bravely weathered a storm of resentment from family, friends, the state legislature and Phog himself.

Members of the state House of Representatives started the tide of sentiment for Phog in 1955, when they passed a resolution requesting the board of regents to amend its retirement policy for Phog and permit him to coach for three seasons beyond his 70th year, through 1958-59. That would cover the Chamberlain era. Phog entered the 1955-56 season believing he'd have a chance to remain on and spent much practice time working with Wilt, who, as a freshman, couldn't play with the varsity. Freshman games were huge draws at Allen Field House, while the varsity team stumbled to a 14-9 record. That season the frosh defeated the varsity by 10 points, ironically on Phog's 70th birthday. Wilt scored 42. Phog called him "the greatest player alive."

Phog lost what proved to be his final home game, to Kansas State, and his final game, at Colorado. A few weeks earlier, he had coached his 1,000th game. But the real action of the 1955-56 season started after the last game. Would the school allow Phog to remain? Should it? Phog said he wanted only one more season. Opinions in state newspapers were divided. Pro Phog editorials criticized the mandatory retirement rule. Those against, like the *Daily Kansan*, cited other distinguished members of the faculty who were physically and mentally prepared to work beyond 70 but abided by the rule.

Phog believed he had a solution. He had continued to carry a teaching load as a physical education instructor. He offered to retire

Phog poses in Allen Field House before his team's final practice of the 1956 season. A month later, he was forced to retire. (Photo by Rich Clarkson)

as a teacher and remain the coach. Kansas had made exceptions to its retirement rule, and Phog noted former athletic director Ernest Quigley was given a contract that took him through a mandatory retirement age. The pressure mounted on Murphy after the 1956 season. He had until a board of regents meeting in the final week of March to make a decision. Phog kept silent and let the media volley the issue throughout most of the season. But on March 14, he called his friends in the press to the field house and read a statement.

> *"I am enjoying splendid health. And if it should be the will of the people as expressed through the duly constituted governing authorities of the University of Kansas that I continue as basketball coach for another year, it would be the thrill of my life to be able to end a long coaching career with a truly great team."*

But Murphy had made up his mind, and presented his case in a March 28 letter to Phog's daughter, Jane Mons.

> *"First of all, I think the whole Allen family must understand the personal bias and affection I have for*

*your father. Since I have been Chancellor, your father
has been warmly understanding of some of my problems
and has never once failed to cooperate completely in
helping to solve them.*

*"It was there with a good deal of personal concern
on my part that, long before the terminal pressures
began to mount as regards to naming the field house, I
had received informal assurance from the Regents that
my request that the building be named after your father,
would, at the appropriate time, be granted, irrespective
of traditions about naming of University buildings.*

*" . . .I had thought that the naming of the building
and the magnificent ceremony attached to it . . .would
represent the capstone to a great and unique career. And
I must say, in all candor, that at that time I could not
conceive of any greater gift in which the University could
bestow.*

*"Within the last two years, veteran, dedicated,
beloved and distinguished members of this faculty came
to retirement at age 70 and have been retired. Most, if
not all of these men, have not wished to retire, and in
most instances they have been quite capable of carrying
on. The same will hold true again this July when six or
eight additional first class people will be retired.*

*"There can be no doubt that to make an exception
in your father's case and not to do so in other cases
would create resentment toward the administration, the
Board of Regents, and the University, to say nothing of
resentment toward your father on the part of not only
many of the retired faculty but other members of the
faculty, who would feel that in the last analysis the
University is more concerned with its athletic fortunes
than with its academic program.*

*"I am sure you realize that this whole matter has
not been an easy one for me. I am a great sports fan, and
I love to see successful teams . . .Come what may, the
Allen family will always have a very warm spot in my*

Phog's most famous recruit was Wilt Chamberlain. Because of retirement, Phog never got to coach the future NBA star and Chamberlain was never able to lead Kansas to a national title. (Photo courtesy of University of Kansas Sports Information)

heart, and I shall always be especially proud of the fact that it was on my recommendation that the greatest building that this campus will ever have will forever bear the name of one of the greatest men that has ever served it — your father."

On March 29, the athletic board met to make recommendations for next year's staff. The board had its orders from Murphy. Phog was out. There was no coaching search. Dick Harp was elevated to head coach. Jerry Waugh, the Lawrence High coach, was named his assistant.

"He would have been no different at 71 than he was at 70," Harp said. "And to coach Wilt would have given him an opportunity to start talking about the rules again."

Precisely. Phog's true motivation for wanting an extra year wasn't winning a national championship. Oh, he wanted to win as badly as anybody. But ultimately, Phog wanted to prove to the basketball world that he was right about the 12-foot goal. In a June 7, 1956, letter to several friends, Phog made it plain that he wanted one year with Wilt to make a sham of the rules. It would be Phog's last laugh to those who laughed at his incessant pleas for the raised basket.

"Frankly, I wanted my last chance to show the Basketball Rules Committee that their continued stubbornness in holding to the rule for the ten-foot height for college and independent baskets was silly and ineffectual. Wilton Chamberlain can jump and reach 24 inches above a ten-foot basket. And I wanted him to throw that ball right through the Rules Committee's collective ten-foot basket teeth.

"Soon Wilton will have the rules makers sitting up all night looking for new solutions and perhaps proposing that they either let the air out of the ball when he has possession or prohibit him from shooting when he's within 20 feet of the basket . . . Wilton could make a successful coach out of anyone. Lucky is the man who inherits Wilton for three fairy tale years.

"I declare Chamberlain coming to KU an emergency for the rules makers. These rules makers will need a tight, top-lid for the Chamberlain ten-foot basket."

Assistant coach Dick Harp with Phog. Harp succeeded Phog as coach and took the Jayhawks to the 1957 national championship game. (Photo courtesy University of Kansas Sports Information)

Turns out, Wilt did change the rules. Because of him, players could no longer leave the free-throw line immediately after releasing the ball. Wilt used to tap in his own free-throw misses. He's also responsible for offensive goaltending. Before Wilt, it was legal to guide a teammate's shot into the basket. But there was no 12-foot goal.

Phog didn't take defeat well. He wrote to Murphy three days after the decision.

"May I say that I have always held you in very high esteem — both as a gentleman and a fine administrator. Our relationships have always been of the highest and the friendliest. I assure you that this situation has in no way changed my opinion of you.

"I cannot, however, forget that the inflexible rule of the Board of Regents was badly broken not too long ago when the Board, with the present acting chairman as a member, hired Mr. Quigley as Director of Athletics when he was past the age which makes prohibitive the continuing as head of any department of the university. Naturally, this mandatory rule which is often stressed does not impress me too highly. But I honor you and your position."

Two weeks later, Phog seemed resigned to his fate at his final team banquet at the Eldridge Hotel. He talked for 50 minutes, remembered Naismith who "did more than twice as much for basketball as I've ever done," and ended his speech declaring his loyalty to Kansas.

"There should be no sad note here," Phog said. "I have some wonderful friends and everything is OK."

19

RETIREMENT

Phog stepped down with what was believed to be a career record of 771 wins and 233 losses, which included his games at Kansas, Central Missouri, Baker and Haskell. But in 1990, the record was revised to 746-264.

For years it was thought Phog had coached three schools — KU, Baker and Haskell — during the 1908-09 season, but that wasn't the way it happened. Phog had left Baker by then. And Phog's Central Missouri record wasn't right. He'd told people it was 107-7, and that's what showed up in stories about his retirement. Actually, it was 84-31.

If Kansas had this knowledge in 1956, it would have celebrated Phog's 1,000th game after a Jan. 14 victory at Kansas State instead of a Feb. 17 loss at Oklahoma. And the publicity that surrounded Adolph Rupp when he passed Phog on the career victory list would have happened two seasons earlier. Rupp recorded his 771st triumph over LSU on Jan. 27, 1968. Little did anyone know that the actual changing of the guard took place toward the conclusion of the eventful 1965-66 season, that ended in the Wildcats' NCAA title game loss to Texas Western. Rupp actually tied Phog with Kentucky's Mideast Regional championship victory over Michigan and passed him the next week in the national semifinal triumph over Duke.

Surely the comments Phog made in 1968, when Rupp caught him, would have created more of a stir at the Final Four.

Phog with his four grandsons after what was thought to be his 1,000th career game as a coach. From left are Bob Allen Jr., Milton Allen Jr., John Allen and Allen Glenn. (From the University of Kansas archives)

"If I said he was a great player I'd only be indulging in professional courtesy," Phog told the *Daily Oklahoman*. "The only reason Adolph went into coaching is because he was offered $10 more a month if he would. He really hates money — he hates for anybody else to have it."

The comments were tongue-in-cheek, of course. Phog said he was happy for his old substitute guard. "Bless his bones. Rupp had a great mind for the game and has become an outstanding coach. I've always said he is the only Kansas hayshacker who can roll his R's like a Kentucky Colonel."

It's natural to wonder what Phog thought about his former pupil during Kentucky's darkest hour. Nobody was more vociferous about gambling's evils than Phog, and no higher profile program suffered more than Kentucky. Phog said during the scandals that maybe a coach can't tell his boys are shaving points, but he knows the type of boy he recruits. If Phog ever felt disappointment in Rupp, he never let it be known publicly. Rupp made it back to all the reunions of the 1923 team, shared laughs and paid homage to Phog.

Phog hardly slowed down in the early years of his retirement. He and Mitt renovated the old Kansas Public Service Co. building on East 8th Street and opened an office where Mitt practiced law and Phog ran a body shop, his first osteopathic clinic since 1919. Phog no longer had to worry about what the university's medical community thought of him. A procession of ballplayers filed through the office, and the town buzzed when a Mickey Mantle or Ted Williams dropped by for a treatment. One of his first patients was Phillies shortstop Granny Hamner, who wanted Phog to check his bum shoulder. Most patients were friends, former players, even opponents. Athletes Phog had treated for years would drop by for an adjustment and a dose of charisma. Phog reveled in the stories of the past, but you also got his take on the political situation in Russia or the price of eggs. His medical practice branched out to Kansas City, where he opened the Phog Allen Health Center, an ahead-of-its-time fitness center for businessmen.

Phog remained a regular on the banquet circuit and was always popular at a high school awards dinner or commencement. He spoke to the Lions Club in Bushton, Kan., the night Wilt Chamberlain made his varsity debut and Dick Harp coached his first game. During an intermission, people filed into the lobby to tune in the game. Wilt was on his way to 52 points, but Phog pulled them away from their transistors after the break. "I never will and I do not intend to attend KU games when going will interfere with what I consider to be of more benefit to all concerned," Phog told the *Daily Tribune* of Great Bend. "I'll only go if it's convenient."

For the most part, Phog stuck to his word. He rarely showed up at a KU practice and had little to do with the program in retirement. He attended games, usually with his sons, but after Chamberlain's first year, the Jayhawks' dominance in the conference started to fade. Oh, there were more league titles. Harp won one in 1960 and his successor Ted Owens won six in his 19 seasons.

Before he died, Phog saw plenty of quality players: Wayne Hightower followed Chamberlain out of Philadelphia, Bill Bridges, Walt Wesley, Jo Jo White and Dave Robisch. But there were no Final Fours between 1957 and 1971 and in 1965, average attendance in his building was down to 8,500.

Phog never criticized the Jayhawks to the press, not even after the 1957 title game loss to North Carolina that caused as much heartache in Lawrence as it did joy in Chapel Hill. Kansas, with the greatest player the game had seen and a more than adequate supporting cast, fell in triple overtime at Kansas City. Harp had been a favorite of the players as an assistant, the one they went to first with their problems. It wasn't that Phog had lost touch, but Harp was younger and had recruited many of them. For the 1956-57 season, he was thrust into the impossible position of succeeding a legend and inheriting a giant. Nothing less than a national championship would suffice.

When it didn't happen, Harp was blamed for his strategy against the Tar Heels. Kansas had overcome a seven-point halftime deficit to take a three-point lead with 10 minutes left. The Jayhawks stopped attacking and stalled for much of what remained in regulation.

Kansas made one more trip to the NCAA Tournament in Harp's final seven years. Maybe Phog would have beaten North Carolina with "Wilt, two Phi Beta Kappas and two aggressive coeds," as he said before the season. But such talk has hurt Harp through the years.

"There were a lot of other ways I'd like to have seen that time unfold," Harp said. "There was no question in my mind that Wilt was going to have a great career as a pro, although I probably thought he'd have won more than two NBA championships. He wanted to win that (North Carolina) game as much as anybody, but I've always been sad for the rest of the kids on that squad. It would have been great for the kids. There's no virtue in second place. There just isn't."

In retirement, Phog couldn't avoid talking about Chamberlain. He created a ruckus in Kansas during a speech at Canisius College in Buffalo, where Phog said Wilt was leaving after the 1957 season. Phog had to retract his comments. When the NCAA handed Kansas its probation in 1960, Phog told a radio station in Los Angeles that Wilt had received $50 to $100 for speaking engagements as a student, and that while Wilt was a freshman, companies regularly called to line up Chamberlain. This wasn't part of the NCAA's investigation. Kansas athletic director Dutch Lonborg was placed in the embarrassing position of having to defuse the issue by calling the remarks of his former mentor "absurd."

Harp had to have cringed on the evening in 1964, at his retirement dinner, when Phog took the podium and asserted that Ralph Miller, and not Harp, would have been his choice to succeed him. Harp deserved better. "Dick was extremely loyal to Doc," Dean Smith said. "My junior year we had beaten Creighton in Omaha and then had dinner. Doc got on the bus then checked the receipt. He thought

Phog (right) on his pregame radio show. In 1956 Phog provided color analysis for the Big Seven Holiday Tournament and hosted a 15-minute TV show for a Kansas City station. (Photo by Rich Clarkson)

he had been overcharged, so he went back into the restaurant. He was looking at the receipt as he was leaving and instead of getting back on the team bus walked onto a city bus. We were all laughing. Dick got up and said if any of us had anything to say, say it to him. It was very quiet when Doc got on our bus.

"Then there was a time in a game when Doc said he wanted us to weave against a zone. I said he doesn't want that. Dick told me to shut up and do what Doc says. I don't think anyone ever understood the love and admiration and the loyalty Dick had for Doc."

After years of giving away his thoughts, Phog found a buyer. In 1956 he provided the color analysis role for the 1956 Big Seven Holiday Tournament and was hired by WDAF-TV in Kansas City to host a 15-minute *Phog Allen Show* highlighting his career, former players and thoughts on the game.

If anybody could fill 15 minutes of air time, it was Phog. Bill Grigsby, one of the Kansas radio voices in the final two years of Phog's career, remembered taping the pregame show as one of his easiest tasks.

"It was a 15-minute show," Grigsby said. "But it wasn't much of an interview. I'd say something like, 'Doctor Allen, you're playing your old rival Hank Iba tonight, it's going to be a tough game.' Then he'd grab the mike and I'd go downstairs, get a Coke, walk around the building and come back in 15 minutes, get the mike back and say 'Thank you, Doctor Allen.'"

Retirement did not turn down the volume on Phog's verbal sparring. Before he stepped down, Phog dropped a load on one of his favorite targets, the AAU and the chairman of the Olympic basketball committee Col. Harry Henshel. The AAU had suspended Kansas miler Wes Santee for accepting excessive expense allowances for some meets.

The group withdrew the punishment but not before Phog sunk in his teeth. He compared the AAU's secret meetings to the Ku Klux Klan, then assaulted Henshel's character, calling him a "Colonel in a Brooklyn band." In fact, Henshel had won a bronze star combat medal in 1945 and earned five campaign stars in Europe during World War II. A few days after Phog was retired, Henshel sued him for $35,000.

"I'm surprised it was for only $35,000 because what I'm going to say about him is going to be worth at least $100,000," was Phog's reaction to reporters. "The AAU is a lousy bunch of rats that don't even own a hurdle. No, I'll go farther than that. They don't even own a toothpick. I like the AAU like a fellow likes garlic for dessert."

Phog, represented by Mitt, countersued for $225,000. The combatants apologized to each other and the suits were dropped in 1957. But Phog never backed off his attacks of the AAU, especially in Olympic years.

The banquet circuit kept alive Phog's harangues. The NCAA ("Nationally Confused Athletic Absurdity") needed a czar — Tennessee Sen. Estes Kefauver was now his choice — baskets should be 12 feet, the game no longer rewarded the fundamentally sound and would benefit by the return of the center jump, and he should have been able to coach another year.

One night was different. On his way to a speech in Kansas City, Phog's Cadillac broke down. He got a ride to town, junked his prepared text and delivered a scathing speech about the unreliability of Cadillacs. As was usually the case when Phog spoke, a newspaper man attended and reported the event. Cadillac told Phog they'd fix his car for free if he'd shut up.

Never lucky with cars, Phog caused his 1956 Cadillac to catch fire in the Allen Field House parking lot when he left a burning cigarette on the front seat. (From the University of Kansas archives)

Phog unquestionably possessed some of the greatest motor skills in coaching history. And some of the worst. With cars, Phog was plain unlucky. His Studebaker was stolen by joyriders, and he seemed to have mechanical problems with just about every one he owned. Toward the end of his career and into retirement, you didn't want to be his passenger. There was the time he missed a curve, drove off the road through a billboard and returned to the highway without missing a breath in his conversation.

Once, driving in western Kansas, a former player recognized Phog as he slowly approached. When Phog didn't respond to a wave, the player turned around, pulled up beside Phog and found him asleep at the wheel.

Phog could be a menace in his own driveway. The Allens were having their house painted when Phog backed out of the driveway. Bessie frantically waved at Phog, who waved back before plowing into the scaffolding, spilling the painters and paint.

When the Jayhawks practiced at Robinson, Phog parked right behind the building. One winter, he continued to complain that he no longer could ride in his car without crushing the top of his hat. Phog

Phog and Bessie just before their 50th wedding anniversary in 1958. When Bessie died at the age of 82 in 1970, the Allens had been married for 61 years. (From the University of Kansas archives)

couldn't figure it out. Harp went out back and noticed Phog had parked under an overhang and a large icicle had dented the roof.

Phog's attendance at KU games dwindled as the years passed and so did his rounds of golf. In his early 70s, Phog played 18 at least four times a week at the Lawrence Country Club. Toward the end of the 1960s, he was walking with a cane and eventually ended up in a wheelchair. When he turned 77 in 1962, Phog wrote a letter to Don Pierce for publication. The birthday was significant to Phog because he was approaching another stage in life.

"I never felt better or had less. I feel pretty lucky. Seven is lucky and so is 11. Here are my lucky stages:

"(Age) 7, the end of infancy; 14, puberty; 21, manhood; 28, the family circle, rearing of children; 35, semi-maturity, financially; 42, durable competence; 49,

winning of civic and financial rewards; 56, durable
satisfactions; 63, philosophical adjustments; 70, convic-
tion not to retire and rest on past accomplishments but to
open new frontiers; 77, overhaul the old machine and
adjust the physical and mental according to the power
the machine can generate.

   "There are many more challenges in the work I am
doing now. I got a kick out of my coaching career but I
get even a greater kick out of endeavoring to eliminate
the suffering of some poor unfortunate. And you always
see someone who is much worse off than you. Then
you're always thankful that you are as well off as you are
at present."

   Every year, the *Lawrence Journal-World* reminded its readers
of Phog's birthday with a story or editorial. His 78th was celebrated
at the Lawrence Quarterback Club meeting, his 82nd was spent quietly at home. In 1968, at 83, Phog was an honorary coach for the
West in its victory over the East in the NABC All-Star game at Indianapolis. The East's honorary coach was Art Schabinger, the NABC's
first secretary-treasurer.

   Phog, who always preferred cars to airplanes, had driven himself to Indiana for the game. A week earlier, he had motored to Los
Angeles to watch UCLA defeat North Carolina in the NCAA championship game. The trips had aggravated his infirmities, and on July
1, unable to walk without pain from arthritis in his knees, Phog closed
his osteopathic office.

   Mary Hamilton, the Allens' oldest child, died in 1969, and Bessie
passed away a year later at 82, ending 61 years of marriage. Phog
continued to greet reporters on his birthday or during the NCAA
Tournament, but some who came around weren't old enough to remember him. And where his old newspaper friends protected him by
not printing the foolish statements, the new ones didn't. A 1972 story
by the Associated Press was brutal.

   "(Basketball) will never replace football and base-
ball as the most popular spectator sport. There aren't
enough players hurt in basketball. Spectators, especially
women, like to see people hurt. They say they don't but
they do.

An aging Phog greets Adolph Rupp, center, and Paul Endacott in 1973. (From the University of Kansas archives)

"It's a reprehensible thing the ABA is doing, trying to lure college players out of school before their eligibility is completed. Mostly, they take advantage of the black boys. The black boys want to get the money as soon as possible because they have been hungry so long. The ABA doesn't care."

More soothing to Kansas fans were interviews like the one by Ted O'Leary, who had spent most of his post-playing days as a newspaper journalist and *Sports Illustrated* reporter. In the last lengthy piece on Phog before the coach's death, O'Leary found him mostly alert for a man of 86. Phog told him he believed John Wooden was the greatest coach of all time ("An All-America man and coach"), that a young Chamberlain was better than a young Lew Alcindor,

Phog makes a point during a classroom session. He was buried in the Olympic USA sweat suit that he is shown wearing. (Photo by Rich Clarkson)

and that he regretted not being able to successfully recruit this young Missouri coach.

"That fellow, (Norm) Stewart, their coach, he's outstanding. He was a good player, too. We tried as hard as we could to get him to come to Kansas but we lost him. He played for my good friend Sparky Stalcup. A few years ago, he invited me to Columbia for his daughter's wedding. Of course, Sparky was glad to see me but the rest of those Missourians there looked at me like Jesse James had come back."

Phog died on Sept. 16, 1974, at 88. About 450 attended the funeral three days later at Plymouth Congregational Church. The Kansas basketball team attended the services as did Harp, Rupp and

Kansas State athletic director Ernie Barrett. Among the casket bearers were Clyde Lovellette and Paul Endacott, the best players on his greatest teams.

Endacott delivered the eulogy, repeating one of his coach's lines often used in correspondence to his athletes during war. "To my men, wherever they are. To the memory of my pupils and those who died in World War I. They are the ones who are fit to live and not afraid to die."

Phog was buried in his Olympic USA sweat suit. The service ended with the singing of the Kansas alma mater. The day's sentiment was best summed by Rupp.

"He'll go down in history," Rupp said, "as the greatest basketball coach of all time."

EPILOGUE

They played nearly three decades apart, but Adolph Rupp and Dean Smith have never been closer than they are entering the 1996-97 season. With 851 career triumphs, Smith needs 25 to tie Rupp's record of 876. Smith isn't impressed with the prospect of becoming No. 1.

"I don't think there should be coaches' records," Smith said. "I like to say last year's team did this, and I was their coach. People say it's a coach's record, but it's really the team's record."

And something of a Kansas record. For the past 70 or so years, the winningest coach in college basketball coached or played at Kansas, starting with Phog. The record may not mean much to Smith but it does to fans of the program. They're especially grateful to Smith for recommending his assistant, Roy Williams, to replace another North Carolina guy, Larry Brown, in 1988.

Rupp and Smith saw Phog near the beginning and end of his Kansas career. Phog turned 37 as Rupp's senior team prepared for its 1923 championship season. It was a time when a jump ball followed every basket and one player shot all the team's free throws no matter who was fouled. It had been less than 10 years since the rules required the bottom of the net to be left open. Athletic scholarships were unheard of.

Phog was 66 when Smith played for the 1952 NCAA champions. By then, teams were traveling by airplane, the Jayhawks had played their first game on television and the sport was becoming integrated.

Phog, and the fact that neither Rupp or Smith was a starter for Kansas, were common denominators.

Phog (left) with Kentucky coach and former Kansas player Adolph Rupp in 1949. The two coaches had agreed to play each other in the dedication game of Allen Field House. It didn't work out, however, and Kansas had to play Kansas State instead. (From the University of Kansas archives)

The starters played nearly every minute of every game in 1923, and Rupp was a backup to Paul Endacott, the team's best player. Rupp did play extensively in one game that season, at Drake. The team was on a three-game Iowa swing and Drake was one of the roughest teams in the area.

From Phog, Rupp learned the importance of fundamentals. The Jayhawks spent two hours a day the first two weeks in practice on drills, working on such mundane matters as the pivot or bounce pass. It paid off; Phog's teams were usually better trained.

The Kansas teams of Rupp were some of the first exposed to Phog's zoology. Even then, he was teaching a defensive fundamental he called the ape-man stance. Players would guard in a crouching position, head up and pretend not to have arms. Make the feet the biggest weapon, and be prepared to shift into any position. No telling whether Rupp heard Phog's dog theory. A kid can't catch a playful pup because it stays low, constantly shifting its feet, dodging capture, never unbalanced. Now, you try that boys.

Rupp never saw Phog's favorite, a short film called *Killing the Killer*. His later teams, including Smith's, watched the tape of a quick and clever mongoose darting around a deadly cobra, who dodges the snake's quick thrusts. The mongoose waits for the opening, then strikes at the cobra's throat. Phog loved the mongoose.

Rupp did use some of the same out-of-bounds plays he practiced at Kansas, but most of his offensive and defensive sets were his own creations.

Smith's influences are diverse. Some of North Carolina's defensive drills Smith learned at Kansas. But there's also some Hank Iba, Frank McGuire, Bruce Drake and Dick Harp in Smith's philosophy. Harp, who spent three years on North Carolina's staff in the 1980s, doesn't see much of Phog in Smith, certainly not as much as he sees of Smith in Williams.

"It's hard to make a comparison between Doc and Dean," Harp said. "The circumstances were different when they coached. Throughout most of Doc's time, he was the only coach there. He didn't have assistants."

Rupp was moved by the spirit of his alma mater in 1962, when he called Smith looking to line up a series with North Carolina. "I should have guessed he'd do it," Smith said. "It was our first year and we weren't any good. He said 'Dean, you're a '53 graduate and I'm a '23 graduate, and we both played for the same coach. I think we need a 10-year series. Now, a lot of teams wait until they get a good player to play me, like Ohio State when they got (Jerry) Lucas. So let's just play a 10-year series, home and home.' I said yes. We beat them up there. It was a huge upset. He never came to Chapel Hill."

Smith was well on his way to a coaching career as a Kansas underclassman. As a junior, he helped Harp coach the freshman team. He and Harp were the Jayhawks' chief scouts, and Smith would coach the reserves as the opponent's team against the starters in practice. "He was one of the smartest players I'd ever seen," Kansas teammate Clyde Lovellette said.

More than tactics and strategies, Rupp and Smith and so many others took from Phog the idea of coaching. Smith's father was a high school coach, but with his attendance at several coaching clinics conducted at Lawrence, he too was influenced by Phog.

The Hall of Fame is loaded with his coaching protégés: Rupp, Smith, Ralph Miller, Dutch Lonborg and John Bunn. John McLendon didn't play or coach for Phog, but credits him with helping shape his Hall of Fame coaching career. Plenty of others, like Harp, Louis Menze of Iowa State, Ray Sermon of North Carolina State, Andy McDonald of Southwest Missouri State and Frosty Cox of Colorado aren't in the Hall of Fame but are recognized among their school's best coaches.

Another who got into coaching but didn't stay long was Ted O'Leary. After finishing in 1932, O'Leary coached George Washington for two seasons before returning to Kansas City and beginning a long career in journalism. Coaching wasn't for him, but not because of Phog.

"I never stepped on the court with anything but anticipation of a great experience," O'Leary said. "I always loved the game, but playing for him made it so much more fun. I wouldn't have not known Phog Allen for anything."

PHOG'S CAREER COACHING RECORD

Basketball

Independence (Mo.) High School

	W	L
1906-07	5	1

Baker

	W	L
1905-06	18	3
1906-07	14	0
1907-08	13	6

Central Missouri State

	Overall		Conf. Championships	
	W	L	W	L
1912-13	11	7	6	0 (MIAA)
1913-14	15	4	9	1 (MIAA)
1914-15	13	4		
1915-16	9	4		
1916-17	13	2		
1917-18	9	4		
1918-19	14	6		

Haskell

	W	L
1908-09	27	5

Kansas

	Overall		Conference		
	W	L	W	L	
1907-08	18	6	6	0	Missouri Valley
1908-09	25	3	8	2	Missouri Valley
1919-20	11	7	9	7	
1920-21	10	8	10	8	
1921-22	16	2	15	1	Mo. Valley, Helms
1922-23	17	1	16	0	Mo. Valley, Helms
1923-24	16	3	15	1	Missouri Valley
1924-25	17	1	15	1	Missouri Valley
1925-26	16	2	16	2	Missouri Valley
1926-27	15	2	10	2	Missouri Valley
1927-28	9	9	9	9	
1928-29	3	15	2	8	
1929-30	14	4	7	3	
1930-31	15	3	7	3	Big Six
1931-32	13	5	7	3	Big Six
1932-33	13	4	8	2	Big Six
1933-34	16	1	9	1	Big Six
1934-35	15	5	12	4	
1935-36	21	2	10	0	Big Six
1936-37	15	4	8	2	Big Six
1937-38	18	2	9	1	Big Six
1938-39	13	7	6	4	
1939-40	19	6	8	2	Big Six
1940-41	12	6	7	3	Big Six
1941-42	17	5	8	2	Big Six
1942-43	22	6	10	0	Big Six
1943-44	17	9	5	5	
1944-45	12	5	7	3	
1945-46	19	2	10	0	Big Six
1946-47	16	11	5	5	
1947-48	9	15	4	8	
1948-49	12	12	3	9	

1949-50	14	11	8	4	Big Seven
1950-51	16	8	8	4	
1951-52	28	3	11	1	Big Seven, NCAA
1952-53	19	6	10	2	Big Seven
1953-54	16	5	10	2	Big Seven
1954-55	11	10	5	7	
1955-56	14	9	6	6	

Phog Allen vs:

	Kansas	CMSU	Baker	Haskell	Total
Colorado	18-13				18-13
Iowa State	62-18				62-18
Kansas	—	0-3	2-0		2-3
Kansas State	73-26	1-1	2-0	0-1	76-28
Missouri	66-34	0-1		0-1	66-36
Nebraska	64-20				64-20
Oklahoma	53-28	2-0			55-28
Oklahoma St.	24-17				24-17

Phog Allen vs. Coaches

Adolph Rupp, Kentucky 0-1
Doc Meanwell, Missouri 0-4
Jack Gardner, Olathe AAB, Kansas St. 18-16
Henry Iba, Oklahoma St. 18-17
Frosty Cox, Colorado 13-12
Sparky Stalcup, Missouri 17-8
Bruce Drake, Oklahoma 22-15
Tex Winter, Kansas St. 3-1

Career

School	No. Years	W	L
Kansas (1907-09, 1920-56)	39	590	219
Central Missouri (1912-19)	7	84	31
Baker (1905-08)	3	45	9
Haskell (1908-09)	1	27	5
Total	**48**	**746**	**264**

Note: Phog coached at two different schools simultaneously for three years (1906-09).

Football

Independence (Mo.) High School

	W	L	T
1906	3	4	1

Central Missouri State

	W	L	T
1912	6	2	
1913	7	2	
1914	5	4	
1915	4	2	2
1916	6	3	
1917	1	4	

Kansas

	W	L	T
1920	5	2	1

Totals

School	W	L	T
CMSU	29	17	2
Kansas	5	2	1
Total	34	19	3

Baseball

Central Missouri State

1913-19	Record not available

Kansas

	Overall			Conference	
	W	L	T	W	L
1941	3	10		3	10
1942	3	7	1	2	4
Total	**6**	**17**	**1**	**5**	**14**

APPENDICES

In the 1930s, Phog conducted a 15-minute radio program on campus station KFKU that usually covered health and physical education topics. His guests often included members of Kansas' physical education department. At least twice, James Naismith was a guest of the program. These are excerpts from the dialogue of those programs.

January 6, 1938
Basketball's Place in the Physical Education Program

ALLEN: Dr. Naismith, we have chosen for our subject of discussion tonight "Basketball's Place in the Physical Education Program." Since you originated basketball and since you were trained in the pioneer school of physical education, namely Springfield, Mass., YMCA College, it seems to me that this subject is an especially fitting one on which you can speak authoritatively. Do you think, Dr. Naismith, there is a danger of the physical educator today neglecting the body-building part of physical education and depending entirely on games for a system of physical education? This, of course, has reference to basketball as well as some of the other games.

NAISMITH: Absolutely yes! A great many of our physical educators are looking at it from the standpoint of the interest of the authorities and of spectators, rather than the benefit that can come to the boy, and a good many of these physical educators have been brought up and have received their appointments largely because of their ability in playing games rather than in their technical knowledge of the development of manhood.

ALLEN: Dr. Naismith, I find myself agreeing with you very emphatically in this statement. However, I can also see how an expert in the games would have a basic knowledge of a particular sport. This exceptional knowledge and splendid skill that he has developed in the sport is only systematic of his interest in the larger program of play and physical education. Most of these coaches who are now teaching physical education undoubtedly had a basic yearning for play in physical education. This, of course, caused them to continue their study to the point where they specialized in their life's work.

NAISMITH: Dr. Allen, don't think for a moment that I do not appreciate the skill that these boys get in learning a game and in devoting their time to it, both the fundamentals and the mechanism of the game; but I do lament the ignorance of a lot of our directors of physical education in the real science of developing the boy into a man. Take, for instance, a man who had been appointed to head of the physical education in a city of 80,000, who came to me and told me he didn't know a single thing about anything but football and basketball, and he wondered if I could help him out in making a program. It is the employment by principals of men of this type that has particularly done away with the real physical education program. I was very glad, as I visited your gymnasium the other morning, Dr. Allen, to see the large class of majors who are beginning at the bottom and learning the gymnastic side as well as recreative side of the development of the body. Now you are developing the men who are going out to head departments of physical education. Is your program, as it is arranged at the present time, comprehensive so as to include all these different parts?

ALLEN: Well, doctor, we're not sure about that, but we are endeavoring to find out. By asking men of your caliber who certainly know physical education, and then by doing a job analysis program . . .we are endeavoring to find out from superintendents and principals in the state of Kansas just what is needed for this state. We are asking those questions and when the survey is completed we believe we will know.

NAISMITH: Why do you go to superintendents and principals to ask them? Why don't you tell them? For instance, a year or so ago a man told me, "I have looked this thing over, spent 30 minutes studying the setup." And I returned, "I have spent 30 years studying the situation, and yet you think you know more about it than I do."

ALLEN: Well, Dr. Naismith, you really put me right on the grill, and I like this. I don't mean that we are going to shape our course exactly like all those fellows would suggest, but we want to know what they think the needs are for the schools of the state.

NAISMITH: Doctor, can you tell me this? In my early days almost every man who was director of physical education was an M.D. Now, why is it that physical education has gone from the medical profession to the educational?

ALLEN: That is a very excellent point, Dr. Naismith. The only answer that I could give that seems logical would be that the men with an M.D. degree can earn very much more than the professor of physical education. The health program of the country has called the doctors of medicine, and then, too, there has been such an expansion of the physical education program that the colleges have established a curriculum for physical education majors. That curriculum calls for a study of the basic sciences, and most of these physical education majors that are going out now have passed satisfactorily courses in anatomy, physiology, biology and chemistry. Of course, it would be fine if they could have a medical background, but that would require a much longer course than a four-year college course.

NAISMITH: Then you consider there is a trend backward to a study of the operations of the body, and that it is a necessity that they understand part of the human body in order to develop a real physical education program?

ALLEN: By all means, Dr. Naismith. I do not see how any intelligent physical education director or athletic coach can do a good job unless he definitely understands the structure and functions of the human body. Diet, fatigue, training, as well as fundamental body building, must of necessity be understood by this individual before he can do justice to the boy. And do not forget this point — a coach who has never had a course in psychology will not have the best understanding of his subject — the boy.

NAISMITH: Doctor, I would like to ask you one question. Do you know, or do you think there is a high school superintendent or principal who wouldn't accept "Whizzer" White as head of a department of physical education, even if he never had a day's study of psychology, or anything of that kind?

ALLEN: Well, doctor, you are hitting right in the middle. I believe most of them would take him. And there is weakness there. But you brought up the name of a wonderful young man who perhaps is not trained in physical education and maybe wouldn't take the job. We both know that he is a Phi Beta Kappa and has been selected as a Rhodes Scholar from Colorado. They tell me he is everything that you want in a young college graduate. Don't you think if "Whizzer" White should take a job like that that he would go ahead and get a major in physical education if he stayed in the field very long?

NAISMITH: Well, I don't believe that he would need it. He would be so busy with his football and basketball and his track that he wouldn't have the time to think along in terms of real physical development.

ALLEN: But, doctor, don't you think he really would get it?

NAISMITH: He ought to have it, certainly. I think that is the trouble. We ought to have lots of things but we can get along without them. But what of the athletics and physical education department? Athletics have a great appeal not only to the instructor but to the public, and also to the principal or superintendent.

ALLEN: Yes, doctor, but I remember a conversation I had with John Bunn over twelve years ago. He came into my office and said to me, "Doc, I am thinking about changing from what I thought was my life work into another field." John also said, "You know, I have received me degree in engineering. I would like to ask you what my future is in education?" I said, "John, there is a great future in physical education. If a man will get his M.D. and his Ph.D. degrees, a $20,000 salary in the next twenty years will not be an unheard of thing for the man who prepares for it. John, there will be a lot of small jobs for fellows who particularly prepare, but there will only be a few big jobs for men who fit themselves for it." I believe if "Whizzer" White went into coaching he would use that only as an introduction to the plumbing of a deeper life's work. And, doctor, we do not have to think of (just) "Whizzer" White. There are a great number of other fine athletes who have been brilliant scholars — John Bunn, Junior Coen, Ted O'Leary. And you remember, doctor, your own football player, Hubert Avery.

NAISMITH: But those men are not in physical education.

ALLEN: That is right, doctor. Our majors course in physical education was not started in any of our American colleges, in the main, until after the World War. The exception, of course, applies to Columbia, New York University and Wisconsin. Now there are hundreds and hundreds of colleges in America offering this course. In fact, I do not know of a single college in the state of Kansas, of that matter, in the land, that does not offer a course in training young men and women in physical education.

NAISMITH: Do you think that most of these colleges that are offering this course are equipped to give a coach a real thorough training in the basic fundamentals for the development of individuals?

ALLEN: Not a fulsome course, doctor. But there is a demand for this type of work in all the high schools, and many of the graduates from the smaller colleges will accept a position at a salary that gives them employment as a teacher in academic subjects and as a part-time coach. Most of our varsity athletes are engineers, lawyers, journalists and graduates of the school of business. It is the business of the university to train professional men, and for that very reason we have not turned out many coaches. However, this newly organized department of education (at Kansas), in the School of Education, will supply to the high schools many teachers in physical education and athletic coaching. This has not been true heretofore.

NAISMITH: Now, doctor, you have touched upon a subject that has been a hobby with me for a number of years. That is each institution should have a man to look after the physical welfare of the students as head of the department of physical education, employing the instructors in other departments to coach the several teams. Then, when the students or the alumni demand a new coach for teams this man simply returns to his teaching work, and the department of physical education goes on without interruption.

ALLEN: Perhaps sometime the various boards of education of the high schools will accept your splendid theory and obtain both a director of physical education and an athletic coach. Wyandotte High School in Kansas City, Kansas, and in fact, all the high schools in Kansas City, Kansas — Argentine, Rosedale and Wyandotte, have this scheme in operation and it is highly satisfactory. Too many educators and laymen confuse the spectacular phase of athletes with the mere prosaic development of the individual. It is very seldom that a coach who is the high-tension, inspirational type of fellow is concerned with the more serious business of building a department and devotes all his energies to developing the young men under him. When you get a combination of the both, the young man you have is ideal. Then if he can originate, deputize and supervise, this setup is truly a wonderful organization.

NAISMITH: Well, here now, Dr. Allen, you have a basketball game tomorrow night between Oklahoma and the Kansas varsity, opening the Big Six Conference, and you have that old team of ever-victorious Big Six Champions of 1936 coming in to play the superlative performers — the freshmen of this year. Aren't you going to say a word about that?

ALLEN: Well, Dr. Naismith, our time is just about up and we'll let Nelson Sullivan, our sports announcer atop Mount Oread, tell you about this. Thank you very much Dr. Naismith.

Jan. 13, 1938
The Tip-less Game of Basketball

ALLEN: Dr. Naismith, I would like to ask you a question. After 45 years of starting your game of basketball with the center tip, this rules committee last April eliminated the tip after field and foul goals. In your opinion, why did they do this?

NAISMITH: Well, in originating the game, after considerable thought as to how the ball would be put in play, the center tip seemed the only reasonable way of giving each side an equal chance of obtaining the ball. Now, the only objection that I can see to it is that the tall player monopolizes the tip-off because of his height and the assistance of the referee who tosses it up in such a manner that the tall man has a better chance of obtaining it than the short man. There are several ways in which this might have been corrected. Now that is my idea. Doctor, what is yours? You are on the rules committee, and attended the meeting in which the national rules body voted it out. Why did they do this?

ALLEN: Well, Dr. Naismith, I find myself agreeing with you on the center tip-off. I have always believed in it. I have always contended that in football we have the kickoff at the start of the game. I feel that the tip-off at the start of the game of basketball,

goals, the playing situation would have been identically the same as this year.

NAISMITH: Well, now, according to the wording of the new rule, how can the game be speeded up on account of the rules? Is it not in spite of the rules that the game has speeded up?

ALLEN: Well, doctor, as far as the speeding up of the game is concerned, that is entirely up to the play of the two opposing teams. The so-called new rules have not been in the books long enough for the teams to get thoroughly adjusted, as yet. If the side scored upon really desires to delay the game, that side may hold the ball five seconds out of bounds by rule at the end line before they throw the ball in, and then they may take 10 seconds in addition before the players on that side are forced by the rule to pass the center line of the court, or the division line. In other words, it is possible to withhold the ball from the offensive court for 14 seconds after a goal is made. So you can see that they can play the slow break just as well as they can play the fast break, and personally I think that some smart team is going to try that. I noticed by Sunday's paper that Iowa State used the slow break against Kansas State and beat them 41 to 30. So you see, doctor, all teams are not going in for this fire department basketball. In another year I predict that many teams will be using the slow break and then you will have 5 seconds to pass the ball in from out of bounds and 10 seconds to get it across. Then after they get across they are going to use a play that many people call "stall," and it will be a dreary game. Don't you think so?

NAISMITH: Yes, I certainly agree with you. That is the real objection to the whole thing, and that has been my objection to the tipless center. It gives the team that has been scored upon an opportunity to delay the game.

ALLEN: Well, then, doctor, you did indicate that since football rules went back to the kickoff there may be a return to the center tip-off in basketball in a year or two. Don't you think there is a possibility of rotating the jumpers in basketball just as they have a batting order in baseball? The coaches could instruct their players during practice, so it would be an easy matter to handle the game situation.

NAISMITH: And another thing, Dr. Allen — if there was a deviation of this practice by any one team, the opponent would quickly recognize it and call it to the attention of the referee.

ALLEN: Why, certainly, they would. No difficulty would be encountered in this regard. But doctor, I see that our time is fast drawing to a close.

NAISMITH: But wait a minute — at least we have time for another question, haven't we?

ALLEN: Surely.

NAISMITH: A great deal has been said about the injurious effects of the fast break, especially in league games among junior high schools. Don't you think that they are putting too much stress upon the contest rather than upon the recreative sport and educational factors for the young boys?

ALLEN: Yes, doctor. Instances of this have come up often in the national rules discussion. I remember distinctly that Floyd Rowe, director of physical education of the public schools of Cleveland, Ohio, submitted a research finding that was done in Cleveland. This research showed that organized league competition actually affected the nervous system of these boys to such an extent that the normal growth was influenced. One group was taken with no special emphasis upon league play and the other group indulged in regular league competition. According to the findings in Cleveland, the regular league competition was very detrimental to high school boys under the old rule, and under the new rule the strenuosity of the game would be increased. I am sure that the authorities who are making surveys would certainly be against this new game on that principle.

NAISMITH: Well, now, isn't this league contest a strain upon the nervous system rather than upon the muscular? And, for my part, I think that it would be very much better to limit the league playing or the interscholastic competition in the junior high schools.

ALLEN: Yes, doctor, you have hit the nail right on the head, because isn't it true that the nervous system controls the glandular system, and the glandular system determines the growth of the individual?

NAISMITH: That's my idea of it.

ALLEN: By the way, we have Nelson Sullivan, our sports announcer atop Mt. Oread. Sully, you tell the wide world the news, will you?

This is a standard letter Phog used in the 1930s and 1940s to respond to those inquiring about trying out for the team.

Dear _____,

I am very glad to know of your interest in the University of Kansas, but as you know, we do not have any special scholarships of any kind for athletes here at the University. As a consequence we do not make any special offers to athletes on account of their athletic ability.

I tell all the boys that a good athlete can get propositions from many schools, but if I were you I would pick out a school that you really want to attend, and then go to that school regardless of whether you make $15.00 or $30.00 a month. I know that you do not want to sell your academic birthright for a mess of pottage.

If you have saved enough money to pay for your books, tuition and incidental expenses, then I am sure that you will have no difficulty in making the grade here at the University of Kansas. I do not want to appear to preach, because no one is converted very much after preaching. I tell the boys that the first thing they must get is their academic work. That is the thing you go to school for, and you will find that your degree from the University of Kansas will amount to just as much as you think it is worth, or as much as you put into it.

It is necessary for you to make definite progress toward graduation to establish yourself as a student in the University. There are three things besides academics which a student may indulge in here on Mount Oread — athletics, politics and social life. A boy who works his way through, either partially or wholly, can only choose one of those three and still make a go of his academic work and his chosen avocation or hobby. About 15 percent of the students at the University participate in athletics, about 15 percent take part in politics as their hobby, and about 15 percent are active in social life. To endeavor to do more than one of these three prime non-necessities of student existence is a sure debacle as far as your academic work is concerned.

You will find that I am not trying to entice you here as a student because you played basketball. I have never contacted basketball players, because I think that any coach who offers a boy a job on account of his athletic ability is doing the boy a real injury. I tell each athlete that he cannot help the University on account of his athletic skill. The

University helps him. When I think of the great scientists here —
such as Dr. Cady who discovered helium gas — and other great men
of science, then I am reminded of the insignificance of the contribution of athletes to this university. Of course, people come to see the
game in which you or I are playing, but if you or I had never been
born they would still go to see the games where other boys play.

So, when you consider the University of Kansas, please do not
think that I am endeavoring primarily to entice you to the University
of account of your basketball ability. If you should decide to attend
the University I would be glad to help you help yourself, but I cannot
promise anyone assistance until he has definitely made up his mind
to enroll at the University of Kansas.

Very sincerely yours

Forrest C. Allen
Director of Physical Education,
Varsity Basketball Coach

NOTES

Unless otherwise indicated all direct quotes were taken from interviews by the author.

CHAPTER 1: Independence Days

"Bess Wallace Truman lived": *Jayhawk Rebounds* newsletter by Phog Allen, Aug. 31, 1945.

"My father would say": *Kansas City Star*, Nov. 22, 1931.

"You're a disgraceful site": *Kansas City Star*, April 20, 1952.

CHAPTER 2: The Amazing Allen Brother

"No athletic event ever took place": *Kansas City Star*, March 21, 1905.

"The Convention Hall series will be among": *Kansas City Star*, March 24, 1905.

"Never has such a well played": *Kansas City Star*, March 28, 1905.

"Unfortunately in both games already played": *Kansas City Star*, March 29, 1905.

"Games in which he officiated": *Arkansas Gazette*, April 18, 1937.

"After the Blue Diamonds won that series": Ibid.

"The Buffalo team will go back": *Kansas City Star*, April 1, 1905.

"If the Athletic Club should play": Ibid.

"Especial credit is due Manager Forest (sic) Allen": April 4, 1905.

"We played at old Convention Center": Phog Allen Biography, Masters thesis, by Donald W. Elston, University of Kansas, 1967.

"much like the front room of a governor's mansion": Alton, Ill., *Evening Telegraph*, Sept. 18, 1974.

"Life is a paradox, isn't it boys": correspondence archives, University of Kansas.

CHAPTER 3: Here a Coach, There a Coach

"Forrest Allen made his first appearance": *University Daily Kansan*, Oct. 18, 1905.

"NAISMITH: I've got a good joke on you": Phog Allen, *Phog Allen's Sports Stories for You and Youth* (Lawrence, Kan.: Allen Press, 1947), page 175.

"We found you, as I remember,": correspondence archives, University of Kansas.

"Yes, I do remember now very clearly": correspondence archives, University of Kansas.

"He is a steady, consistent player": *University Daily Kansan*, March 21, 1906.

"A rosy-cheeked blond male of 21": *Topeka Daily Capital*, Feb. 20, 1955.

"The great difficulties in developing the team": *University Daily Kansan*, Dec. 20, 1906.

"Being faced with the problem of all white man officials": Allen, *Sports Stories*, 147.

"He was clean as a hound's tooth": Allen, *Sports Stories*, 127.

CHAPTER 4: Mending Friends and Foes

"I came out of the series with a cracked elbow": interview with University of Kansas publicist Don Pierce, 1965.

"The way you describe it": correspondence archives, University of Kansas.

"Dr. F.C. Allen, miracle man": *Warrensburg Star-Journal*, Dec. 30, 1916, reprint of story that appeared in *Champaign*, Ill., *Daily News*.

"I sure wouldn't be here if I couldn't throw": *Topeka Daily Capital*, July 23, 1950.

"I have them come to me from all over": correspondence archives, University of Kansas.

"Seems too bad that in a country like ours": correspondence archives, University of Kansas.

"Personally, I'm not ashamed of it": correspondence archives, University of Kansas.

"A youth athlete should watch for the three B's": Allen, *Sports Stories*, 71.

"Dr. Allen's wonderful personality": *Pittsburgh Press*, July 30, 1927.

CHAPTER 5: *Normal Phog*

"Athletic prospects took a great boom": *The Normal Student*, Sept. 21, 1912.

"Whether we should call him Dr. Allen": *The Normal Student*, Oct. 5, 1912.

"This Mercury-footed flyer": Allen, *Sports Stories*, 148.

"We hope that the Normal has fired their coach": Lawsuit filed in Johnson County, Mo., Circuit Court, Feb. 1915, Forrest Allen vs. Drury College and Emmett Thomas.

"Be it resolved,": *Warrensburg Star-Journal*, Dec. 9, 1914.

"I remember distinctly the first day I arrived": correspondence archives, University of Kansas.

"His last year at Warrensburg was terminated": *Warrensburg Star-Journal*, Sept. 18, 1974.

CHAPTER 6: *Dreaming Touchdowns and Stadiums*

"I never have looked over my left shoulder": Allen, *Sports Stories*, 44.

"Was it magic or hokum": Ibid, 46.

"Swooping down from the North": Ibid, 23.

"Pandemonium broke loose": Ibid, 26.

"When I returned to Kansas in 1919": correspondence archives, University of Kansas.

"He had some unique ideas": Phog Allen Biography, Masters thesis, Donald W. Elston, University of Kansas, 1967.

"Like a majestic prelude to a powerful symphony": Allen, *Sports Stories*, 27.

CHAPTER 7: 1923 - The Legend Begins

"I was none too favorably impressed with Wisconsin's playing": correspondence archives, University of Kansas.

"True to the traditions of the South": Allen, *Sports Stories*, 50.

"Erroneously, Tus felt that some member of the Missouri football team": Allen, *Sports Stories*, 54.

"I'm glad to be here because this group means": correspondence archives, University of Kansas.

"Dr. Allen does not hold that his is the first word, nor the last, on basketball": *Chicago Herald and Examiner*, June 20, 1925.

"In my opinion, Northwestern University": *University Daily Kansan*, Feb. 18, 1925.

CHAPTER 8: Dr. Naismith

"I have no sympathy with it": correspondence archives, University of Kansas.

"I even saw the casket which Uncle Peter": correspondence archives, University of Kansas.

"gets into the players' hearts": Phog Allen, *My Basket-Ball Bible* (Kansas City, Mo., Smith-Grieves, Co., 1924), page 314.

"Had Dr. Naismith patented some of his paraphernalia": *Time* magazine, March 13, 1933, page 36.

"Being an M.D., Dr. Naismith was always intrigued": Dr. Henry A. Shenk, from a paper, Dr. Naismith — The Man, 1970.

"He imbued his students": Ibid.

"This game, the only international game": correspondence archives, University of Kansas.

"The whole deal smacks of a publicity stunt": correspondence archives, University of Kansas.

"I have been to Lawrence a number of times": correspondence archives, University of Kansas.

"Twelve years before Dr. Naismith passed on": correspondence archives, University of Kansas.

CHAPTER 9: The Entrepreneur

"I get a cheer out of watching my boys": correspondence archives, University of Kansas.

"I have never sold my name by way of endorsements": correspondence archives, University of Kansas.

"They brought a pair of Converse makes": correspondence archives, University of Kansas.

"The thought occurred to us": correspondence archives, University of Kansas.

"You are the only one to whom we sell": correspondence archives, University of Kansas.

"You can rest assured that I would not": correspondence archives, University of Kansas.

"New Game Sweeps City": *Sioux Falls*, S.D., *News Argus*, undated.

"Cage Coach Becomes Inventor of New Sport": *St. Louis Star-Times*, Dec. 5, 1939.

"Goal-Hi, New Game Developed by Noted Basketball Authority": *The Athletic Journal*, December, 1939, page 37.

"Se trata del Goal-Hi parecido al basketball": *El Diario* (The Daily), Montevideo, Uruguay.

"(Phog) thinks so much of the sport that he put about as much effort": *San Francisco Examiner*, Dec. 16, 1937.

CHAPTER 10: Rules, Rules, Rules

"Out West football is king": correspondence archives, University of Kansas.

"Men 6-10 tall are getting to be quite commonplace": correspondence archives, University of Kansas.

"Next season is 1935": correspondence archives, University of Kansas.

"The 12-foot basket is coming": correspondence archives, University of Kansas.

"Few young lives have held greater promise than his": *Crete,* Neb., *News*, July 5, 1928.

"'Phog' Allen Gets Another Brain Tantrum": *Lafayette,* Ind., *Journal and Courier*, undated, 1940.

"To show your utter incompetency": correspondence archives, University of Kansas.

"Why shouldn't this be all right": *University Daily Kansan*, March 19, 1948.

"Sure thing, why not?": *Kansas City Times*, Dec. 12, 1948.

CHAPTER 11: Olympic Rise and Fall

"I talked with the manager of the McPherson Oilers": correspondence archives, University of Kansas.

"Personally, I feel that there will be so much objection": correspondence archives, University of Kansas.

"The Los Angeles Organizing Committee which is concerned": correspondence archives, University of Kansas.

"With further reference to our former correspondence": correspondence archives, University of Kansas.

"I was somewhat surprised inasmuch as": correspondence archives, University of Kansas.

"There was no doubt in the minds": correspondence archives, University of Kansas.

"That farcical exhibition Thursday night": *Topeka Daily Capital*, April 11, 1936.

"In the early days of American Sport": *Topeka Daily Capital*, Aug. 28, 1936.

CHAPTER 12: Phog's Folly

"The football season is over now and the *University Daily Kansan* can do no more harm": letter from Allen to *University Daily Kansan*, Dec. 2, 1936.

"To get Kansas out of the fog": letter to *University Daily Kansan*, Dec. 3, 1936.

"Your talk before the game was an inspiration": correspondence archives, University of Kansas.

"Dr. Allen refuses to build great castles": correspondence archives, University of Kansas.

"I have arrived at an age that convinces me": correspondence archives, University of Kansas.

"Three years ago certain incidents happened here": correspondence archives, University of Kansas.

CHAPTER 13: Saving the Tournament

"I knew many schools were angling for Miller's services": correspondence archives, University of Kansas.

"I own a farm in Kansas and pay taxes": *Topeka Daily Capital*, Aug. 28, 1938.

"I think this would be a very interesting experiment": correspondence archives, University of Kansas.

"This committee is to communicate with and petition": correspondence archives, University of Kansas.

"You give me this tournament in Kansas City": correspondence archives, University of Kansas.

"(Iba) assures me that without any question of doubt": correspondence archives, University of Kansas.

"I want to build character": NABC newsletter, Dec. 1940.

"The Kansas City Auditorium . . .is tops": Ibid.

"My motive has been to sweeten the pot": correspondence archives, University of Kansas.

"I told them that when an individual makes certain promises": correspondence archives, University of Kansas.

"Such a procedure gives Wisconsin an 8- to 10-point advantage": *Lawrence Journal-World*, March 7, 1941.

"He's a toe-dancing, shadow-boxing politician": correspondence archives, University of Kansas.

CHAPTER 14: The Patriot

"He cleared up many things and he helped me get a better perspective": Bob Dole, *The Congressional Record*, Sept. 19, 1974.

"Somehow this is the most difficult letter that I have ever attempted": *Jayhawk Rebounds* newsletter by Phog Allen, Sept. 12, 1944.

"These are the words for it - ": correspondence archives, University of Kansas.

"When we started out we didn't think we were going to win a ball game": correspondence archives, University of Kansas.

"Football the game will be with us": *Kansas City Star*, Feb. 1, 1942.

CHAPTER 15: Smelling a Rat

"What do you look for in the way of post-war athletics?": correspondence archives, University of Kansas.

"Judge Landis is fighting betting in professional gambling": correspondence archives, University of Kansas.

"It has not taken a statement from Lawrence, Kansas": correspondence archives, University of Kansas.

"He's been doing this thing for years now": *Denver Post*, Oct. 24, 1944.

"Dr. Phog Allen, who made a career out of proving": *Philadelphia Record*, Oct. 25, 1944.

"Each year for many years this bumpkin of no particular standing": *San Francisco Call Bulletin*, Oct. 25, 1944.

"deplorable lack of faith in American youth": *Kansas City Star*, Oct. 25, 1944.

"Phog Allen has thrown down the gauntlet,": *Denver Post*, Oct. 24, 1944.

"Whether Coach Allen was right or wrong": *Lincoln, Neb., Star*, Oct. 26, 1944.

"No matter what the Allen episode proved": *Saturday Evening Post*, Dec. 23, 1944, page 3.

"(T)he fact is, if (Irish) stepped out gambling": *Stars and Stripes*, Dec. 27, 1944.

"The head of the department can do nothing about it": correspondence archives, University of Kansas.

"Now who's the bumpkin?":*University Daily Kansan*, Jan. 30, 1945.

"You should be ashamed of yourself": correspondence archives, University of Kansas.

"They are there for every youth to see": correspondence archives, University of Kansas.

"Some of the boys around New York think": correspondence archives, University of Kansas.

"Western players wouldn't last in a tough league": *The Sporting News*, Feb. 6, 1943.

I am thinking of a man with college ideals": correspondence archives, University of Kansas.

"Some are in the athletic business": correspondence archives, University of Kansas.

"Horse racing, former king of sports, is a sideline": correspondence archives, University of Kansas.

CHAPTER 16: Friends and Enemies

"Missouri has a slush fund of $15,000 a year": correspondence archives, University of Kansas.

"'Absurd,' Tigers athletic director and football coach Don Faurot said": *Kansas City Star*, Nov. 24, 1945.

"I was told that Bobby Reynolds was offered $10,000": *Lawrence Journal-World*, March 30, 1951.

"have been dull, multiple-fouling contests.": correspondence archives, University of Kansas.

"What we would get is chicken feed": correspondence archives, University of Kansas.

"I'm for Oklahoma A&M 100 percent plus.": *Lawrence Journal-World*, April 30, 1947.

"The University of Missouri enjoys this rivalry": *Kansas City Star*, Dec. 30, 1951.

"The night will never be too dark or stormy": *Daily Oklahoman*, April 25, 1972.

"Clair Bee of LIU, Nat Holman of CCNY and Adolph Rupp of Kentucky": correspondence archives, University of Kansas.

CHAPTER 17: Brass Rings and Gold Medals

"to silly to bother with.": *Lawrence Journal-World*, Jan. 15, 1952.

"It was an exact copy of the stall and freeze game": *Lawrence Journal-World*, Aug. 11, 1952.

"Maybe enough hollering like such people as Dr. Allen": *Kansas City Star*, Nov. 3, 1952.

CHAPTER 18: Wilt and Statutory Senility

"My 1954-55 team would consider it a privilege": *Lawrence Journal-World*, April 2, 1953.

"How can there be any other answer?": *University Daily Kansan*, April 16, 1953.

"The only drawback so far": *Lawrence Journal-World*, March 4, 1955.

"Of course I used everything we had to get him.": *Life* magazine, Jan. 28, 1957, page 113.

"Gee that's great news. I hope he comes out for basketball": *Kansas City Star*, Sept. 17, 1974.

"I am enjoying splendid health": *Lawrence Journal-World*, March 14, 1956.

"First of all, I think the whole Allen family must understand": correspondence archives, University of Kansas.

"Frankly, I wanted my last chance to show": personal archives of Paul Endacott.

"May I say that I have always held you": correspondence archives, University of Kansas.

"did more than twice as much for basketball": *Lawrence Journal-World*, April 12, 1956.

CHAPTER 19: Retirement

"If I said he was a great player": *Daily Oklahoman*, June 2, 1968.

"Bless his bones!": *Kansas City Star*, Jan. 31, 1968.

"I will never and I do not intend": *Kansas Daily Tribune*, Dec. 4, 1956.

"Wilt, two Phi Beta Kappas and two aggressive coeds": correspondence archives, University of Kansas.

"Colonel in a Brooklyn band.": *Lawrence Journal-World*, Jan. 4, 1956.

"I'm surprise it was only for $35,000": *Kansas City Star*, April 3, 1956.

"I never felt better or had less": correspondence archives, University of Kansas.

"(Basketball) will never replace football or baseball": Associated Press story, no newspaper identified.

"That fellow, (Norm) Stewart": *Kansas City Star*, March 26, 1972.

"He'll go down in history": *Kansas City Times*, Sept. 20, 1974.

Epilogue

"I want to touch it tonight": correspondence archives, University of Kansas.